CARRIER DOWN

THOMAS BRADSHAW

ibooks
new york

DISTRIBUTED BY SIMON & SCHUSTER

An ibooks, inc. Book

All rights reserved, including the right to reproduce this book
or portions thereof in any form whatsoever.
Distributed by Simon & Schuster, Inc.
1230 Avenue of the Americas, New York, NY 10020

ibooks, inc.
24 West 25th Street
New York, NY 10010

The ibooks World Wide Web address is:
www.ibooks.net

Reprinted with permission from Eakin Press.

Copyright © 1990 by Thomas I. Bradshaw and
Marsha L. Clark

First ibooks, inc. mass market printing April 2005

ISBN: 0-7434-9342-7
10 9 8 7 6 5 4 3 2 1

Printed in the U.S.A.

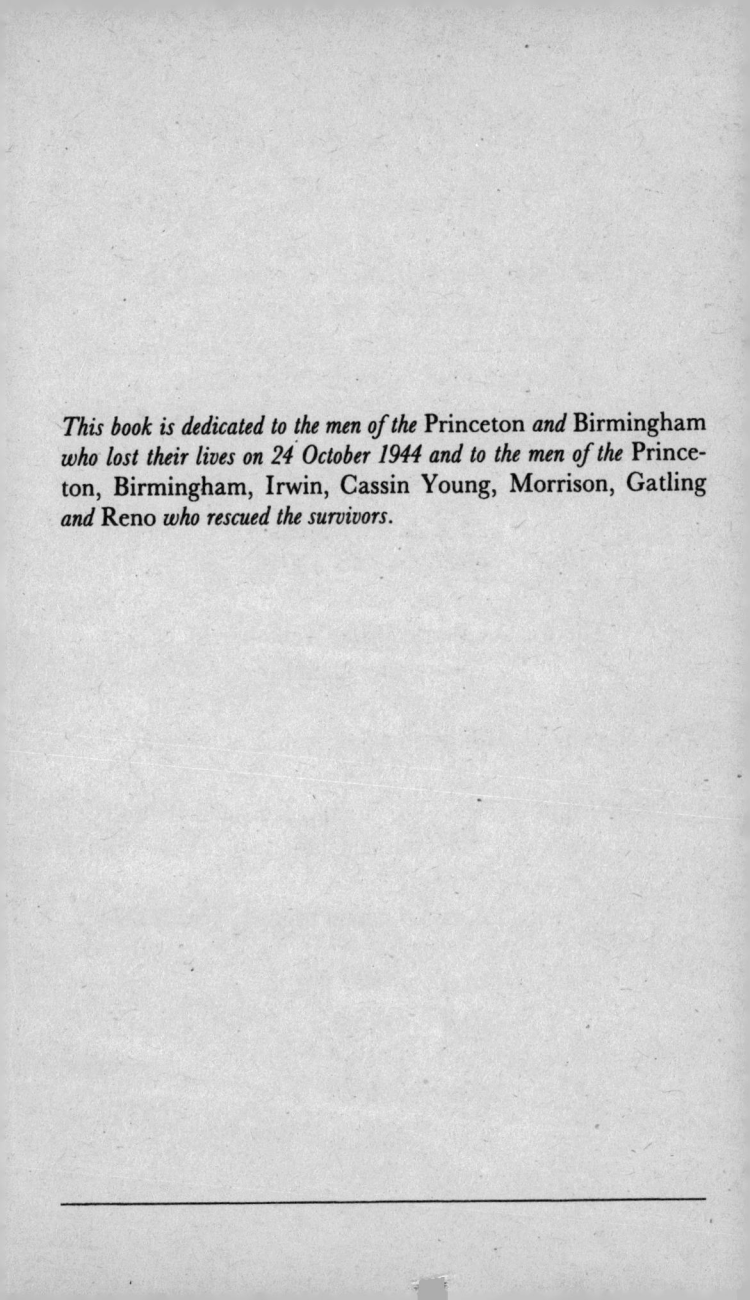

This book is dedicated to the men of the Princeton *and* Birmingham *who lost their lives on 24 October 1944 and to the men of the* Princeton, Birmingham, Irwin, Cassin Young, Morrison, Gatling *and* Reno *who rescued the survivors.*

Contents

Foreword by Vice Adm. Thomas B. Inglis		vii
Preface		ix
Acknowledgments		xi
I	Legacy By Name	1
II	From Cruiser to Carrier	5
III	Shakedown Cruise	13
IV	Time to Go	19
V	The Real War	25
VI	Target Hopping	33
VII	Changing of the Guard	42
VIII	Spirits Afloat	47
IX	Air Group 27 Takes Shape	53
X	Into Japan's Backyard	61
XI	Marianas Turkey Shoot	68
XII	The Great Chase	75
XIII	On to the Philippines	81
XIV	Fighter Pilots' Day	88
XV	One Plane, One Bomb	96
XVI	Fire and Water	110
XVII	Devastation Below Decks	125
XVIII	On Their Own	137
XIX	So Near to Winning	147
XX	Fatal Blow	154
XXI	The Hatchet is Buried	170
Epilogue		183
Casualties		189
Index		219

Foreword

The beginning of our war with Japan was their attack on Pearl Harbor. We remained on the defensive until the Battle of Midway. That marked the end of the beginning. We went on the offensive. The Pacific Fleet, including the *Princeton* and *Birmingham*, advanced westward, either conquering or neutralizing Japanese-held islands in the Central Pacific. The conquest of the Marianas, including our former possession of Guam, was a marked victory. The "turkey shoot" materially damaged Japanese naval aviation.

There were differing opinions as to the best strategy for prosecuting the war. Admirals King and Nimitz favored a direct, concentrated assault on the Japanese home islands, by-passing the Philippines. General MacArthur preferred a campaign deliberately island-by-island, re-conquering first the Philippines. "I shall return" was an emotional issue with the general.

The general's strategy prevailed, and all U.S. forces, including Nimitz's Central Pacific Fleet and MacArthur's Southwest Pacific Command, concentrated in the assault at Leyte in central Philippines. The Battle of Leyte Gulf was a crucial contest. Our victory there was the beginning of the end of the war. Much remained to be accomplished, including Okinawa and the holocaust of Hiroshima and Nagasaki.

Princeton and *Birmingham* met their fate as America's chief sacrifice in winning the Battle of Leyte Gulf.

As captain of the *Birmingham*, I welcomed the orders to assist the *Princeton*. We were enthused by the navy's tradition to "save the ship," and by the expectation of an exciting adventure. Little did we expect the adventure to turn into a terribly heart-rending misadventure.

This narrative of the dramatic events on the *Princeton* is unique in disclosing details of the personal actions and emotions of scores of individuals. It is intensely interesting.

The authors have told the story of the *Birmingham* with just commendation of the courage, unselfishness, organization, training and efficiency of that wonderful crew. In my farewell to the crew I said:

> "It was my good fortune to be entrusted with the high honor of commanding the *Birmingham* from 11 August 1943 to 22 November 1944. Those were months filled with action, excitement, and high adventure. The trials and triumphs, which we faced together; the knowledge that the success of the ship, and the safety of all, depended upon the devotion to duty of each the understanding that the team was more important than the individual; and the mutual respect and affection among all of us; all of these things made us 'shipmates' in the finest sense of the word.
>
> "In the face of exhaustion, danger, and grimmest tragedy there was no grumbling, no shirking, and no flinching. Young America need concede nothing in fortitude to other races or other generations. Our steel ships, too, are served by iron men.
>
> "Never in history had a captain the good fortune to command a finer crew."

The *Princeton* presented to the *Birmingham* a plaque with a quotation from the Bible, "Greater love hath no man than this, that a man lay down his life for his friends." (John 15:11).

— Vice Adm. THOMAS B. INGLIS

Preface

In the early hours of the greatest naval battle ever, a lone Japanese plane pierced the defense perimeter of the U.S. fast carrier task force cruising east of the Philippine Islands. On that squally morning of 24 October 1944 the enemy pilot dropped a single bomb on the aircraft carrier *Princeton*.

The 550-pound bomb penetrated the flight deck, passed through the hangar deck, where it started raging gasoline fires, and exploded on the second deck. Although the resulting hole in the flight deck was enough to divert the *Princeton*'s airborne planes to other carriers, the damage did not initially appear fatal.

However, the eventual results were unbelievably destructive. In less than a half-hour, the *Princeton* was rocked by a series of internal explosions that blew first the after, and then the forward, elevators out of position and left them cocked at crazy angles in their openings.

While the bulk of Task Force 38 went on to attack the Japanese fleet attempting to destroy Allied landing forces at Leyte, the stricken *Princeton* was left to fight its fires with the help of two cruisers, the *Reno* (CL-96) and the *Birmingham* (CL-62), and four destroyers, *Irwin* (DD-794), *Morrison* (DD-560), *Gatling* (DD-671), and *Cassin Young* (DD-793).

When that day was ended, the *Princeton* had gone down in the deepest waters of any ocean. The *Birmingham* had sustained devastating damage in a blast that tore away the *Princeton*'s stern, and suffered more casualties than the *Princeton* itself. Three of the four destroyers were so badly damaged in the firefighting effort they required stateside repairs before they could return to battle.

On the *Princeton,* 309 were killed or wounded. On the *Birmingham,* 653 were dead or wounded. Among the *Princeton*'s casualties was Capt. John M. Hoskins, aboard to relieve Capt. William Buracker as commanding officer. In the final explosion of bombs and other munitions stowed outside the *Princeton*'s after magazine, Hoskins lost the lower part of his right leg.

Hoskins later was to convince navy examiners his newly acquired artificial foot was no reason to prevent him from commanding a combat vessel.

The *Princeton* was a proud ship because of the record established by those who served aboard her.

When the carrier went down in the Battle for Leyte Gulf, her officers and crew felt a loss much more personal and far-reaching than just so many tons of wood and metal. They had lost a haven on which they depended. They had lost individual belongings, which, in the remoteness of sea duty, can become all the more vital.

Most importantly, they had lost friends because of the vulnerability of the ship they had come to consider invulnerable.

These same factors, however, served to bring survivors together. Many of those who lived beyond the carrier's end have banded together to keep the *Princeton*'s memory alive — not merely because the ship had been lost; but because they felt a certain pride in having helped do something they considered good during a very bad period of the world's history.

At their reunions, some of these survivors have put on record their memories of the *Princeton* and the ship's sinking. This book draws on those unique accounts to tell the story in the words of those who lived this dramatic chapter in U.S. naval history.

Acknowledgments

In the course of researching this book, I was helped by many people. Several deserve special mention.

George Green, who stimulated my initial interest, wanted a short story written about the sinking of the *Princeton*, dedicated to the men who lost their lives. The "short story" kept growing and became a book.

JO1c Bill Trent, of the Naval Office of Information in Los Angeles in 1980, put me in touch with Anna C. Urband, assistant for Magazines/Books Media Services Division, Department of the Navy. Anna always was there when needed. If she didn't have specific material, she found out who did and how it could be obtained.

A search of the pages of the *Navy Times,* at the Moreell Library at the Port Hueneme Naval Base, turned up an announcement of a reunion of shipmates for the USS *Princeton* (CVL 23). This led to contacts with hundreds of those who served on the carrier.

Larry Morgan, president of the Princeton Association, and many association members, provided stories and pictures. Without them the book couldn't have happened.

Tom Mooney of VT 27 has been an advisor, friend, and personal pilot providing transportation to various sources of research information.

John Fitzgerald of VF 27 has been very helpful, especially by establishing contact with the author, Tom Bradshaw, who served on the *Princeton* as air combat intelligence officer with VF 27.

Vic Moitoret, navigator of the *Princeton*, provided pictures, stories, and valuable advice while helping to keep the book as factual as possible.

Adm. Henry Miller, who was Air Group 23 commander, supplied a history of that group along with pictures.

Leo Ghastin, editor of the Air Group 27 newsletter, and Carl Brown, fighter pilot, air tactician and author, worked with Tom

Bradshaw in recreating the story of Air Group 27.

Adm. Thomas Inglis, captain of the *Birmingham*, provided the story of the gallant effort by the cruiser's crew to save the *Princeton*.

Not everyone who helped me was connected with the U.S. Navy or the USS *Princeton*. To these people I give a special thank you. Tom Batten drove me several hundred miles to Lowell, MA, so I could meet with Tom Bradshaw and show him my research on the *Princeton*. As publication grew closer Tom Batten assisted in getting me to the National Archives and to get better photographs for *Carrier Down*.

Sam Messiter was invaluable in the quest for an agent. When his friend, Tom Mooney, asked him to help, he steered this stranger around New York, provided advice on what was needed to sell a book and then arranged a meeting with Richard Curtis. This outstanding agent stuck through eight years of ups and downs while the project was completed, providing encouragement and advice throughout.

Don Knox, senior editor at Harcourt Brace Jovanovich, gave support and encouraged me to continue when it seemed the project was at a dead end.

Many thanks to my good friend, Kurt Van Laar, for all his help in creating the index for the book.

Most special thanks to my husband, Daryl. He did drawings for the book, taught me to use a word processor, and was my emotional support and encouragement through nine years of research.

I sincerely thank Tom Bradshaw for blending my research with his own memories and information in creating this book.

— MARSHA L. CLARK

CHAPTER I

Legacy By Name

A SHIP AND NAME CAN be inseparable for better or worse. If the name is well-chosen, the lasting image of the vessel can be greatly enhanced. Should the ship have a lackluster career, or come to an inglorious end, the name may or may not be carried forward.

The name *Princeton* has been borne by six U.S. Navy ships. The original source has been attributed variously to the battle fought at Princeton, NJ, during the revolutionary war, and to the town that was the birthplace of *Princeton* number one's captain, Robert F. Stockton.

The initial *Princeton* was the navy's first steam-powered, screw-propelled warship. The keel was laid 20 October 1842 at the Philadelphia Navy Yard. Eleven months later, the 164-foot, three-masted vessel was launched, and within a matter of days placed in commission.

Although bearing a full complement of square-rigged sails, the *Princeton* was equipped with a pair of engines to drive a six-bladed screw, which measured fourteen feet in diameter. A trio of boilers burned anthracite from Pennsylvania's hard coal mines.

After a trial run on the Delaware River, with Stockton in command and carrying a crew of 166 officers and men, the new ship left Philadelphia for a sea trial, which included a speed contest with the

British steamer *Great Western,* off New York.

Following her return to Philadelphia for basic outfitting, the *Princeton* sailed to New York on New Year's Day 1844, to be equipped with two large guns. One of these bore the name "Oregon." The second, weighing more than 27,000 pounds, was considered an improved version of Oregon and was named "Peacemaker."

So armed, the ship was ordered to Washington, DC, where considerable interest was aroused both in official circles and among the general public. Three special trips were arranged for high-ranking guests, and on each occasion Peacemaker was fired several times, to the wonder of the civilians aboard.

One such cruise was arranged for 29 February — 1844 being a leap year — for the entertainment of President John Tyler, members of the cabinet and other guests, including a former New York state senator, Col. David Gardiner, and his attractive daughter, Julia. Miss Gardiner had caught the eye of the widowed Tyler, who wished very much to make her his First Lady.

It was later reported that Julia Gardiner, on the night of 27 February, had a frightening dream that while she was aboard a warship a pair of white horses came toward her, each bearing a skeleton as its rider. One skeleton had her father's face.

Julia went to her father that morning and told him of her nightmare. The vessel of which she had dreamed resembled the new *Princeton* closely. Terrified by her experience, she begged Colonel Gardiner not to take the planned cruise. He brushed aside his daughter's fears as the result of "overwrought nerves," and refused to change their plans.

A similar dream caused Anne Gilmer, wife of the recently-appointed secretary of the navy, Thomas Gilmer, to plead with her husband to forego the trip aboard the *Princeton.* He also rejected the idea of staying ashore on such an important occasion. Further pleas by Anne Gilmer, even after she and her husband were aboard the ship, failed to change his mind.

That day, 29 February, the *Princeton* sailed down the Potomac River on a combination pleasure and trial run, carrying President Tyler, members of his cabinet and some two hundred other guests.

When the ship was well under way, Secretary Gilmer requested that Peacemaker be fired, as it had on the three previous Potomac junkets. Captain Stockton issued the order — as he later testified, against his better judgement, because he felt the gun was still overheated from previous test firings that day.

The giant cannon burst. When the smoke had cleared, the dead scattered about the deck included Abel P. Upshur, secretary of state; Secretary Gilmer; Beverly Kennon, chief of the navy's Bureau of Construction, Equipment and Repairs; Rep. Virgil Maxey of Maryland; David Gardiner; and a sixth victim, a servant of the President. Twenty others, including Captain Stockton, had been injured.

Julia Gardiner, who survived the disaster unhurt, later married Tyler.

The *Princeton* saw service with the navy's Home Squadron until 1847 before being assigned to duty in the Mediterranean. When the ship returned to the United States, in June 1849, she was relegated to inactivity at the Boston Navy Yard and eventually was scrapped.

Princeton number two came into being less than two years after the demise of her predecessor. Designed with the racy lines of a clipper ship, the 177-foot vessel was laid down in June 1851, at the Boston Navy Yard. Timbers salvaged during the scrapping of the first *Princeton* were used. The original engine designs were employed, with new boilers and propellers added.

Fitted out for duty with Commodore Perry's squadron in the Far East, the *Princeton* sailed out of Baltimore 18 November 1852 with orders to join the *Mississippi* off Annapolis. However, the *Princeton* developed boiler trouble and was forced to pull into Norfolk, Virginia, while the *Mississippi* continued on to the Pacific. The *Princeton* was not destined ever to make it to Perry's command.

For a portion of 1853, *Princeton* II was the flagship of the navy's Eastern Squadron, with the assignment of protecting the fisheries off Nova Scotia. After a stint of operation out of New York, in October 1854, the vessel was ordered to the Gulf of Mexico and the West Indies for patrol duty.

In June 1855, the *Princeton* returned to Norfolk, and in 1857 was stationed at Philadelphia as a receiving ship. In 1866, she was ordered sold.

Princeton number three was listed on naval records as a "composite gunboat." Unlike her two previous namesakes, she had a considerable wartime career.

The ship was laid down in May 1896, and commissioned at Philadelphia a year later with Comdr. C. H. West as skipper. Soon after acceptance trials, conducted off Delaware Bay, the gunboat set sail for Key West to join the North Atlantic Fleet at the outbreak of the Spanish-American War.

The *Princeton's* wartime service began with patrol duty off the Yucatan Peninsula, Guatemala, and Florida through the final months of 1898. Early in 1899, the gunboat passed through the Mediterranean and the Suez Canal to join the Asiatic Fleet in the Philippine Islands.

When the Spanish-American War ended, the *Princeton* sailed throughout the Philippine Islands, distributing the peace proclamation to towns and villages. Actual peace was slow in coming there, however, and the *Princeton* at various times served to blockade the Lingayen Gulf ports of St. Vincent and Musa.

When local disturbances broke out on the island of Luzon, the *Princeton* carried troops to San Fabian, took cavalrymen from Vigan to Lingayen, and filled a number of other roles ranging from picking up surrendered arms and conveying dispatches, to taking stores to U.S. Marines at Subic Bay.

During the balance of the *Princeton's* Philippine tour, the ship took formal possession of the Babuyan and Bataan Islands, patrolled off Luzon, and served as station ship at Iloilo and Cebu.

From the Philippine area, the *Princeton* was ordered to cruise Chinese waters during the Boxer Rebellion, operating between Hong Kong and Woosung. Returning to the Philippines in December 1900, she continued on duty there until July 1902.

Serving as a survey ship at Zamboanga and Dumanquilas Bay, and visiting Japan, the *Princeton* returned to the U.S. for decommissioning in June 1903. Two years of inactivity were ended by recommissioning at the Mare Island Navy Yard in California and attachment to the Pacific Squadron.

From May 1905 to March 1907, she patrolled the West Coast before being dispatched to Nicaragua to protect American interests in that country. Then back to Bremerton, Washington, for a second decommissioning.

Again recommissioned, *Princeton* sailed 28 November 1909 for duty with the Nicaraguan Expeditionary Squadron, "showing the U.S. flag" off Nicaragua and El Salvador until March 1911. Next came nearly four years as station ship in American Samoa, then a period as a training vessel at Seattle before her final decommissioning in 1919. In June that year, *Princeton* number three was struck from the navy's roster and ordered sold.

CHAPTER II

From Cruiser to Carrier

FOR DECADES THE NAME *Princeton* lay dormant. Then, with World War II already in progress and the United States close to military involvement, the keels for nine cruisers were laid down at the New York Shipbuilding Corporation, Camden, NJ, not far from the site of the Battle of Princeton, as well as the town and the university of the same name.

Designated light cruisers (CLs), the planned warships were to be named, according to naval custom, after various U.S. cities. Work on the first of the vessels got underway 1 May 1941 — seven months before Pearl Harbor.

While the hulls were only partially completed, a critical need for aircraft carriers in the forward areas of the Pacific brought a shift in plans. The nine cruisers were ordered to be finished as light carriers (CVLs). This necessitated a change, again in keeping with naval custom, that flattops be named after battles or former navy vessels.

Thus the first of the new carriers was altered from USS *Amsterdam* to USS *Independence*, which in turn gave that name to the nine-ship class. Other members of the Independence class were: the *Princeton* (started as the *Tallahassee*), the *Belleau Wood* (*New Haven*), *Cowpens* (*Huntington*), *Monterey* (*Dayton*), *Langley* (*Fargo*), *Cabot* (*Wil-*

mington), *Bataan* (*Buffalo*), and *San Jacinto* (*Newark*).

With the lines and engine powers of cruisers, Independence class carriers were capable of thirty-two knots, which placed them on a par with the biggest carriers in the U.S. fleet, from a speed standpoint. By contrast, other carriers, which were created by converting freighter hulls and became known as "baby" flattops, were slower and more vulnerable.

The ships of the Independence class displaced 11,000 tons, or 15,800 tons fully loaded. The overall length was 623 feet. While the basic beam was 71 1/2 feet, the width of the flight deck itself was 109 feet. They were designed to carry a complement of 1,569 men and operate with a total of 45 aircraft. Initially, the plane "mix" included dive bombers as well as fighter and torpedo planes, but the dive bombers were removed from all Independence class carriers early in their careers.

Ships with broader beams, in relation to their length, are inclined to pitch in heavy weather — bob on their longitudinal axis — while vessels with greater relative length have a tendency to roll from side-to-side. The Independence class carriers were "rollers."

All nine in the group saw extensive action during the war in the Pacific.

Wartime pressures served to appreciably shorten shipbuilding timetables and cut down on the normal frills of launching.

The *Independence* slid into the Delaware River in August 1942, and the *Princeton* followed suit in October. A newspaper account said the *Princeton* was launched "with informality" and the accompanying twenty-five dollar affair was in keeping with the cost limit prescribed by the navy.

Mrs. Harold Dodds, wife of the president of Princeton University, christened the new carrier by cracking a traditional bottle of champagne against the chrome yellow-painted hull. The ship's gray "battle dress" was applied later.

There were no formal speeches during the launching ceremony, and the hundreds of shipyard workers within eyesight paused only long enough in their work to watch the *Princeton* become waterborne.

With the *Princeton* pulled into a fitting dock, members of the outfitting detail began reporting to the New York Shipbuilding Company yards and were assigned to nearby living quarters. The initial group consisted of about 300 enlisted crew members who had survived the 26 October 1942 sinking of the USS *Hornet*, as well as officers who had served on the *Hornet* or other carriers, including the *Wasp*, the *Saratoga*, and the *Enterprise*. Among the ex-*Hornet* officers assigned to the *Princeton* was the new carrier's designated skipper, Capt. George R. Henderson, who had started his navy career as a "white hat," or enlisted man, and who attained the three-star rank of vice admiral before his eventual retirement.

In addition to the nucleus of carrier veterans, there were a number of officers who had seen combat duty in the Pacific on battleships and cruisers.

These war-experienced officers provided invaluable counsel on more than one occasion during the later stages of the *Princeton*'s completion. One such incident involved the 5-inch, 38-caliber single guns to be mounted on the carrier's forecastle and fantail. Captain Henderson and Lt. Comdr. Walt Phaler, the *Princeton*'s gunnery officer, who had served on the cruiser *Chester*, insisted that 40-millimeter quad mounts, with four barrels each, would provide much better anti-aircraft protection than the slower firing, single-shot weapons. There was resistance to the shift on the grounds that the change would ruin the morale of shipyard workers who had been laboring around the clock to finish the *Princeton* ahead of time. Henderson and Phaler won their point, and the 40-millimeter quads proved their worth many times later in the Pacific.

While the conversion of cruiser hulls provided sorely needed carriers, there were unique problems. Gun turret armor, ammunition hoists, and other cruiser equipment had to be removed and/or designed out of basic cruiser plans. Smoke stacks had to be retrunked to the starboard side. Heavy bulkheads to wall off the carrier's high octane gasoline storage areas had to be erected in sections, because already built decks prevented easier one-piece installation.

The biggest problem was that of overall ship balance. The original hull was not designed to carry a towering structure topped by a massive flight deck. To prevent the altered vessels from being top-heavy, naval architects considered the use of ballast to make the ships ride lower in the water and, therefore, more stably. Probable loss in speed, stemming from the 6,000 tons of added weight, ruled out that approach. The answer came in the form of blisters, or bulges, on each side of the hull. The weight of the carrier superstructure on the starboard side was overcome by pouring cement into the port blister. An all-out effort was made to eliminate all possible weight above the water line to enhance stability. No possible sacrifice was deemed minor — down to the replacement of all doors to officer's quarters by much lighter cloth curtains.

On every warship, personnel attached to the vessel itself make up the "ship's company." On a carrier, those serving the squadrons are a separate entity — the "air group."

The term "ship's company" was a particularly fitting designation, because an efficient cruiser, battleship, or aircraft carrier must be operated in a business-like manner. The crew is organized into various departments with specialized assignments — engineering for example. Each unit in turn is divided into two watch groups — nautically titled port and starboard — to provide alternating duty staffs.

In the three months following the *Princeton*'s launching, arriving officers and men were dovetailed into the organization wherever their individual talents appeared best-suited. The *Princeton*'s navigator and quartermasters busied themselves making hand corrections to literally hundreds of navigational charts in the ship's allowance, inserting data provided by the Navy Hydrographic Office. With no routine duties to be performed until the ship was ready for them, the crew underwent training and instruction. The Camden YMCA made its facilities available so the non-swimmers could be taught and the swimmers could exercise.

As the time for commissioning the carrier drew near, there were some 600 crew members on board the *Princeton* and an additional 450 at the receiving station in Philadelphia.

Meanwhile, a few miles north of Philadelphia at the Willow Grove Naval Air Station, Air Group 23 was commissioned with orders to begin training as the *Princeton*'s first flight unit. Philadelphia provided more than enough entertainment for all hands, but foul wintry weather cut flying time and ground training to a minimum. As a result, the decision was made to shift the group to the marine base at Parris Island, South Carolina.

The move was carried out 6 January 1943 with the first plane taking off from Willow Grove at 1000. By 1700, the last of the F4F fighters, TBM torpedo bombers, and SBD dive bombers were tied down at Parris Island.

With the *Princeton* due to be commissioned 25 February training was stepped up sharply — ground school, aircraft and fighter direction procedures, and enemy plane and ship identification. W. L. Curtis, then a lieutenant and the new *Princeton*'s landing signal officer-to-be, arrived at Parris Island to conduct field-carrier landing practice. This consisted of landings on the airfield with procedures and conditions resembling, as much as possible, those on a carrier.

Curtis also was a survivor of the *Hornet* sinking and, like Henderson, reached the rank of vice admiral before retiring.

Lt. John J. Becker was to be in charge of the *Princeton*'s V-4 Division. He put in an appearance to establish contact with the squadron personnel he would be working with to keep the planes airworthy — no matter what operational or combat damage they might encounter. The necessary intermingling of personalities and talents — between the ship's company and air group — was taking shape.

Tragedy struck the air group in the second month at Parris Island. Two pilots, Albert W. Robbins and Richard P. Selman, were killed when the SNJ training and utility plane they were flying crashed at Hilton Head Island, not far from their home base. Just a short week later, Ens. Robert Jefferson Young was killed when he made a forced water landing. His F4F fighter plane turned over and trapped him in the cockpit.

The other members of the group had little time to dwell on these sad losses. They were involved in carrier landing qualifications at Norfolk and catapult takeoff checkouts at Philadelphia, where the *Princeton* was being given her final touches.

From the Camden yards of the New York Shipbuilding Company, the carrier was towed across the Delaware River to the Philadelphia Navy Yard on the morning of 25 February. Almost as soon as the ship was tied up, the 450 men who had been quartered at the receiving station went aboard and were assigned their berths. The operation went off so smoothly that the first meal on the new *Princeton* was served that day. All hands were fed within one hour.

The formal commissioning took place that afternoon. George A. Brakeley, vice-president of Princeton University, was on hand to present a silver ladle, tray, and punch bowl on behalf of alumni and friends of the school. The silver set was described as a replica of one made by Paul Revere and later displayed at the Boston Museum.

Plans had called for the *Princeton* to be ready to depart on her shakedown cruise six weeks after the commissioning. However, a number of leaks were discovered when the ship's fuel tanks were tested and the timetable had to be altered accordingly.

A continuing topic of discussion was the raid on Tokyo by Col. James Doolittle's group, who launched their Army Air Corps B-25 bombers from the carrier *Hornet*. Lt. Comdr. Henry L. Miller, commanding officer of Fighting 23, gave his squadron and members of Torpedo 23 an "educated" account of the Doolittle exploit. Miller had trained the air corps pilots in carrier takeoffs and had been aboard the *Hornet* as an advisor.

Shortly thereafter, the Air Group 23 commander, Lt. Comdr. George B. Chafee, was detached to become air officer on the new carrier *Cabot*. Miller was named to succeed Chafee.

Flight training centered around night missions and night carrier landings. The pace was stepped up to a point where the marines on the Parris Island base complained their sleep was being interfered with and guests at the base officer's club — particularly the ladies — expressed their fright, if not outright terror, at the constant flow of air traffic low over the club roof. The night-flying schedule was curtailed, but by then most of the necessary training had been accomplished.

"In spite of occasional differences between the marines and the air group," said Commander Miller, "we gave the marines a party at the officers' club to show our appreciation for our use of their facilities. Memories of that occasion lingered long afterward."

In mid-April, President Franklin D. Roosevelt visited Parris Island. All planes of the air group were flown in parade formation while the commander in chief inspected the balance of the group's personnel on the ground.

In the final two weeks of their stay at Parris Island, pilots of Fighting 23 experienced a series of crash landings.

"First, it was Ens. Walter J. Kirschke, who was forced down on a swamp on Hunting Island," Commander Miller said. "Then Ens. Robert S. Tyner went down on the Hunting Island beach, and within two days ensigns William G. Buckelew and Jack D. Madison had the bad experience of making forced landings in swamps. Fortunately, none of the pilots was injured."

As their scheduled rendezvous with the *Princeton* neared, three pilots — Madison, Tyner, and Jack Abell — became newlyweds in ceremonies performed at the marine base chapel.

"On May 18 we received orders to leave Parris Island and

proceed to Pungo, an auxiliary field near Norfolk," Commander Miller said. "Pungo turned out to be quite a spot. Virginia Beach was only a few miles away. The boys became acquainted with a navy nurse rest facility, so there were frequent travelers to the beach in the Pungo milk wagon."

At the Navy Yard in Philadelphia, the pre-shakedown period was put to good advantage with crew training in a variety of subjects. A majority of the officers and enlisted men never had been to sea before.

The *Princeton* crew was deep in a variety of trials: a test run underway down the Delaware River and back, firing of dead weight shots while alongside the dock to test the two catapults, a wide range of drills — man overboard, fire, collision, abandon ship — and the tremendous task of loading provisions, stores, ammunitions, and fuel into a new and previously empty ship.

On the social side, all hands welcomed a three-section liberty schedule, which meant both officers and men could go ashore in Philadelphia three nights out of four.

"This was a strenuous period for the personnel officer, chaplain and division officers," said Lt. Comdr. Edward L. Clifford, aide to the ship's executive officer. "The men found plenty of trouble, although most of it was relatively harmless.

"Two parties were held which were worthy of note. On March 17, a beer party was given in one of the base buildings, to which Ilona Massey, Arthur Treacher and other cast members of the Ziegfield Follies — then in a pre-New York opening run in Philadelphia — were invited. The Follies girls performed, danced with the men and generally provided a pleasant evening for all. Then in April, the ship's officers held a party at the Warwick Hotel in Philadelphia, attended by wives, sweethearts and other guests. This was the first time the officers had gotten together socially as a group, and proved a great success," Commander Clifford said.

The *Princeton* left Philadelphia 19 May and headed down the Delaware River. At the mouth of Delaware Bay, off Cape May, the carrier was joined by a pair of destroyers, the *Stockton* and the *Stevenson*. They escorted her to Chesapeake Bay — a run which took just one day, but which was marked by a rash of seasickness among the officers and men who were experiencing their first real taste of wind and wave.

For the next four days, the *Princeton* cruised up and down Chesapeake Bay to enable the air group pilots to practice landings and takeoffs. There were the expected number of barrier crashes and other mishaps, but no injuries occurred. With this vital operation completed, the carrier tied up at Norfolk to take aboard supplies needed for the shakedown cruise.

CHAPTER III

Shakedown Cruise

RAPIDLY THE BULLET AND GUN approached the point of union. The air group pilots and crewmen were fine-tuned in their airborne military skills as the ship's company became a working team prepared to take the carrier into combat.

From Pungo, the planes were flown to Norfolk, and loaded aboard the *Princeton* on 27 May. The following morning, the carrier sailed out of Hampton Roads and headed down the Chesapeake Bay bound for Trinidad. The final step in the training process had begun — the shakedown cruise.

The West Indies island of Trinidad was selected because it lay on the Gulf of Paria, a body of water sixty miles long and thirty miles wide. Most importantly, the gulf has only two entrances — somewhat dramatically named the Dragon's Mouth and the Serpent's Mouth — both of which could easily be protected against the entry of enemy submarines. This made the gulf an ideal spot for U.S. carriers and their air groups to "shake down," to discover any flaws that might need correction.

The *Princeton* was joined by three escorting destroyers — *Pullam*, *Ringgold*, and *Wadsworth* — for the trip to Trinidad. On 2 June the four-ship flotilla reached the gulf and anchored at Port of Spain.

In the following four weeks, the pilots and air crews were put through a grueling six-days-a-week schedule, literally from sunrise to sunset — and, in the case of night carrier landing qualification, well into the hours of darkness.

An all-out effort was made by officers and petty officers to emphasize the need for caution in the hazardous carrier operations. The first edition of the ship's newspaper, christened *The Tiger Rag* after the Princeton University mascot, carried a plea by the ship's skipper, Captain Henderson, himself a *Hornet* survivor. The newspaper was circulated as the *Princeton* entered the Gulf of Paria to commence the shakedown trials. Henderson wrote:

> This is a fast-moving war. Everyone must keep his eyes and ears alert. It has been said before but cannot be repeated too often: one or more among you, because of carelessness, will not return from this cruise. The experience of other carriers on their shakedowns indicates this.
>
> Dangers aboard a carrier are more numerous than aboard most naval vessels. Planes continually landing and taking off render a careless person unsafe on the flight deck. Elevators without guards are a constant hazard. Plans-of-the-day have emphasized the dangers of propellers in motion.
>
> Handling ammunition, ascending and descending numerous ladders, and working at our various jobs with potentially dangerous equipment, calls for eternal vigilance. While we keep our conscious mind on the immediate task at hand, let's keep our subconscious on the goal for which we fight.
>
> It is our obligation to do our work safely.

Aircraft carrier landings and takeoffs were particularly awe-inspiring to non-flying personnel, a precision performance that seemed to ask more of those involved than should be expected of any human.

Takeoffs were divided between down-the-deck runs and catapult launches. In either case, the carrier was turned into the wind and sufficient ship speed attained to create a thirty–thirty-two knot air flow over the deck from bow to stern. This gave the planes being launched enough lift to become airborne, and those coming in for landings the proper conditions to approach the bobbing and rolling deck at a minimum speed, leading up to the final instant of flight.

More often than not, takeoffs immediately preceded the landing sequence, with one group of planes heading skyward moments before those they were relieving came back aboard. Always the emphasis was on swift execution, since the carrier and escorting vessels were more vulnerable to enemy sub attack when cruising on a predictable course.

Key figures in the carrier landing operations were the pilot and the landing signal officer. Each had to have complete confidence in the other.

The landing signal officer, or LSO, invariably was a pilot himself. As such, the LSO fully understood the problems faced by the flier, and the demands placed upon him. Whenever possible, the LSO would spend pre-cruise time with the pilots he would be working with later at sea. During their tour of duty together, the LSO and the airmen would exchange thoughts and suggestions in an effort to make a highly risky business as safe as possible. If a pilot made a landing the LSO considered poor enough to have endangered the carrier and deck crews, as well as putting the pilot and plane in jeopardy, the signal officer would visit the ready room to lay it on the line.

On carriers like the *Princeton*, the landing signal officer's duty station consisted of a seemingly flimsy platform jutting from the aft end of the flight deck on the port side. Standing there, his job was to guide each incoming plane by means of a pair of paddles, one in each hand. In night operations, the paddles were replaced by a pair of lighted wands. The LSO followed the course of the plane with the help of the wingtip and other plane lights.

Basic signals showed the pilot whether he was coming in too high (paddles raised from the horizontal position to form a V), or too low (paddles forming an inverted V). If the plane was too slow, the signal consisted of a paddle motion resembling a swimmer's breast stroke. The need for an increased angle of bank was indicated by tilted paddles.

The most crucial signals of all were those for a wave-off and landing go-ahead. The former — paddles criss-crossed repeatedly over the LSO's head — was an order to the pilot to add speed fast and turn to port, then go around in the landing pattern for another attempt.

The landing go-ahead involved a chopping motion with the right paddle across the LSO's chest. At that sign, the pilot cut the throttle and put the plane in a nosehigh attitude to catch a deck cable with the craft's extended tail hook. The cable permitted the plane to continue only a few yards. If the cable was not engaged, the plane crashed into the cable barrier forward on the flight deck.

When the cable was successfully caught, members of the flight deck crew scrambled to the plane's tail as fast as possible to disengage the hook, permitting the pilot to taxi out of the way of the next incoming plane.

The wings were folded as the pilot taxied, and then the plane either was parked on the flight deck or was sent down on the forward elevator to the hangar deck for refueling, rearming, and any needed repairs.

Understandably, mishaps were not uncommon. The flight deck scene at best was one of strong wind, a rolling or pitching deck, powerful airplanes carrying live ammunition and highly volatile fuel, and — during times of combat — the handling of aircraft coming back bullet-riddled or flak-damaged, perhaps with a wounded man in the cockpit. There were barrier crashes aboard the *Princeton*, but no serious damage or injury resulted.

On the second day in the gulf, three of the fighter pilots lost their way, but managed to land at Carupano, Venezuela, the nearest point on the mainland. None of the trio, Ensigns Abell, Tyner, or William Buckelew, could speak Spanish. But they were able to communicate with those in charge of the Venezuelan airfield, and got word back to the *Princeton* that they were safe.

Two days later, Ens. Oscar Cantrell failed to return to the carrier after a routine flight. He was not found, and no reason could be established for his disappearance.

The grueling pace set during the month-long stay in the gulf was indicated by the number of landings made — 1,242, which long stood as a record for any comparable carrier during a shakedown cruise. The squadrons became the first to qualify in night carrier landings.

Mondays were designated rest and relaxation days. Half of the air group, and the same percentage of the carrier crew, were given shore liberty between the hours of 1100 and 1800. The fortunate ones on any given Monday took off at 1100 sharp to head to the Maqueripe Beach Club for a swim, basketball, or baseball. Others zeroed in on Port of Spain itself and the Queens Park Hotel Bar, famed for its Planter's Punch.

An important side benefit of the shakedown was the rapport

that developed between the ship's crew and air group personnel. The former came to realize they were to go into the combat area with well-trained and highly competent squadrons.

"Everyone was well pleased with our group," said Lieutenant Commander Clifford. "It should be noted also that Air Group Commander Miller had really done a job in selling the *Princeton* to the pilots during the forming period. They were as enthusiastic about being attached to the *Princeton* as the ship's officers themselves."

That spirit carried over to the men on the *Princeton*'s escort destroyers. At one point, a fight broke out ashore between sailors from the *Ringgold* — a member of the *Princeton* flotilla — and bluejackets from the carrier *Belleau Wood*. Their difference of opinion concerned the relative merits of the two flattops.

As a final exercise before the *Princeton*'s departure from Trinidad, a realistic abandon-ship drill was staged, in which one-third of the men literally went over the side. A six-knot running tide provided an added element of excitement as motor launches picked the life-jacketed figures out of the sea. A few newer members of the crew were nonswimmers and had to be retrieved from the end of the fantail lines, which they had refused to relinquish.

As June drew to a close, the *Princeton* steamed out of the Gulf of Paria, headed for Philadelphia, and escorted by two destroyers, the *McKee* and *Dashiell*. Off Trinidad, the carrier made a high-speed run, reaching thirty-three knots in a choppy sea — a performance deemed more than acceptable.

Nearing Delaware Bay, the *Princeton* and her destroyers were joined by the *Belleau Wood* and that carrier's escorts. Together, they engaged in gunnery practice, attempting to down a target drone. The gunners on the two carriers missed on each try, and the drone went down eventually under fire from one of the destroyers.

One hundred and fifty miles from landfall, the *Princeton* launched all planes, with their destination the Willow Grove Naval Air Station, as the carrier continued on to the Philadelphia Navy Yard.

"Willow Grove had changed since our departure in January," said Commander Miller. "There were trees, lawns, and paved streets, instead of the mud and slush we experienced earlier in the year."

As the *Princeton* was being provided with gear and equipment the shakedown cruise had indicated were needed, one-half the crew was given a five-day leave, with the others going on leave when these returned. Similar leaves were granted to the personnel of the air group.

The fighter squadron was supplied with new F6F Grumman Hellcats, replacing their F4F Wildcats, the plane which had established such outstanding records at Guadalcanal and elsewhere. The pilots had been checked out in the F6F while at Trinidad, and were able to adapt to the change readily.

Advent of the F6F represented a considerable improvement. The F4F was driven by a 1200 horsepower engine and had a top speed of about 300 miles per hour. The F6F had 2000 horsepower and a top speed of over 400 miles per hour. The latter also had a considerably higher landing speed, a difference of prime consideration in the case of pilots operating on the smaller CVLs.

By 21 July the *Princeton* and Air Group 23 were deemed ready to go to war.

CHAPTER IV

Time to Go

AIR GROUP PERSONNEL WERE ordered to be back aboard the carrier by mid-afternoon on 20 July, which posed a number of problems with half the squadron members plunged into the pleasures of New York, Philadelphia, and points east and west.

The ship's officers experienced similar difficulties rounding up crewmen, twenty-two of whom either missed the sailing time accidentally, or jumped ship intentionally. All of these were rounded up, eventually, and disciplined to varying degrees, depending on their intent and explanations.

At dawn on 21 July the *Princeton* sailed down the Delaware River and Bay with orders to join the *Belleau Wood,* then proceed to the Panama Canal. Passage through the Canal was made on 26 July and that night liberty parties were put ashore to take in the attractions of Balboa, Canal Zone, including a drink known as the Blue Moon, which cost the whistle-provoking price of one U.S. dollar, and consisted of a lot of orangeade and very little, if any, alcohol. These were usually consumed by the local bar girls while their male companions were being served cheap whiskey.

The Panamanian constabulary was rated less than understanding in dealing with several problems involving members of the

Princeton group, all of which were ironed out by the time the carrier sailed.

The two CVLs, *Princeton* and *Belleau Wood*, were joined by the new big carrier *Lexington* as they left the Canal Zone on 28 July under directive to proceed to Pearl Harbor. Providing escort were six destroyers, *Guest, Stevens, Sigsbee, Wadsworth,* and *Harrison*, as well as the *Princeton*'s Trinidad compatriot, the *Ringgold*.

As this squadron-in-transit moved into the open Pacific, the war suddenly seemed soberingly close. The protested training-grind of the immediate past took on a new meaning.

Adding to this feeling was the introduction of censorship. It was no longer permissible for those aboard to write home details of where they were, where they were headed, or what they were doing militarily. Editing of homeward-bound letters written by crew members was done by ship's officers, while air group mail was bluepenciled by squadron officers. This resulted in some embarrassment and resentment all around at the outset, but soon faded into a state of inconsequence. In time, censorship became such an accepted part of shipboard life that censors were put in a position of sharing the most intimate details of many a marriage and other relationships. Few, if any, such mail monitors ever violated their position.

The 3,000-mile voyage from the western mouth of the Canal to Hawaii was conducted in keeping with wartime conditions. The three carriers — all new and as yet untried in combat — and their escorting destroyers operated as a task unit in enemy territory. The seas around them were, in fact, just that — a hunting ground for enemy submarines.

During the long trip, exercises were conducted to familiarize fighter pilots with the process of being directed into battle by the carrier's fighter direction team in the combat information center. Pilots from the *Princeton* also took turns flying combat air patrols with their counterparts from the *Lexington* and *Belleau Wood*.

A friendly, and at the same time valuable, rivalry developed between the pilots of the *Princeton* and *Belleau Wood*. If the *Belleau Wood* air patrol became airborne even a few seconds faster than the *Princeton* group, the *Princeton* air officer called a pilot's meeting and expressed his disappointment in more than a few well-chosen words. Usually, the launch rate showed considerable improvement the next time around.

Newer members of the ship's company for the first time had an opportunity to practice keeping station in a cruising formation — maintaining the proper distances from neighboring ships, and following precisely the speed set by the lead vessel in the group.

The ship's gunners were also given a chance to brush up on their marksmanship, including night firing, which was received by some of the air group as an entertaining, Fourth-of-July touch.

Two days out of Pearl Harbor, the *Princeton* and her air group received orders to carry out, along with the squadrons on the other two carriers, a series of simulated air attacks against various targets on the island of Oahu. The pilots and air crewmen welcomed this development, because it meant they would be ashore immediately after the attack exercise was completed.

"The simulated attacks were carried out successfully," said Miller, "with no interceptions by army fighters, and our planes landed at Barber's Point at 0900 that morning. This naval air station recently had been completed, consisting of 26,000 acres, with runways thousands of feet in length.

"Transportation was readily available, the beds had Simmons mattresses, and the officers' club was quickly given a favorable rating, except that other air groups were already on the base and it was sometimes a bit hard to get by them to the bar."

Arrival of the *Lexington, Belleau Wood* and *Princeton* brought to seven the number of combat carriers at Pearl Harbor, the most that ever had been there at one time. In addition to the newcomers, the carriers on hand were the *Yorktown, Essex, Independence* and the Royal (British) Navy's *Victorious*. Allied capabilities were drawing close to the point of a gigantic Pacific rebound.

The newly arrived fighter squadrons were placed under the jurisdiction of the Army Interceptor Command. This meant that one division of four planes from Fighting 23 was on alert daily, and more often than not scrambled to check an assigned area, or to take a look at an incoming plane or ship.

The days and nights were rife with rumors — the scuttlebutt mill was in high gear. Stories about the air group's immediate future ran the gamut of human imagination; but for three weeks there were only the everyday routine flights, fuel consumption tests, gunnery hops, and the inevitable pre-dawn combat air patrols.

Wherever possible, liberty groups were given an opportunity to visit Honolulu. The immediate Waikiki area was ruled out-of-bounds, however, because of a local outbreak of dengue fever, a highly infectious viral disease and one of the many medical problems encountered by service personnel during wartime. This particular illness causes severe joint pains, headaches, and a rash.

Twenty-one August brought another medical development. *Princeton* and Air Group 23 personnel were informed they were about to head for the combat zone and needed tetanus shots. This done, all hands were ordered aboard the carrier, and the planes were loaded. One notable change was made — the SBD dive bombers were removed from all CVL rosters, and additional fighter planes, with a dozen pilots transferred from Fighting Six, were added to replace them. The *Princeton* now carried twenty-four F6F Hellcat fighters and nine TBF torpedo bombers.

For some reason, which was never really set forth, the carrier's complement of armor-piercing bombs — used primarily by dive bombers — remained on board throughout the *Princeton*'s career.

While the ship's officers and crew were being briefed separately, air personnel were called together and told they were to operate with the *Belleau Wood* in supplying air cover for the occupation of Baker Island. A U.S. possession since 1936, the deserted atoll, located more than 1,200 miles southwest of Pearl Harbor and a short distance above the equator, had been abandoned in 1942. Now, the United States planned to construct an airfield there for land-based bombers to carry out raids on Japanese installations, including Tarawa, 700 miles away, in the Gilbert Island group.

For pilots and air crewmen, who had been in training so long for this moment, the word that Japanese planes might well be encountered during the Baker operation was intriguing news.

The *Princeton*'s first war mission began 25 August. The carrier left Pearl Harbor with the *Belleau Wood*, six transports carrying troops and supplies, and four escorting destroyers: *Spence, Trathen, Boyd* and *Bradford*.

The task group commander was Rear Adm. Arthur W. Radford, who came aboard with his staff, taking over the captain's quarters and the navigator's sea cabin in the *Princeton*'s island structure. Admiral Radford later was to become chairman of the Joint Chiefs of Staff.

A full schedule of combat air patrols was flown from the two CVLs during daylight hours. For those not in the air, briefings were the order of the day. The air combat intelligence officers used slides, charts, and maps to give the fliers as much information as possible about Baker Island, its surrounding waters, the planned occupation, and enemy aircraft that might put in an appearance.

While the six-day voyage was generally uneventful, there was one mishap on the *Princeton*. Lt. (jg) Dixie Loesch, in attempting to land, instead went over the carrier's port side into the sea. Loesch escaped without major injuries, but his F6F, which had been the air group commander's favorite aircraft — he had dubbed it "The Imp" — was lost.

On 31 August the two carriers left the convoy to provide air cover while the transports continued on to the landing areas. The following dawn the first troops moved ashore, with *Princeton* planes overhead. The morning was without incident, but an hour after Loesch's division of four Hellcats had taken over the patrol duties, a four-engine Japanese patrol plane — designated by U.S. intelligence as the Emily type — was intercepted by Loesch's group. Loesch and his wingman made a single pass each at the intruder, and the Japanese plane went into the water, the first "kill" of this type of plane by any U.S. aircraft.

While the *Princeton* was being refueled on 2 September the *Belleau Wood* took over the air patrol assignment. The day passed without circumstance. The next day, with the *Princeton* back as "duty" carrier, things were different.

"At 1200 Lt. Sandy Crews took off from the *Princeton* with a six-plane flight," said Air Group Commander Miller. "An hour later another Japanese plane was intercepted and, after a running fight, hit the water. The *Princeton* had two to its credit and the *Belleau Wood* none.

"It looked as though the Japs were very regular and prompt about arriving over the same area on odd days about 1300 hours," Miller said. "Consequently, everyone wanted the noon flight, and the *Belleau Wood* fighter squadron indicated they thought the *Princeton* squadron was being favored.

"The admiral allowed the *Belleau Wood* pilots to take the Baker Island patrols. As luck would have it, on September 8 — an even day — two *Princeton* pilots, Lt. Harold Funk and Lt. (jg) Leslie Kerr, were patrolling the offshore area miles from Baker when, lo and behold, a Jap plane approached from a different direction than the earlier two. Number three hit the water in short order."

The Baker Island operation lasted until 16 September as far as the *Princeton* was concerned. It was a far different "ballgame" from amphibious landings yet to come in the Pacific theater. Baker had been unoccupied, except for scores of gooney birds, the black-footed albatross that can be so graceful in flight but a laughable lummox on the ground. The goonies at Johnston Island, west of Hawaii, at Baker Island, and elsewhere through the Pacific, became the butt of soldier and sailor alike, who got their kicks out of stretching trip wires across the area where the gooney birds made running attempts to become airborne. The result was a cartwheeling albatross, which usually just shook it off and tried again.

While operating in the Baker Island area, the *Princeton* crossed the equator — but the traditional initiation ceremony for neophytes had to be put off until another time.

Before the *Princeton* departed from Baker Island, a plane was flown to Canton Island to pick up mail. In this, the VF-23 executive officer, Lieutenant Funk, received orders to report to San Diego to assume command of a fighter squadron of his own.

There were "hot" rumors afoot at the time that the *Princeton* would be involved in upcoming attacks on the Japanese stronghold of Tarawa. Funk, who also had learned from his new orders that he had been promoted to lieutenant commander, didn't want to miss an action such as Tarawa promised to be. His orders were "forgotten" for the moment.

CHAPTER V

The Real War

VERY QUICKLY, SCUTTLEBUTT BECAME fact. Tarawa was to be the next target in the resurging U.S. drive back across the Pacific.

Again, the squadron air intelligence officers broke out maps, charts, and slides for briefing sessions as the *Princeton* and *Belleau Wood* sailed north to rendezvous with a task group capable of far more clout than was available in the Baker Island occupation.

The two CVLs joined the bigger carrier *Lexington*. Further enhancing the task group's firepower were three light cruisers, the *Santa Fe*, the *Birmingham*, and the *Mobile*; and ten destroyers, including the *Princeton*'s shakedown companion, the *Ringgold*, as well as the *Stevens*, the *Shroder*, the *Harrison*, the *Hazelwood*, the *John Rogers*, the *McKee*, the *Bancroft*, the *Caldwell*, and the *Coghlan*. The navy's ability to field a major striking force was growing impressively.

As the task group approached Tarawa, it was decided Makin Island also would be a target.

For the Makin Island strike, two *Princeton* fighter pilots, Lieutenant Crews and his wingman, Ens. "Junior" Godson, volunteered to accompany the torpedo bombers. With launch at 0330, the mission was a success. Japanese installations on Makin were bombed and strafed, and four enemy float planes were set afire and listed as destroyed.

The strike against Tarawa, launched an hour later, also culminated successfully. Returning pilots reported heavy anti-aircraft flak as they raked ground fortifications with their machine guns.

A combat air patrol in the early afternoon tallyhoed a lone Japanese torpedo plane. In a matter of seconds, a pair of *Princeton* pilots, Jack Madison and James Syme, joined forces to score Fighter 23's fourth "kill." The squadron had destroyed every one of the Japanese planes encountered to date.

The air group sustained its first combat loss during the Tarawa mission. One of the *Princeton*'s torpedo planes, piloted by Lt. (jg) Charles M. Bransfield, was seen making a forced landing in the sea, five miles off the island's shoreline. Bransfield and his men were observed getting out of the damaged plane before it sank and getting into a rubber life raft.

Unfortunately, at that point in the Pacific war, air-sea rescue techniques had not been developed to pick up survivors. After the occupation of Makin in 1944, it was learned from a Catholic priest on the island that the downed air crew had come ashore, been captured, and sent to Japan as prisoners-of-war.

As the carriers and their escorting warships pulled away from Tarawa, the task group commander messaged: "Congratulations to all hands. Your alertness in meeting the enemy highlighted the day. Well done!"

Next order of business: return to Pearl Harbor for repairs to the *Princeton*'s catapult, which had broken down during the raids on Makin and Tarawa. The trip back to Hawaii gave crew members with previous equator-crossing credentials a chance to initiate anyone who did not.

In the lore of the sea, those who have been duly inducted by King Neptune and his royal court after a crossing of the equator are designated shellbacks. Before their initiation, they are lowly pollywogs.

"Events leading up to Neptune's appearance were hectic," said Commander Miller. "For days before the actual ritual, a wide variety of haircuts could be observed about the carrier. It seems shellbacks would catch an unwary pollywog and treat him to a less than artistic hair trim. However, the worm turned.

"The evening before the scheduled convening of Neptune's court, Lt. Chuck Kenyon of the fighter squadron was called on the ship's loudspeaker to report to the flight deck. Kenyon and some fellow pollywogs realized this was actually a summons to a shellback-administered haircut. Kenyon and his companions holed up in the pilot's ready room and sent out word they were ready to receive any and all shellbacks.

"A band of shellbacks accepted the invitation, and the result was a real melee with chairs, coffee mugs, backpacks, chartboards, and even bodies flying every which way. Fortunately, the captain happened by the ready room, and quiet was restored for the time being."

The following morning, in the final moments of the induction ceremony, the shellbacks formed two lines on deck, with paddles in hands, and had their inning as all new hands ran the gauntlet before receiving cards attesting to their shellback status.

With catapult repaired and fresh supplies aboard, the *Princeton* was made ready for sea while the squadrons engaged in field carrier landings and gunnery drills — in between visits to Honolulu attractions.

On the quiet, lovely Hawaiian morning of 10 October Air Group Commander Miller received a telephone call. He was summoned to the *Princeton* by the ship's air officer. Things were happening "down south" — in the combat area of the Pacific.

Events moved at a rapid pace. The squadrons were recalled from the outlying airfield at Kaneohe to Ford Island, and the planes were loaded aboard the *Princeton*. Seven new pilots, all ensigns without combat experience, were put ashore and attached to Fighter Squadron One. In exchange, VF-23 received twelve of the other squadron's experienced flyers, two lieutenants, one lieutenant (jg), and nine ensigns.

By midnight 10 October — the same day Commander Miller had been called back to the *Princeton* — all personnel and equipment were aboard the carrier. Somehow, plane repairs, which had been expected to take days, had been accomplished in hours.

The following morning, 11 October, the *Princeton* left Pearl Harbor with a lone destroyer, the *Edwards*. As the two ships moved out to open sea, the task group that had just completed an attack on Wake Island was entering the harbor. The *Princeton* would have been part of that operation if it had not been for an inoperative catapult.

The *Edwards* served both as an anti-submarine escort and as a rescue vessel during flight operations. In the latter capacity, the destroyer cruised astern the carrier. In the event a plane went into the drink on takeoff or landing, the fast and highly maneuverable *Edwards* was there to pick up any surviving pilots or air crewmen.

Off Hawaii, all new pilots who had not been qualified were checked out in landing and takeoffs from the CVL. With this accomplished, the *Princeton* and *Edwards* turned to the southwest, bound for Espiritu Santo, largest island in the New Hebrides archipelago, recently renamed the Republic of Vanuatu. Espiritu Santo had become a major Allied staging base. During the nine-day voyage, the *Princeton* crossed the equator for the thirty-fifth time, and all pollywogs aboard were given a necessarily shortened welcome into King Neptune's realm.

On Sunday 17 October the two ships crossed the International Date Line, which meant the following day was Tuesday. Monday had been leap-frogged in the process. More than one Christmas day, or other normally important date, was lost this way at sea, but in wartime it didn't seem to matter that much.

Upon arrival at Espiritu Santo on 20 October Captain Henderson received orders teaming the *Princeton* with the carrier *Saratoga* — already at Espiritu — and other warships supporting the impending invasion of Bougainville, in the Solomon Islands. For two days the *Princeton* and *Saratoga* cruised offshore to give pilots, airmen, and ship's crew experience in working together.

Air group personnel were given orders by the *Princeton*'s first lieutenant to send home any gear not absolutely essential to the upcoming operation. Members of the ship's crew had gone through a similar "house-cleaning" earlier.

After five frenzied days of loading supplies and provisions, the *Princeton* and the *Saratoga* sailed from Espiritu on 29 October. They were accompanied by two anti-aircraft cruisers, *San Diego* and *San Juan*, and a half-dozen destroyers: *Hazelwood, Wickes, Lansdowne, Lardner, Farenholt* and *Meade*.

This task unit was directed to neutralize the Buka and Bonis airfields, at the northwestern tip of Bougainville, during the crucial first hours of invasion. The trip to the Solomons was uneventful except for a forced water landing by fighter pilot Syme, who experienced engine trouble while chasing after an unidentified plane. A destroyer was dispatched to look for Syme, and found him in his rubber raft, sampling some of the emergency rations from his back pack.

Throughout the first two days of November, bombing and strafing attacks were carried out against the two airfields. At the same time, troops and their supplies were being put ashore at Empress Augusta Bay, on the southern part of the island.

On the first day, one *Princeton* plane was lost in an emergency water landing, but the pilot was rescued. The following morning, a second plane went down during a strafing run and the pilot was lost.

The navy's high command was happy with the results of the two-day operation. The ships involved received this message: "Admiral Halsey has congratulated the task force on the strikes at Buka and says well done. As a result, Buka is not now contributing to the Jap war effort."

The *Princeton* and escort vessels pulled back to await further orders. On the evening of 4 November things were sufficiently calm to permit the showing of a movie on the carrier's hangar deck. While the film was still running, the air officers were called to the captain's quarters. A short time later other officers, including the squadron intelligence officers, were summoned. The word they received and quickly passed along to their groups: Attack Rabaul in the morning!

This was the "big time" Commander Miller had talked of with his men on more than one occasion. Rabaul, one of the enemy's principal western Pacific bases, now was serving as an anchorage and supply point for a task force of Japanese heavy cruisers and destroyers. This armada had been sent down from Truk to attack the invasion site at Empress Augusta Bay. Allied intelligence sources also had indications the Japanese were in the process of sending additional warships to Rabaul for the planned onslaught.

Led by the air group commander, five divisions of fighter planes — twenty Hellcats — took off from the *Princeton* at 0900 on 5 November, followed shortly thereafter by the bomb-carrying Torpedo 23. The order of the day: attack anything and everything in the Rabaul harbor or ashore!

Located at the northern end of New Britain Island, Rabaul, at that moment, was harboring a major segment of the Japanese Imperial Navy, with sufficient seapower to thwart the Bougainville landing.

Commander Miller described the scene as the *Princeton*'s fighters approached their target.

"The harbor was protected by an umbrella of terrific anti-aircraft fire, the like of which our boys had never experienced before and hope never to see again," he said. "Japanese fighter planes swarmed the skies — Zekes, Tonys, Haps, everything the enemy could make airborne. Hell had broken loose, literally, and planes seemed to fill every inch of the sky."

The *Princeton* and *Saratoga* pilots did their job so satisfactorily that the Japanese were unable to put enough ships into action to seriously interfere with the amphibious operation at Empress Augusta Bay.

In the dogfights that developed, *Princeton* fighter pilots shot down ten Japanese fighters. Two others were listed as "probables," and eight additional enemy aircraft were damaged. When the Hellcats and TBFs left Rabaul, Miller said, "the place was an inferno. Cruisers and destroyers were hit, some sunk, while Japanese planes were scattered all over the place, total wrecks."

The aerial battle cost Fighting 23 three pilots — J. D. Madison, J. A. Smith, and Richard O'Connell. The bombing raids saw three Torpedo 23 planes go down under the heavy anti-aircraft barrage. The planes lost were flown by George Scott, Charles Dyer, and William Fratus.

Many of the planes making it back to the carrier had been extensively damaged. Stanley Crockett, who was wounded while flying cover for the mission's air coordinator, the *Saratoga* air group commander, managed to land on the carrier in his Hellcat, which had been riddled with 277 bullet and shrapnel holes.

Crockett, and the man he had been assigned to protect, were jumped by a flight of Japanese planes. Though wounded and flying a badly shot-up plane, Crockett managed to shoot down one of his attackers. Later, he was unable to recall any details of his landing back on the *Princeton*.

The *Saratoga* air group commander sent the following message to be given to Crockett in sick bay: "Your courage, determination and loyalty will be a lasting inspiration to me. H. H. Caldwell."

Pilots' brushes with death in the skies sometimes prompted realizations of belief, of faith, which probably surprised the individual involved as much as, if not more than, the chaplain to whom they were declared.

"These were not the reactions of soft, sentimental, and certainly not effeminate, men," said Chaplain O. K. Olander. "They bespoke the inward feelings of the virile, red-blooded manhood of which our fighting forces are made up."

A flier who returned to the carrier from Rabaul with 185 bullet and shrapnel holes in his plane had nine Japanese Zeroes on his tail at one time, yet he still managed to successfully defend a *Princeton* torpedo bomber. Wounded in the head, wrist, leg, and foot, he landed on the *Princeton* and collapsed. He told the chaplain:

"Today, I became a humble man. All I can say is 'Thanks to God.' "

Another pilot was forced down with his crew of two in enemy territory. There wasn't time to break out the emergency rubber raft. The pilot's life jacket wouldn't inflate because the carbon-dioxide bottles had been jarred loose in the crash. He felt one of his crew slip from his grasp and disappear beneath the water's surface. After the pilot and the other crewmen were rescued, the former told the chaplain:

"Padre, I saw the Man. I'll never be closer to Him than I was then. I have no right to be here talking to you this minute except He was with me."

Chaplain Olander recalls many such solemn statements after combat missions. None were less flippant or more reverent than the brief comment of one aviator in describing his reaction to a close encounter with death: "I prayed like Hell."

While the task group had been operating off Rabaul, not a single Japanese plane was able to penetrate the combat air patrol perimeter and approach the carriers or their escorts.

As pilots and air crewmen were downing a welcome issue of brandy to settle their nerves, aerial photographs and pilot debriefing reports were scanned in great detail. They helped confirm preliminary indications that the bombing raids and air-to-air encounters at Rabaul had resulted in a clear cut victory for the U.S. Navy's air arm. The findings were relayed through the chain of command, and back by radio came enthusiastic congratulations from Adm. Bull Halsey, Gen. Douglas MacArthur, in the Philippines, and the Army Air Corps' Gen. Hap Arnold.

In addition to the beatings administered to the enemy ashore, afloat, and in the air, the Rabaul-Bougainville ventures brought a U.S. carrier task force closer to the prime air attack target in the western Pacific — Truk — than at any previous point since the tides of war began to turn. Moreover, what was described as the toughest engagement involving naval air units since the Battle of Midway had been carried out by a task unit dwarfed in size by those which followed. The members involved, and the results achieved, were not lost on either the Allied high command or the war lords in Tokyo.

CHAPTER VI

Target Hopping

BEGINNING IN EARLY NOVEMBER 1943 the *Princeton* and Air Group 23 went through a five-month period of hopping from one operation to another. The carrier and its squadrons were involved in combat strikes, support missions, and reconnaissance flights at Rabaul; Nauru; Wotje; Taroa; Palau Islands; New Guinea; and Truk.

The perimeter of war was moving steadily closer to the Japanese mainland.

Because there were indications the enemy planned to send additional warships to the Rabaul area, the *Princeton* hastily took aboard fresh supplies, munitions, and new aircraft at Espiritu, and then headed back to the Solomon Islands.

While Armistice Day, 11 November, was being observed in the U.S., the fighter and torpedo squadrons of the *Princeton* and *Saratoga* launched strikes against Rabaul. The weather was poor, but post-mission reports noted that the target had been saturated.

"Anti-aircraft fire was just as heavy as on our earlier strikes at Rabaul," said Commander Miller. "The Japanese had planes in the air everywhere, but we had learned from our previous experience."

Admiral Halsey expressed his satisfaction with the results: "You have dealt severe blows to the enemy. Your first attack on

Rabaul was another shot heard around the world. Your second was equally effective, although hampered by insufficient targets. I know you will carry out successfully future central Pacific operations. Good hunting and good luck."

Again hurriedly provisioned at Espiritu, and with fresh pilots brought aboard to fill out squadron rosters, the *Princeton* steamed toward new targets — enemy installations in and near the Gilbert Islands.

Nauru, an island just south of the equator which had been occupied and turned into an air base by the Japanese early in their drive across the Pacific, was attacked 19 November by a joint *Princeton-Saratoga* strike force. All the U.S. planes returned safely, and at least two Japanese fighters were destroyed in aerial combat over the target.

That night, Japanese aerial "snoopers" trailed the U.S. force, but were driven back by heavy anti-aircraft fire from the cruisers *San Juan* and *San Diego* and the nine destroyers, or "small boys," protecting the two carriers.

While cruising near the Gilberts, the *Princeton* developed an intense shaft vibration. The carrier was ordered to return to Pearl Harbor. The long trip was made in convoy with the battleships *Colorado* and *Tennessee*, five destroyers, seven transports, and a Landing Service Dock, most of them going back for repairs or alterations to prepare for upcoming operations.

Hawaii was reached 7 December, the second anniversary of the Japanese sneak attack on Pearl Harbor. Before the *Princeton* could settle in, word was received that the carrier's assigned berth would be needed by the *Lexington,* which had just been torpedoed near the Marshall Islands. The *Princeton* was ordered to proceed to the navy yard at Bremerton, Washington.

To the dismay of air group personnel, the squadrons were put ashore in Hawaii to await the return of the *Princeton* from Bremerton. All planes were off loaded at Ford Island, then flown to the island of Maui, where the lush pineapple and sugar cane fields had been interspersed with military installations, including operating and auxiliary airfields.

Some of the pilots' disappointment at not getting a trip back to the mainland was compensated for by a chance to visit the ranch of Mr. and Mrs. John E. Russell. There they were able to ride horseback and hike in the lava-red Maui hills when they weren't busy with routine training at the air base.

Before the *Princeton* left Pearl Harbor, the ship's well-liked executive officer, Comdr. John B. Moss, was detached to become chief of staff for Carrier Division Three. He was replaced on the *Princeton* by Commander John Murphy, an Annapolis grad who had some flight and shipboard experience, but most recently had been "flying a desk" stateside. Shifts in such key personnel on a combat vessel in wartime frequently resulted in unhappiness among crew members who had felt "comfortable" with the departing officer and weren't sure how they would react to the newcomer. Murphy's advent was no exception; but he was to establish himself later as a worthy addition to the carrier's company.

After three weeks of work on a top priority basis, the *Princeton* left Bremerton 3 January 1944 with its shaft repaired and with additional anti-aircraft weaponry topside — both 40- and 20-millimeter guns.

The carrier sailed short-handed. Sixty-seven crew members who had been given shore leave either overstayed their leave or jumped ship.

As the *Princeton* steamed westward, the log showed that in the 225 days since the start of the shakedown cruise, the carrier had been at sea 147 days.

The five-day trip from the mainland to an 8 January landfall at Pearl Harbor was marked by very heavy seas. Occasionally rolling as much as 33 degrees, and even taking some water over the flight deck, the carrier still performed well.

First order of business at Hawaii was a two-day joint operation with the *Langley*, a sister CVL whose key officers had been counselled, and to some extent trained, by their *Princeton* counterparts before the latter left Philadelphia for the Pacific.

The operational plan was two-fold — to enable the crews of the two carriers to practice working as a team and to check out new pilots in CVL landings and takeoffs. The planes flew aboard the carriers from Hawaii. One of the *Princeton*'s torpedo bombers struck the carrier's mast in taking a wave-off. The pilot was lost as the plane crashed in the sea. The two crewmen aboard managed to free themselves from the sinking aircraft and were rescued.

On 19 January the *Princeton* departed from Pearl Harbor with the impressive array of warships forming the Northern Task Force 58. In addition to the *Princeton*, there were two more carriers (*Sar-*

atoga and *Langley*), three heavy cruisers (*Baltimore, Boston,* and *Canberra*), and a screen of eight destroyers.

This group was assigned the job of protecting the northern flank of the main task force by neutralizing enemy airfields at Wotje and Taroa while U.S. troops and their supplies were put ashore at Kwajalein atoll.

The first amphibious move into the Marshall Islands came on 31 January with the invasion of Kwajalein and Majuro atolls. Air strikes began two days earlier.

Sixteen fighter planes left the *Princeton* at dawn on 29 January in the first of three bombing and strafing attacks on Wotje that day. Anti-aircraft fire was not as heavy as anticipated, and was even lighter after the first mission. In between these sorties, Fighting 23 provided combat air patrol coverage for the task group. No enemy plane put in an appearance.

After a "battle breakfast" of steak, eggs, fruit, and coffee the following morning, the *Princeton* launched planes at 0545 to revisit Wotje and also to attack the Japanese installations at Taroa. Before the day was over, *Princeton* pilots had flown six missions over the Wotje airfield to make certain no enemy aircraft became airborne, and also had carried out four strikes against Taroa. On the last flight of the afternoon, one four-plane division of VF-23 Hellcats provided spotting guidance for the three cruisers while they bombarded Taroa.

As the 31 January landings were being made at several points on Kwajalein, air strikes raked both Wotje and Taroa in coordination with intense surface bombardment by the cruisers. Air Group Commander Miller, who spotted for the warships during his last mission, brought back reports that both Wotje and Taroa were "a shambles."

The fighter squadron sustained one combat casualty at Wotje.

"Lt. (jg) W. G. Buckelew, while carrying out daring strafing runs against an enemy gun emplacement he had spotted, was struck by anti-aircraft fire which disabled his plane and forced him to make a water landing," Miller said. "Buck, himself, apparently was not hit. He told his wingman by radio he planned to ditch his plane. When he landed, the Hellcat disappeared almost immediately; and for some reason Buck wasn't able to get out. Our planes circled the area for as long as possible, but without success."

After a day of refueling at sea, which gave the pilots a chance to catch up on much-needed sleep, the task group headed for Eniwetok, the westernmost atoll in the Marshall Islands. Shortly after the carriers arrived there on 3 February, strikes were made against Japanese installations on Engebi Island.

"There were no enemy planes in the air," Commander Miller said, "so a systematic destruction of their airfield was carried out. Sorties were conducted every day. The anti-aircraft fire was reduced to nothing and, as a matter of fact, the torpedo planes were taking passengers, in the form of non-flying personnel, toward the end to watch the bombing and get a look at an enemy target under attack."

With Engebi "out of business," the *Princeton* and her task group companions steamed to the newly acquired base at Roi. Boasting the largest lagoon in the western Pacific, Roi, since its capture during the Kwajalein invasion, in the few short weeks had been turned into a mammoth U.S. anchorage and staging area.

"As we approached," Miller said, "we could see ships and ships in the lagoon. They were of all types and sizes. As we drew closer to shore, we also could spot evidences of our landings with the remains of our tanks and landing craft, as well as destroyed enemy gun emplacements. Marines were everywhere souvenir hunting."

At Roi, three members of the air group were given permission to go ashore to look over the blasted Japanese fortification. The trio consisted of Lt. Claude Schmidt, Lieutenant (jg) Kerr, and Lieutenant (jg) Crockett, the VF-23 pilot who had returned his shot-up Hellcat to the *Princeton,* wounded, after successfully defending the air coordinator at Rabaul. He also downed an enemy plane in the process.

"They came back loaded with souvenirs and colossal stories," the air group commander said. "It seems the marines had cornered the market on Japanese property and demanded terrific exchanges for a flag or sword. What the marines wanted most of all was one of our 45-caliber revolvers. For that you could get a Japanese sword. Next on their list was whiskey. For a bottle you could get practically anything they had. Money meant absolutely nothing in that marketplace."

Also at Roi, the *Princeton* had a change of skippers. Captain Henderson, who had commanded the carrier since the commissioning, was relieved by Capt. William Buracker, who had been on board during the Marshall Islands operation observing and preparing to take over.

Henderson, who had started his navy career as an enlisted man, was promoted to the rank of commodore. He was very well-liked among the *Princeton*'s crew, as noted by Navigator Vic Moitoret.

"When Hank Miller flew aboard with Air Group 23," said Moitoret, "he came up to the bridge to chat with the skipper. He began by apologizing for the fact some of his fliers didn't have a full bag of uniforms, and that for lack of laundry or dry-cleaning at the Parris Island Marine base, the uniforms they did have might not pass Captain's inspection. Henderson smiled and said, 'Hank, I expect you and your boys to do a helluva lot of flying aboard this ship, and I am not going to be too much concerned about how your uniforms look.'

"At another time," Moitoret said, "not long after we were first underway, the Captain was sitting in his chair on the bridge and motioned me over beside him. 'Vic,' he began, 'I know it's an old naval tradition that probably goes back to John Paul Jones for the officer of the deck to send a messenger to me every day at noon to report that it was 12 o'clock and the chronometers had been wound. Well, Vic,' he said, 'I have this very excellent aviator's watch that the U.S. government has supplied and I know without being told that it's 12 noon. Furthermore, I know that as long as you are my navigator those chronometers are always going to be wound. So isn't that one little bit of routine we could dispense with?'

"A bit stunned at first at this suggestion that did such violence to naval tradition," Moitoret said, "I realized how practical the idea was. 'Yes, sir, Captain,' I said. 'I'll instruct the OODs to eliminate that one.' "

Moitoret's assistant navigator at one point was then Lt. (jg) W. T. "Barney" Rapp, who also developed a warm spot in his heart for Captain Henderson.

"Once when Barney was OOD underway, he made a mistake in looking up some evolution in the tactical instructions, which resulted in the *Princeton* making a wrong move," Moitoret said. "When Barney reported the error, expecting a good chewing out, Captain Henderson smiled and said, 'Well, Barney, you know that's why they put erasers on the end of pencils.' "

Rapp went on to the rank of vice admiral and commanded the Third Fleet.

As Henderson prepared to go, a message was received from the commander, Carrier Division Eleven:

"Before the departure of Commodore Henderson, I wish to thank the *Princeton* for its outstanding performance of duty on this operation, as well as on all operations since you have joined CarDiv Eleven. To me, you have no equal in the CVL class. Captain Henderson's superior leadership, and your loyalty and efficiency, have made it so."

With a new commander on the bridge, the *Princeton* rounded out the month of February providing air support for landings at Eniwetok, while strikes hit Truk as well as two new targets — Tinian and Saipan, in the Mariana Islands.

As February drew to a close, the carrier was relieved and sent back to a newly established naval base at Majuro, in the southern Marshall Islands. Air group and ship's personnel enjoyed a long-overdue shore liberty and received their first mail in more than six weeks.

"There were 339 sacks for the *Princeton*," Commander Miller recalled. "Little by little it arrived. The packages were in terrible condition, especially if they contained cakes or candy. No first class mail was included, which meant no letters."

While the carrier was being refueled, rearmed and resupplied, the off-duty personnel in the crew, and from the air group, grabbed a few hours of sun-bathing, impromptu athletics, and letter writing. A Catholic chaplain from another carrier came aboard and conducted services, including memorials to the pilots lost in action. Each evening, the carriers left the lagoon to prevent enemy subs or aerial snoopers from catching them helpless at anchor.

In the initial weeks of March, an awesome U.S. naval force was mustered. Allied sea-born and amphibious strength had engulfed enemy-held island after island in a relentless move westward across the Pacific. Now the time was ripe for a concerted drive to the north — toward the very core of the Japanese empire.

After a shift from Majuro to Espiritu Santo in early March, the *Princeton* sailed 23 March as part of a task group, which also included the carriers *Yorktown, Lexington,* and *Langley;* the battleships *South Dakota, Massachusetts, Alabama,* and *North Carolina;* the cruisers *Louisville, Portland, Indianapolis* (which later was to disappear at sea after delivering the first A-bomb components), and the *San Juan*; along with sixteen small boys.

Jim Large, a transplanted Philadelphia banker serving as air plot officer on the *Princeton*, was among those impressed by the tremendous display of naval strength.

"Ours was only one of three task groups involved," he said. "The overall task force included so much seapower that at one time it was possible to see from the *Princeton*'s bridge sixty-seven major combat vessels."

Air Group Commander Miller had a similar impression.

"The operations plans had come aboard," he said. "We were headed for Palau and Yap. When you got up on the flight deck and looked around you had a strong feeling of security. The greatest fleet in the world lay before your eyes; and we were going out to give the enemy hell."

As the U.S. armada neared its target, the Japanese indicated a nerve center had been touched. On 26 March a Japanese snooper came within thirty miles of the task force but left the area without incident.

All was quiet until noon Wednesday 29 March when one of the combat air patrol pilots spotted an enemy torpedo bomber approaching the task force low on the water and finished it off. In the late afternoon, two more enemy aircraft were tallyhoed and shot down. Just before dusk a third bogey was downed. The Japanese by now were fully aware a major attack force was headed their way. As a result, all the enemy warships based at Palau had left the area by the time the U.S. carrier planes appeared over the target.

The first fighter sweep was launched shortly after dawn, 30 March, to "clear the air of enemy planes." Only a few Japanese Zeroes were encountered, however, and two of these were quickly shot down. Then the torpedo and dive bombers from the carriers moved in. Their attacks were continued through the day, without incident, other than the loss of one *Princeton* fighter plane in a dead-engine water landing. The pilot was retrieved unhurt.

After all the carrier aircraft had been taken back aboard and darkness settled down, the Japanese came to life. Using a flight pattern designed to afford them the most protection, and to confuse the task force gunners, the enemy torpedo bombers skimmed the sea as they made their runs.

"With hundreds of our guns firing, no Fourth of July ever

looked like that scene," said Jim Large. "The tracers were flying everywhere."

The Japanese attacks proved only of a nuisance value. No U.S. ships were damaged before the surviving enemy planes turned back.

The "fireworks" began earlier the following day. Led by Commander Miller, a fighter sweep which took off at 0730 encountered a lone Japanese plane on the way to the target, and swiftly disposed of the Betty.

"Over the target," Miller said, "there were Zeroes all over the sky. Two of our fighters had to return to the *Princeton* with engine problems, but the rest of the flight waded in with guns blazing. Dog fights continued for nearly an hour. One of our divisions, led by Lt. Claude Schmidt, accounted for eight enemy planes. Jack Abell, after shooting down one enemy fighter, accompanied Les Kerr back to the carrier with engine trouble. Earlier, Kerr himself had scored two 'kills.' "

The score for Fighting 23: fifteen enemy aircraft destroyed in the air. One of the squadron pilots, Frank Muhlfield, was wounded in the fighting and another, Syme, was lost over the target. Although one of his fellow fliers reported seeing a parachute going down, a prolonged search failed to turn up any sign of the missing Syme.

No enemy low-level attacks occurred that night; and the air crews got sorely-needed sleep.

A fighter sweep took off the morning of 1 April to attack Woleai, east of Palau. Radar indications of unidentified planes in the area resulted in a fruitless search, and the *Princeton*'s Hellcats never reached their planned target.

As the carrier turned away from Palau to resupply at Majuro, a dispatch arrived detaching Henry Miller as air group and fighter squadron commander. Orders naming him air officer of a "baby flattop" (CVE) had come through two months earlier, but Miller had been putting off his departure as long as possible.

As the *Princeton* dropped anchor at Majuro 6 April, the question was how much longer could Miller delay reporting to the CVE.

CHAPTER VII

Changing of the Guard

EASTER SUNDAY, IN THE WAR year of 1944, fell on 9 April. Sunrise services were on the flight deck at 0630 and a Catholic Mass was celebrated on the hangar deck at 0800.

Many members of the air group, and some of the ship's crew, had an opportunity in the afternoon to go ashore for a swim and a can of beer or two on the beach.

After four days of stepped-up preparation, the *Princeton* steamed out of the Majuro lagoon on 13 April with a fleet-sized task group including three other carriers, five battleships, three heavy cruisers, and seventeen destroyers. Their destination was New Guinea, their mission to support landings at Hollandia.

In addition to the *Princeton*, the three other carriers were the *Langley*, the *Lexington*, and the *Enterprise* with Adm. J. W. "Black Jack" Reeves aboard as task group commander. Each flattop left a pilot contingent on shore to fly out new planes after the fleet was well under way. Lieutenant Commander Miller and three VF-23 flyers were assigned from the *Princeton*.

Making up the battleship force were the *South Dakota*, the *Indiana*, the *Massachusetts*, the *Alabama*, and the *North Carolina*. The heavy cruisers were the *Canberra*, the *Portland*, and the *Louisville*. In the destroyer screen were: *Taylor, Converse, Spence, Thatcher, Pritchett,*

Charles Ausburn, Dyson, Albert W. Grant, Caperton, Cogswell, Ingersoll, Knapp, Cotton, Dortch, Gatling, Healy, and *Cassin Young.*

As the mammoth task group cruised the Pacific, the officers developed their strategy for the air attack on New Guinea. Each air group and squadron commander took turns visiting their counterparts on the other carriers, making detailed plans for the invasion. Pilots and air crewmen were briefed on their intended targets, the enemy strength anticipated and the operational schedule. En route the *Princeton* crossed the equator for the forty-fifth time.

On 19 April, when the task group was still two days from New Guinea, an unidentified plane was detected. All hands went to general quarters until the bogey disappeared from the radar screens. In the early morning hours, a tanker rendezvoused with the warships to refuel them. A *Princeton* fighter division on combat air patrol, led by Lieutenant (jg) Kerr, was vectored after another enemy snooper in mid-afternoon. The invader turned out to be a twin-engine Japanese patrol plane, which was shot down by the Hellcats just after being spotted.

On the day before the scheduled amphibious landings, Fighting 23 was assigned three strikes against the Japanese airfields at Hollandia, Cyclops, and Sentani. Despite heavy cloud masses over the targets, the first two missions were carried out. Led by Air Group Commander Miller, the fighters raked the earth-bound enemy planes and the airfield installations.

The third strike had to be cancelled because the *Princeton*'s forward elevator became jammed with a fighter plane spotted on it. The flight deck couldn't be used until the elevator had been repaired.

D-Day at Hollandia was 22 April. The *Princeton,* along with the other carriers, sent air patrols to fly cover over the landing areas. The fighters were not called on to provide any direct support of the ground troops.

"The Japanese evidently had moved into the hills," Miller said, "from which they could venture forth later."

As the Hellcats began their return to the carriers, the landings were virtually completed and roads already were being constructed for the supply trucks and other rolling stock being put ashore. The weather closed in to near zero ceiling conditions as Miller and his companions landed back aboard the *Princeton*.

On the second day of the operation, the Fighting 23 pursued

an occasional enemy aircraft, but failed to score any "kills." In between a series of frustrating chases, they made strafing runs ahead of the advancing U.S. troops.

"Our planes got back to the *Princeton* after sundown," Miller said. "The landing signal officer had to resort to lighted wands as darkness closed in. Just as the last of our fighters were retrieved, the Japs appeared over the task group and we went to general quarters again. Our night fighters from the bigger carriers shot down one bogey, but others got into Hollandia to bomb our forces there."

After three days of combat air patrols and attack missions, the task group retired for refueling. During this operation, a lone Japanese bomber approached the formation. The enemy plane was shot down and four survivors were picked up. They were put aboard the *Enterprise* for interrogation by intelligence officers on Admiral Reeves' staff.

During the Hollandia operation, members of Air Group 23 gained a new appreciation of the *Princeton*'s captain, Bill Buracker.

Two four-plane divisions of Hellcats were launched on the morning of 26 April to fly a routine combat air patrol over the task group. One division was led by Joe Webb and the other by Bob Tyner, neither of whom had any enemy planes to their credit, and both of whom wanted very much to gain that distinction.

A snooper put in an appearance shortly after the *Princeton* fighters had been launched. It so happened the enemy aircraft was closer to Webb's division than to Tyner's. Webb and his three companions located the Japanese plane and disposed of it jointly.

Meanwhile, Tyner's division was flying directly above the task group, hoping another opportunity would arise. A second snooper came on the scene — but once again closer to Webb's division.

The chase began, and for over seventy miles, Webb and his fellow fighter pilots followed the bogey before catching up with him. The enemy proved to be a new type twin-engine aircraft with good speed, but not enough to escape. Webb's division accounted for a second "kill."

As the Japanese plane plunged into the sea, Webb and his companions realized they were dangerously low on fuel and about 100 miles from the *Princeton*. Webb radioed the carrier with a report on their status.

"Captain Buracker immediately requested permission from the admiral to be detached from the task group in order to speed to the assistance of the distant and nearly fuelless planes," Miller said. "Permission was granted and the captain ordered the carrier crew to pour on the coal. He really produced when our boys needed help. When the *Princeton* met the returning fighters, one Hellcat's fuel gauge indicated empty. Luckily, the ship was already headed into the wind and that pilot came straight in, followed by the others, without any waveoffs or nervous landings. When all four were safely aboard, everyone on the flight deck and bridge let out a loud cheer."

Later in the day, three more Japanese snoopers were shot down near the task group perimeter, but the kills were registered by fighter planes from other carriers flying combat air patrol at the time.

As evening settled over the western Pacific, Admiral Nimitz radioed his "congratulations on another job well done." The Task Force 58 commander, Adm. Marc Mitscher, added a "well done." And from his task group command on the *Enterprise,* Admiral Reeves told the *Princeton* "good work. Your boys are right on the job."

On the strength of the results at Hollandia, and the expectations of a few days shore leave, spirits were high on the *Princeton*; but new orders arrived calling for a two-day onslaught on Truk. With thoughts of a rest from combat flying temporarily pushed aside, pilots and airmen returned to their ready rooms for briefings on Truk targets and strike plans.

After receiving mail, which had been brought by a newly arrived member of task force — mail delivered only three hundred miles from Truk — the carriers and their screening ships moved in close enough to spot the islands around Truk on the horizon.

For the final two days of April, VF 23 carried out strafing runs against land targets and shipping in the harbor as the torpedo pilots made bombing runs. Lieutenant Commander Miller's fighter division shot down one Japanese plane during these attacks.

While the Japanese presence was still evident, in the form of moderate to heavy anti-aircraft fire and on two occasions nighttime snoopers over the U.S. ships, the enemy fortress at Truk was being reduced to rubble.

On the return voyage to Majuro, battleships accompanying the carriers made a slight "detour" to shell the Japanese base at Ponape. Arrival at Majuro came on 4 May, and on 6 May the

Princeton, as well as the *Yorktown* and the *Monterey*, set sail for Pearl Harbor to take aboard new squadrons.

During the period from 19 May 1943 to 26 May 1944 the *Princeton* had been at sea 243 days, or two-thirds of that year. The carrier had steamed some 95,000 miles over the expanse of the Pacific.

Serving on a cruiser-turned-carrier, Air Group 23 played a prominent role in a dozen major operations as the United States and her allies closed on the Japanese home islands. Fighting 23 and Torpedo 23 were instrumental in establishing the innovative Independence class flattops as worthy participants in the sea-oriented counter offensive against an enemy which had used its own sea power to bite off a huge chunk of the world.

As the old guard was replaced by the new at Pearl, Air Group 23's log showed more than 9,000 hours of combat flying. On the fighter squadron side of the ledger, individual pilots' records listed 325 strikes against the enemy and nearly 300 hours of combat air patrolling.

Thirty-seven Japanese planes had been destroyed in aerial combat by VF-23 pilots. Three others were probably shot down and an additional eleven damaged in dog fights. Eleven enemy aircraft had been damaged on the ground by strafing. The cost had been seven VF-23 fliers killed or missing in action.

The *Princeton*'s torpedo squadron had accounted for another four Japanese planes shot down. VT-23 pilots scored torpedo hits on two enemy heavy cruisers and one destroyer. A dozen other vessels, and a score of smaller craft, were destroyed or damaged in the fifty-two strikes made by Torpedo 23. Five pilots and air crewmen were lost or missing in action.

The *Princeton* arrived back at Pearl Harbor 11 May and immediately prepared to receive Air Group 27, which had been in training on the island of Maui. As Air Group 23 disembarked, more than one member of the ship's company wondered whether their replacements would be as good under fire. All hands were in agreement — it would be a tough act to follow.

CHAPTER VIII

Spirits Afloat

ON THE NIGHT BEFORE Air Group 23 personnel left Hawaii for the States, a farewell party was arranged. This affair was, in the words of Lieutenant Commander Clifford, aide to the *Princeton*'s executive officer, "the type of party you could expect under the circumstances."

Deadly serious as the war in the Pacific was, there were lighter moments and many of these centered around the presence — or absence — of alcohol. One such incident became known as the "Great Beer Heist," a shipboard development which should be considered in the light of the times and the situations in which men found themselves.

"Life on the *Princeton,* as on any carrier at that time, was for the most part a monotonous succession of days," said Aviation Machinist Mate Leo Kieri. "During those periods when we were not in unfriendly waters, one day was pretty much like the rest.

"You retained brief flashbacks of liberties at Pearl Harbor, Panama, or some uninhabited island where we could spend a few hours nursing our allotted two bottles of beer and contemplate a sandy beach with a few scraggly palm trees."

The two bottles of beer were the normal issue given members of the ship's company and air group when they had an opportunity to go ashore between combat operations. On the *Princeton,* the beer supply became an object of unusual interest.

The ship, which had started taking shape as a cruiser and was converted to a carrier, involved some design innovations. The main deck of a cruiser slopes from bow toward the stern. An aircraft carrier's top deck is the flight deck and, to receive and launch planes, this must be level. Consequently, the basic cruiser hull was topped by the necessary superstructure. This created a vacant space, which, on the *Princeton,* was used for storage.

"The beer was in a compartment in this void between the first deck and the hangar deck," said Watertender Larry Brown, a survivor of the carrier *Hornet* sinking. "The cases of bottles were stacked in one area maybe five feet high, with a hatch on one side so that the marine guard could look in to make sure the beer was still there.

"What somebody did was get into the space near the beer compartment," Brown said, "and then cut a hole with an acetylene torch so cases of beer could be taken out from the back of the pile. When the marine checked, he saw cases still stacked near the hatch so he closed the hatch and locked up."

Brown said he was under the impression there were thousands of cases of beer in the storage compartment to begin with. With the "withdrawals" continuing for months, Brown couldn't be sure how much disappeared in all.

"I know an awful lot of it was gone. All this time the marine guard was still making daily checks and seeing full cases right up to the hatch — but the ones that should have been right behind the front row may not have been there at all."

Brown became involved accidentally. He came through the area where the purloined beer was being taken out one night, and when he learned what was happening, joined the group.

"Four or five guys would form a line after some cases had been removed from the storage compartment but left in another section of the void," he said. "Then one case at a time was taken out. Watches were posted down the passageways so we could get the beer to the ice cream cooler at the geedunk [refreshment] stand."

The Great Heist came to an end when too many members of the crew learned that beer could be had. The "supply line" dried up fast when the *Princeton*'s captain ordered a muster of crew members on the flight deck and announced he fully intended to catch the ringleaders of the plot. As chance would have it, Brown, who had reason to believe he was a suspected participant, was transferred off the carrier a few days later.

"My division officer came to me and asked 'how soon can you get your bags on the quarter deck?' and I told him 'five minutes,' " Brown said. " 'That's all you've got,' he told me and then he indicated the captain was hot on my heels."

Yeoman Kermit Dearman, who handled the paperwork in the *Princeton*'s air office, was another who came under close scrutiny as a result of the Great Beer Heist.

"The captain never was quite convinced that I didn't know anything about it, despite repeated denials by me," Dearman said. "I really didn't know who had stolen the beer. Now if the captain had asked about sick bay alcohol — it was great if you covered the bottom of a water glass thinly and filled the glass with ice and fruit juice.

"This all meant, of course, you had to have a consortium of one pharmacist's mate, one chief master-at-arms, one captain's writer and one geedunk operator to supply the ice and fruit juice."

Neither Brown, who went back to the U.S. to attend boiler school, or Dearman, who went on in the navy to become a commander before his retirement, ever learned the final result of the captain's investigation. The *Princeton*'s eventual encounter with a Japanese bomb may have closed the book on the case.

In the unpredictable days of wartime, some individuals managed to cope on a broader scale than others. One *Princeton* crewmember who enjoyed an occasional encounter with "the good things in life" was Ray Arlequeeuw, a ship's cook and another survivor of the sinking of the *Hornet*.

"As a cook, anytime I wanted something to drink I could get some 180-proof alcohol from a plane captain and I'd take care of him with some things from the galley," Arlequeeuw said.

The carrier's post office became Arlequeeuw's happy hour headquarters, along with a few selected friends.

"The only guy allowed inside the post office was the crew member serving as post master and the captain of the ship," Arlequeeuw said. "So that's where we used to hold our get-togethers. The guys from the ice machine would bring ice. The guys from the geedunk machine would bring the cokes, a plane captain would bring some alcohol. Then I would get chicken, maybe olives, and french fries from the galley. It wasn't so bad."

Arlequeeuw said "you had to be careful not to get caught drinking on the ship. The masters-at-arms were like the police aboard and they were always on our butts. One time we knew they were coming to get us so we filled up a gallon jug with water and sat it in plain sight. Well, the master-at-arms came busting in and grabbed the jug — nothing but water for evidence.

"Whenever you got hold of some alcohol," he said, "you took it to a pharmacist's mate to have it tested. I got some stuff once and it had come from a compass or somewhere like that. It was bad, but I tried it anyway. It almost killed me."

Kieri had put in much of one day on the *Princeton* working with another aviation "mech" on an airplane engine.

"It had been hot on the hangar deck; and we were tired from working long hours," Kieri said. "Casually my partner produced a can containing liquid, which turned out to be alcohol. Some of this added to our pitcher of coffee certainly improved our dispositions and mental outlook.

"Suddenly there was the sound of gunfire topside. We ran to an open bay on the starboard side of the hangar deck near the after elevator. We could see a Japanese plane bearing down on us. He came so close we could read his numbers and his torpedo loomed big and menacing. At the last minute our gunners brought him down. My friend and I clapped and shouted something like 'good show.' The real impact of the situation hit us later," Kieri said.

On another occasion, Kieri and two fellow *Princeton* crew members were sent ashore at Espiritu Santo with several airplane engines in need of repair and replacement parts. He returned with a new admiration for the skills of the navy's Civil Engineer Corps, known as Construction Battalions, or "Sea Bees."

"We spent a couple of days living in a quonset hut with some Sea Bees," Kieri said. "They were a colorful bunch, and told interesting stories about landing at Espiritu during the rainy season. One Sea Bee, a mechanic, said he was told to replace the rear axle assembly of a truck, which had become mired in the deep mud.

"This guy said he tried to keep an opening shoveled out big enough to work in but the mud kept oozing in," Kieri said. "When he finally got the job done there was so much mud in the differential he couldn't get any grease in, so he slapped on the inspection plate and the truck was driven away. The immediate objective — to get that truck out of the way — had been accomplished but I wonder how long it lasted."

Kieri said the Sea Bee mechanic not only was a great story teller, but also an excellent host.

"Not only did he entertain us with stories, he plied us with the specialty of the house. This was a slightly cloudy liquid he referred to as 'jungle juice.' There was no set formula for this concoction — sometimes the mash contained more raisins than dried apricots or perhaps the other way around — all depending on the current availability of ingredients.

"When the mixture had duly fermented," Kieri said, "the mash was distilled in a custom-made contraption.

"The whole operation was housed out of sight, beneath the spreading branches of a huge banyan tree. Those guys certainly lived up to the Sea Bee motto: 'Can Do.' "

The same sort of ingenuity was sometimes shown aboard ship. On a major war vessel such as the *Princeton*, the pharmacy was an important and virtually self-sufficient unit. Because many of the medications dispensed here had been put together "in-house," the raw ingredients were available for a smattering of "experimental projects."

Pharmacist's Mate George Pantages said one such venture in particular had a "Rube Goldberg" appearance because of the unlikely components that had been assembled to produce an unlikely product.

"First of all," Pantages said, "there was a hot plate sitting on the lab table upon which was a large beaker filled with a thick syrup of sugar and water, along with a few pieces of orange rind and slices of orange. Suspended from a bunk overhead was a candy thermometer immersed partially in the syrup solution.

"At the proper moment, when time and temperature indicated the process was complete, to the syrup would be added just the right percentage of alcohol to produce one of the most tempting, mouth-watering cordials available. One jigger of my famous orange cordial would make almost anything on the chow line seem delicious.

"Speaking of alcohol," Pantages said, "aside from various medications, this was the one item which didn't hurt my popularity. I could have traded almost anything I wanted — but never did. I really kept a pretty tight lid on the use of alcohol, although there always was an 'excess' available. Being in charge of all the alcohol and whiskey placed me in a somewhat enviable position."

Pantages was responsible for the locker in sick bay, which contained "the best whiskey and brandy money could buy." On the carriers, pilots returning from combat missions were offered two ounces of either brandy or bourbon, depending on the individual's preference.

"Some of the pilots didn't drink," Pantages said, "and the allotment for those who refused it was placed in a 'private stock fund, so to speak.'"

Because alcohol was used to prepare large quantities of a cough syrup widely used on board ship, and the green tincture of soap employed in the operating room, Pantages said "it was a simple matter to detour small amounts." For the good of all concerned, Pantages helped stem what might otherwise have been a more serious problem.

CHAPTER IX

Air Group 27 Takes Shape

AIR GROUP 27 HEADED TOWARD the *Princeton* well-trained, sobered by the loss of comrades along the way and possessed of an invaluable esprit.

The two squadrons, Fighting 27 and Torpedo 27, began taking shape in the fall of 1943 at the Alameda Naval Air Station, across the bay from San Francisco. Pilots, air crewmen, and other personnel reported in on a day-to-day basis.

One of the first to put in his appearance was William "Bill" Lamb, a darkhaired, soft-spoken Annapolis graduate, and, as a full lieutenant, temporarily the senior officer present. The author was another early arrival, reporting in as VF-27 air combat intelligence (ACI) officer. He was joined by another recent "graduate" of the Naval Indoctrination and Air Combat Intelligence Schools at Quonset Point, Rhode Island, Bill Kerr, who was the assigned VT-27 ACI officer. One of Lamb's welcoming gestures was to give the former a demonstration of such basic maneuvers as the inside loop and slow roll using a two-seated SNJ, the air group's utility aircraft for guard mail pickup and other chores.

Lt. Frederic A. Bardshar arrived just before the air group was ordered moved to an auxiliary airfield near Watsonville, California. Bardshar, like Lamb a graduate of Annapolis, assumed command of the fighter squadron with Lamb as his executive officer. Bardshar, before entering flight training, had been attached to the battleship *Pennsylvania* at Pearl Harbor when the Japanese attacked.

When Fighting 27 was initially formed, the planes being used were Grumman F4F Wildcats, the type flown from the beleaguered airfield at Guadalcanal, and from the decks of the carriers *Saratoga, Lexington,* and *Enterprise* in the early stages of the Pacific war.

The landing wheels on the F4F were closer to one another than on some other planes. As a result, the Wildcat had a pronounced tendency to groundloop, or swerve off the runway, if not treated with the proper respect.

Before the shift to Watsonville, the Wildcats were replaced by the newer, faster Grumman F6F Hellcats, a change welcomed by all hands, including Bardshar, whose long frame was ill-suited to the F4F cockpit.

Some members of the air group were not too happy about the move to Watsonville, which meant exchanging the off-duty possibilities of San Francisco and Oakland for a small town where the major attractions were a movie theater, hamburger "joint," and a couple of bars, including the White Swan, which the boys renamed the Dirty Duck.

A few of the married pilots were able to rent houses for their families at nearby Rio Del Mar, on Monterey Bay. The ones not so fortunate settled for rooms on the base, including those in the Bachelor Officer Quarters — rechristened Boystown. The few buildings on the base were constructed of California redwood, creating the impression of a frontier settlement clustered along the two runways.

While the torpedo squadron, under the new VT-27 skipper, S. M. Hadley, was engaged in ground training at the base and flight exercises over the rolling hills to the east, as well as the offshore areas to the west, Bardshar was establishing the operational organization within the fighter squadron. As each new member of VF-27 reported for duty, Bardshar assessed the individual's previous experience and talent. From this process emerged the division assignments.

The U.S. Navy's fighter division consisted of a pair of two-plane sections. After the division leader, the most important member of this team was the section leader. He and the division leader had an accompanying wingman. In combat, the division frequently was forced to break formation, but the leader and his wingman made every effort to stay together, protecting each other from surprise side, rear, or overhead attack.

Among those selected as a division leader was Lt. (jg) James A. "Red" Shirley, who had been involved in early use of four-plane division tactics before this air tactical unit became the navy's standard.

In Shirley and others like him, Fighting 27 was blessed with talent. The division leader, in addition to bringing out the potential of his three division partners, carried on the training process within his group.

Also chosen to lead fighter divisions were Carl Brown, who, like Shirley, was to establish a remarkable combat record; Bob Grove, a soft-spoken and serious type who quietly guided his more exuberant charges; and Dick Stambook and Patty McMahon, a pair of extraordinary fliers who completely enjoyed what they were doing, and who took every opportunity to refer to each other as "Shorty."

As fall turned to winter, a new commander for both the air group and the fighter squadron came on the scene in the person of Lt. Ernest W. "Woodie" Wood, Jr. Short and slight of build, he and Bardshar presented a contrast that earned them the nicknames "Mutt and Jeff."

These two made an excellent team. Woodie, the name he preferred, could not say no to any request, and Bardshar frequently had to "wear the black hat" to prevent Woodie from being taken advantage of. Under Wood, Bardshar became fighter squadron executive officer and Lamb served as operations officer.

Wood soon proved his mastery of the 13,000-pound Hellcat, which seemed to dwarf him in the cockpit. From various sources, members of the air group learned of previous exploits — punching a Nazi sympathizer when the latter attacked an elderly Jew in Berlin before the start of World War II, and shooting down a German ME-109 while flying the less maneuverable F4F during the African invasion.

He was, indeed, a man of many talents. Wood played the piano somewhat the way he flew, as though the instrument possessed a throttle — sometimes soft and low, then swiftly, wildly.

Wood also dabbled with paints. One of his first acts as skipper of Air Group 27 was to institute a coffee mess in the ready room at Watsonville. He painted each officer's name in large red letters on a personal cup, an old barber shop tradition. Among the first so decorated was a cup bearing the name of the non-flying air combat intelligence officer, a gesture that was deeply appreciated.

One of the Rio Del Mar residents was the fighter squadron's flight officer, Lt. Herman Baker, who occupied a house along Monterey Bay with his wife and small son. A onetime flight instructor before coming to VF-27, Baker had logged more hours than a dozen of the younger pilots put together.

One afternoon, four of the fighter pilots returned to the field long before their scheduled landing time. They reported that Baker, whose plane was rigged with a gunnery target sleeve, had failed to rendezvous with them over Monterey Bay. As the squadron office clock ticked away, the weather began to close in and a low overcast forced a temporary end to the search.

Further efforts the following day proved fruitless, and finally a blimp was called in from a nearby lighter-than-air base. This slower-flying craft located the wreckage of Baker's plane high up in the snow-dusted mountains, only a few minutes flying time from the Watsonville airfield.

The next morning a ground party, guided from the air by the blimp, worked its way up the side of the mountain through dense underbrush and snow to the remains of the F6F and its pilot. It appeared the target sleeve had caught some treetops and whipped the Hellcat into the ground.

Amazingly, the plane's 50-caliber wing guns, and much of the ammunition, were not to be found. An intense search, which eventually involved the Federal Bureau of Investigation, tracked down the missing weapons and live ammo. They had been taken by several young area residents, and were retrieved from various hiding spots.

Baker's death cast a shadow over the final days of the air group's stay in California as preparations were completed for departure to Hawaii.

After completing a round of carrier qualifications on a "baby flattop," the *Copahee*, off San Francisco Bay, and three weeks of joint training at Hollister, an auxiliary airfield near Watsonville, the two squadrons were ready to head west.

Twenty-two March saw the air group back at Alameda, where

another escort carrier, the *Barnes,* waited to transport the planes and personnel of AG-27 to Hawaii. The days at sea were occupied with what might be called shipboard ground school — briefings on the Hawaiian Islands, enemy plane identification tests, tactical discussions, and even an account of the Japanese bombing of Pearl Harbor as witnessed by Bardshar, who had been a battleship gunnery officer at the time of the sneak attack.

At Pearl Harbor, Wood passed along the word from navy headquarters that the air group was to train on the island of Maui until the *Princeton* returned to Pearl. Some of the pilots ferried the fighters and torpedo bombers from Ford Island, on Oahu, to the navy fields near Kahului and Puunene, on Maui. Other air group personnel made the trip on a minesweeper.

Highlight of the day-long voyage was a close look at the east coast of Molokai — site of the famed leper colony founded by Father Damien. The coast, in part, is a 1,000-foot sheer drop laced by a series of finger falls. When the wind is from the right direction, the plunging water feathers out in shimmering plumes before reaching the sea.

Kahului and Puunene proved to be typically drab auxiliary military airfields, although in a particularly lush and beautiful setting. The island of Maui is shaped roughly like a dumbbell, with extinct volcanoes at either end. One of the two airfields was situated on each of the two bays at the narrowest portion of the island.

One of the few sources of annoyance on Maui was the all-pervading red volcanic dust. Maui apparently had been pretty much dust free until the navy built the two airfields. The leveling and grading involved in the construction work uncovered enough loose earth so that it was carried everywhere by the constant breeze. Noses and throats were coated by the stuff after a short time.

On the more pleasant side of the picture were the coconut palms, growing in great abundance, and from which members of the air group gathered fruit to test, to taste, or just for the lack of something better to do.

As part of the ground training program, two experts came to Maui from the Bishop Museum at Honolulu to lecture on survival in the South Pacific. The impression was gained that these two could have been dropped off on almost any out-of-the-way spot on the map and lived in relative comfort.

On the stage of the Kahului auditorium, they constructed

small waterproof huts from palm fronds; made shoes, cooking utensils, and eating bowls from the coconuts; and even started a fire the hard way — from scratch. One of the fighter pilots, Van Carter, became so entranced with this last experiment that he tried it himself time and again. He never actually got a fire going, but he did create a fair amount of smoke. He gained the nickname "Castaway" Carter as a result.

Off-duty hours gave air group members an opportunity to get to know one another better, and to share such common problems as homesickness, the pain of being separated from wife, children, or the girl whose picture you were carrying in your wallet.

A frequent pastime was a card game known as "Red Dog," in which each player anted up to create a "pot," was given four cards, and then in turn bet any amount, up to the pot limit, that one of his cards would beat by suit and number the next card turned up by the dealer. The bets sometimes reached surprising levels, but no one was "hurt real bad."

Out of this game came the name for the newly created air group newsletter — the *Redde Dogge Gazette*. When this mimeographed publication first came to Wood's attention, he asked for an explanation of the title. Then he and Bardshar sat in on a Red Dog game to get a first-hand feel. Wood didn't participate again after that, but Bardshar did. The general impression was that he really wanted to keep a lid on the betting to prevent any real problems.

Wood it was, too, who permitted, if not actually encouraged, the painting of Hellcat faces on the VF-27 fighter plane noses. While this type of squadron identification had been used successfully, and with considerable fanfare, by the Flying Tigers in Southeast Asia, the U.S. Navy and Army Air Corps frowned on the practice.

Fighting 27's venture into the world of aviation art came while the squadron was training at Kahului.

"When we were at Maui, prior to the Mariana Islands invasion, we arrived at this ugly face design on our Hellcats," said pilot Brown. "It came about like this. When I was flying F3F-3's in training at Corpus Christi, one of the planes had two big eyes painted on the cowl. I remembered that, and took a piece of chalk to draw a pair of eyes on my Hellcat at Kahului. I tried to arrive at a face, utilizing the braces on the air intake as teeth. I couldn't get anything worth a darn.

"The air station had an ACI officer, Germain Glidden, who was a portrait painter as well as being a topnotch tennis player," Brown said. "A couple of my fellow pilots — Hugh Lillie, Bob Burnell, and one other whose name I can't be sure of — carved a wooden model of that part of the Hellcat forward of the cockpit. They took the model to Glidden, who designed a face and painted it on the carving. Then we painted one plane and our C.O., Lieutenant Wood, said to go ahead and paint the rest of the Hellcats. Ours was the only navy squadron with anything like that on its planes."

The faces remained intact through the squadron's tour of duty on the *Princeton*, with two notable incidents. Once, while the air group was still training at Maui, an admiral from Pearl Harbor came to Kahului for an inspection. VF-27 personnel scrambled to get canvas covers on the painted faces before his arrival. He was told the covers were needed because of a dust problem.

Then, on the *Princeton*'s final day, Frank "Smoke" Kleffner and several other VF-27 pilots were forced to land on the *Essex* because their own carrier was in trouble. The admiral aboard the *Essex* ordered the *Princeton* fighter planes taken to the hangar deck, fast, and the faces painted out.

Early in May, a joint exercise was scheduled involving both the fighters and the torpedo squadron. The idea was for the pilots to make a realistic combined "attack," simulating bombing and strafing runs, without live ammunition being employed. The "target" was the Barking Sands Naval Airfield on the island of Kauai, north of Oahu.

Bardshar agreed to let the VF-27 ACI officer go along as an observer in one of the torpedo planes. The early morning air was surprisingly crisp as the planes took off and rendezvoused, with the aircraft exhaust flashes gradually forming an organized pattern in the dark sky.

The torpedo planes climbed slowly, while the Hellcats S-turned to stay back with the Avengers. The horizon still was not edged with light as the fighters and bombers began their runs.

In the pre-flight briefing, the torpedo pilots had been instructed to come out of their attack dives at 2,500 feet. However, as they reached 4,000 feet, the Avengers pulled up abruptly and began circling. At the far end of the Barking Sands north-south runway was a tremendous blaze which could have only one meaning.

The worst fear was confirmed on landing. Lt. R. P. "Robin" Butler, a lanky Texan and one of the best-liked members of the fighter squadron, had collided with another Hellcat as the two planes approached the airfield from slightly different angles. The second plane managed to recover and land. Butler spun and crashed in trees near the field.

Butler's loss hit the squadron hard, and both Wood and Bardshar realized this. The pilots were given as much time as possible to relax at the beach near the Kahului base.

The last few weeks on Maui boiled down to a lot of marking time. On 14 May the planes were flown back to Ford Island. Nonflying personnel and the air group's gear were transported by air.

Tied up near the Ford Island airfield was the battle-proven *Princeton,* waiting to take an untried AG-27 aboard.

CHAPTER X

Into Japan's Backyard

WITH NEW AIR GROUPS ABOARD, the carriers *Yorktown*, *Langley*, and *Princeton* pulled out of Pearl Harbor 15 May for a two-day exercise off the island of Oahu.

On the *Princeton*, the reaction to the replacement squadrons was voiced by the assistant to the ship's executive officer, Lt. Comdr. E. L. Clifford.

"Air Group 27 proved at once that it was a superior outfit. All hands were satisfied at our good fortune."

The *Princeton*'s air operations officer, Lt. Comdr. James Large, agreed.

"We soon realized our new air group was 'hot.' They looked good, and future events were to prove them among the very best."

Back at Pearl, the *Princeton* moved into the navy yard for nine days of repairs and the application, for the first time, of a black-white-and-grey paint pattern designed to confuse the enemy. The interval made possible rotating shore leaves for the ship's company, most of whom were aware that they would not be seeing Hawaii again for months.

On 29 May the *Princeton* headed out to sea, bound for Majuro and a rendezvous with Task Force 58. The U.S. high command had decided against seizure of Truk in favor of a massive amphibious operation involving the heavily fortified Mariana Islands, just 1,200 miles from Tokyo. Only key military personnel, and a relatively few civilians, knew the Japanese airfields on Saipan and Tinian were sought so they could play a major role in plans to strike Japan with a new weapon of incredible power — the atomic bomb.

The task force left Majuro 6 June Marianas-bound. Whenever the pilots and air crewmen were not flying or occupied with readying their planes for battle, they attended intensified briefing sessions. D-day for the U.S. Marines to land on Saipan had been set for 15 June. Resistance on the part of the Japanese was expected to be as heavy, if not heavier, than any experienced thus far in the Pacific. The enemy air strength in the Marianas was enough to create a major problem for the attacking task force. Moreover, there appeared a strong possibility that the Japanese fleet might steam to the rescue of Fortress Saipan.

Air Group 27 participated in a strike against Saipan shortly after the task force reached the Marianas area 11 June. After flying combat air patrol over the ships for a day, Fighting 27 joined Torpedo 27 in three missions against Saipan's airfield and ground installations 13 June.

In between air attacks by the carriers' planes, other task force ships bombarded shore targets with their heavy guns; all were part of the "softening-up" process before the amphibious landings. The enemy attempted to retaliate, without notable success.

The *Birmingham* was among the warships shelling Saipan on D minus one, 14 June. For two hours, the cruiser steamed 2,500 yards off the beaches, firing at Japanese targets despite a continuing barrage, with dozens of near misses from the enemy's shore batteries.

The *Birmingham*'s skipper, Capt. Thomas B. Inglis, referred to the ship's log to describe the intensity of the Japanese shellfire. In one twenty-five-minute period, the log noted: "shells fell short abeam to starboard fifty and twenty yards. One lands twenty yards over starboard bow. Continue to be straddled. Shells whistle as they pass over. Shells land 400 yards ahead, also over by fifty and twenty-five yards. Shells land on all sides close aboard. Shells land thirty yards over. Picked up pieces of shrapnel on open bridge. Two men injured by shrapnel on 40-millimeter mounts."

Captain Inglis was far more impressed by the performance of his own crew than he was by the enemy's accuracy.

"You may become indifferent to enemy fire," he said, "but

after two hours it does get wearing. I made trips around the bridge to see how the personnel were standing up and they were magnificent.

"Fear is a natural and necessary emotion. Without it no one could live. I noticed that after the novelty wore off, the men who were not busy at their guns were tempted to duck behind any available shelter. Let no man condemn another for suffering fear. The real hero is the man who carries on in spite of fear."

On D minus one and again on D-Day itself, Air Group 27 helped soften up the enemy. The Hellcats strafed ahead of the Avengers as they — with 100-pound general purpose and fragmentation bombs — made low-level attacks on the Japanese gun positions, the enemy tanks, and the Saipan airfield.

Then the marines moved ashore under heavy fire. On the *Birmingham*, again operating close offshore, Captain Inglis observed:

"I was deeply impressed with the planning, training, and execution of the assault. Landing craft literally covered the water's surface. They were in perfect parade formation as they proceeded along the boatlane, over the reef, across the lagoon, direct to the beach."

Inglis said the shore batteries, which had been concentrating their fire on the bigger ships, quickly turned their attention to approaching marine-laden boats.

"It was amazing," he said, "how few hits were scored on the landing craft despite the close formation. The bulk of the shots seemed to land in the water."

As the marines battled ashore, the Hellcats strafed the beach ahead of them. Sixteen of the *Princeton*'s fighters were directed by the support aircraft commander to attack a group of enemy tanks headed toward the landing area from the town of Charon-Kanoa. Pilots later reported a number of hits among the tanks, which took cover along the roadsides and were not observed moving again as long as the planes were within range. On their way back to the *Princeton*, the fighters raked Japanese planes on Saipan's Aslito Airfield with machine gun fire.

While the marine casualties were being treated at aid stations, and in some instances ferried by small craft to ships offshore, their buddies dug in for the bloody defense of their newly gained foothold on the island. Then, from Guam, the Japanese launched a night attack against the task force. It proved the heaviest air onslaught the *Princeton* had experienced thus far.

Twin-engine Bettys, armed with torpedoes, took full advantage of the massive concentration of U.S. warships, coming in low on the water and flying between their intended targets to make counterfire more difficult. The resulting pyrotechnics were breathtaking.

"The Bettys were flying so low," said Large, "they barely skimmed the surface. With every ship in the task force firing, it was a thousand Fourth of Julys in one. As we dodged and weaved at high speed, we had a ring of blazing and exploding enemy planes close aboard. The Japs raced down the columns of ships like great black bats, and the automatic fire from our own forces etched the sky in a criss-cross of flame.

"We were caught momentarily in cross fire," Large said, "and the 40-millimeter missiles produced a roman candle effect as the balls of fire seemed to be arching toward us in leisurely lobs. It was anything but harmless. We had nine people wounded, and were holed below the surface. Miraculously, no ship was seriously damaged and I doubt if any of the Japanese got home."

One Betty flew so close, between the *Princeton* and a nearby battleship, that the Japanese pilot could be seen plainly outlined in the cockpit by the gunfire bursts on the far side. As the torpedo bomber passed abreast of the carrier it suddenly glowed like a giant neon sign, flamed spectacularly, and crashed astern of the ship.

The author at one point ran from the forward end of the flight deck toward the fantail, counting enemy planes burning on the water nearby. There were seven.

A group of *Princeton* crew members on the port catwalk clutched the railing with white knuckles as a torpedo wake streaked toward the carrier and passed under the ship's overhang, just barely astern.

Lt. Frank Bell was at his battle station topside during the attack.

"I have never seen such a display of fireworks. The multi-colored tracers were going all over the place. One enemy plane went between us and two battle wagons, the *Indiana* and *North Carolina*, which were off our port bow about 1,500 yards. I could see by the tracers approaching that we were going to be hit by the fire from one or both of the battleships. I yelled to my crew 'hit the deck.' Almost immediately our ship was struck. A splinter shield near us saved our lives as a large hole was blown only eighteen inches from me. Another shell hit the shield and splattered shrapnel, killing two men, and wounding others directly aft of us at a gun sponson.

"Later," Bell said, "after the ships had secured from general quarters, the alarm was again sounded because a submarine periscope reportedly had been sighted. Strangely, the 'periscope' came closer and closer to the *Princeton*. It turned out to be the upended handle of a mop, which somehow had gone overboard in the confusion surrounding the Japanese air attack."

Pharmacist's Mate Pantages said the night engagement off Saipan was "indelibly engraved on everyone's memory."

During the heart of the action, which lasted less than half an hour, "the sky was completely lit with thousands of tracers, shells exploding, and flares," he said.

"This was our first experience with casualties aboard the *Princeton* as a result of enemy fire. We were caught in a crossfire with our own ships and one 40-millimeter shell penetrated into the officers' wardroom," Pantages said.

"One of the wounded had a considerable amount of intestine torn by a huge piece of shrapnel. After hasty preliminary surgery, it turned out he needed a piece of medical equipment we didn't possess, namely a thing called a Waggonstein apparatus, which is designed to suck the wastes from the stomach through tubes in the patient's nostrils. Necessity being the mother of invention, we were not to be outdone by the emergency.

"By joining two gallon coke bottles with a couple of feet of glass tubing and partially filling one bottle with water, a rapid inversion of the containers provided the necessary suction required to do the job, and fairly efficiently at that."

The Japanese torpedo planes had been repulsed with heavy losses, while inflicting relatively little damage in return. Particularly significant was that the Bettys came from Guam, not from the closer airfields on Saipan and Tinian where, early in the Marianas operation, Task Force 58 squadrons destroyed or damaged the majority of the enemy aircraft present while still on the ground.

While the marines, with 3,500 casualties in the initial 48 hours of fighting, and U.S. Infantry units, which had joined the assault, continued to meet with stiff resistance on Saipan; the Japanese here lacked the ability to pose a serious problem from the air without help from other sources.

The following day — D plus one, or 16 June — the *Princeton*'s Hellcats strafed and set afire two enemy planes on the Ushi Point Airfield, Tinian. They then turned their attention to gun positions in Garapan town, Saipan, and Japanese troops spotted moving south from Garapan toward Charon-Kanoa. On the same mission, VT-27 Avengers laid their bombs in a string 400 yards ahead of the advancing U.S. forces.

During an afternoon mission, Ensign Kleffner had a narrow escape as his F6F was shot down over Guam and in so doing earned a nickname — Smokey Joe. He was flying wing with Air Group Commander Wood.

"Woodie didn't have any sense of the limitations of the plane [Hellcat]," Kleffner said, "and so we made a screeching dive from about 9,000 feet over Guam to look for camouflaged targets. Just he and I. The rest of the air group stayed at altitude.

"We came across the Guam airfield at about 200 feet and doing about 300 knots. As I tried to stay with him I couldn't have seen any targets, camouflaged or not."

The two Hellcats prompted intense ground fire from the Japanese.

"Every kind of fire opened up," Kleffner said, "and caught me instead of him. I don't know what caliber they were using, but there probably were some small arms. One shot the throttle quadrant off in my hand and at the same time I had it on 'full.' The plane started to burn rather well and the oil pressure went to zero. It wasn't long before there was severe sudden stoppage. RPMs went to the peg on the gauge as there was no prop governor. I could read 'Hamilton Standard' [the manufacturer's name] on the propellor blade."

Kleffner said he considered briefly the possibility of jumping, but "I could see the Japs were still shooting as I zoomed up for altitude." Instead of parachuting, he "stayed in the turkey and got out to sea about a mile before flopping in the water." In so doing, he said, "I probably set some kind of record for stretching a glide."

Kleffner scrambled out of the plane, and noted the entire underbelly had melted away, as water poured through the hole. He broke out his emergency rubber boat and inflated his Mae West-style life jacket. As he climbed into the tiny craft, he spotted splashes in the water all around him.

"I figured these coordinated with puffs of smoke I could see on the beach," Kleffner said, "so I sank the boat and went into the water with just my head sticking out. Sea conditions that close to the beach were not particularly rough."

Kleffner said he was told later that one of his flying mates contacted a destroyer and "threatened them with strafing if they didn't pick me up." Whether or not such pressure was involved, a ship appeared on the scene about an hour after Kleffner went into the water.

"When it was still on the horizon and hull down, I couldn't tell right away whether it was one of ours or otherwise," he said. "It really felt good when I saw the Stars and Stripes on it."

A member of the destroyer crew let Kleffner know that they intended to try a running pickup because of their closeness to the enemy-held island of Guam.

"They indicated they were not going to slow down too much, and would throw lots of life rings and I better catch one," Kleffner said. "I did, and damn near jerked my arms out by the roots. The crew ran up the deck and got me alongside without getting me tangled up in the screws."

The destroyer was the *Aylwin*, which had been involved in U.S. forays from Alaska to Guadalcanal.

"Some weird ducks on there," Kleffner said, "but I was happy and slept the clock around. I was in some sort of mild shock. There was a doctor aboard the ship. He couldn't find a mark on me, so I didn't get the Purple Heart.

"All in all, it was rather humiliating, as I hadn't done any harm to the enemy. My forced landing had been spectacular and that's how I got my name — Smokey Joe. I celebrated my twenty-first birthday on March 9 and got shot down on June 16."

Smokey Joe was returned to the *Princeton* when the ships of Task Force 58 next dropped anchor after the Marianas operation.

CHAPTER XI

Marianas Turkey Shoot

RELIEVED BY WORD FROM THE destroyer *Aylwin* that Kleffner had been retrieved and was more or less unhurt, air group members turned to the immediate business at hand.

On 17 June bombing and strafing missions were flown against installations at Rota, north of Guam. The Japanese, now fully aware that the Marianas operation was a full-scale invasion, reacted. That night, after another suicidal enemy torpedo bomber attack out of Guam, with little damage resulting, Task Force 58 received word of Japanese aircraft carriers, cruisers, and destroyers steaming northeast from the Philippine Sea toward Saipan. A massive showdown was in the making.

Initially, Task Force 58's commander, Vice Adm. Marc Mitscher, contemplated driving his powerful armada directly at the oncoming enemy. It was decided, however, not to leave the U.S. forces on Saipan unguarded. The task force turned back to await the expected Japanese attack.

At 0600, 19 June, a lone bogey was tallyhoed by an F6F pilot from the *Princeton*'s sister ship, the *Monterey*. The enemy plane was shot down before it could reach the task force. A second bogey was brought down by gunfire from a screening destroyer. The two intruders did not appear part of a Japanese carrier-based flight.

After a brief lull, plane and shipboard radios crackled with excited transmissions. Fighter pilots from the *Belleau Wood,* flying combat air patrol over Guam, reported a flight of enemy planes coming in from the southwest, believed to be reinforcements from Truk. Fighters from the carriers *Cabot, Yorktown,* and *Hornet* were told to join the *Belleau Wood* Hellcats.

In the resulting dogfights, thirty-five enemy planes were destroyed in aerial combat. The *Princeton*'s F6Fs, on combat air patrol over the task force, could only listen to the tallyhoes and "splash" reports from the other squadrons.

Pausing four hundred miles to the southwest of Task Force 58, at 0830 hours, the Japanese carriers launched an initial wave of torpedo planes, dive bombers, and escorting fighters. Lacking the weighty armor plate that protected U.S. pilots in battle, the enemy aircraft were capable of greater flight range. Their pilots had an additional advantage — they could complete their mission by landing at Japanese airfields in the Marianas rather than make the long, fuel-demanding return to the carriers.

Moments after the first launch, a second wave was on its way. Some 470 enemy planes were headed toward Task Force 58.

While air crews monitored radar screens and radios closely, other personnel on the ships of Task Force 58 relaxed or carried out routine chores. The calm was short lived. At 0959 a radar "blip" indicated the vanguard of the first wave of Japanese carrier planes.

The nerve-tingling bell sounding general quarters was heard on every ship in the task force, literally spread over hundreds of square miles of the Pacific. Crew members donned helmets and life jackets as they ran to their battle stations. Porthole covers and hatches banged shut. Gun crews trained their anti-aircraft weapons skyward.

As the fifteen carriers in the task force turned into the wind, along with their screening vessels, the fighters on combat air patrol or ground support missions over Saipan were called back. Pilots aboard the flattops rushed to their ready rooms for briefing, and to await word to man their planes.

The three divisions of *Princeton* fighters aloft were led by Air Group Commander Wood, Lamb, and McMahon. The eleven Hellcats were instructed to go higher for greater attack advantage when the enemy arrived. A twelfth F6F had been forced to return to the carrier with faulty blowers, which prevented a high-altitude climb. At 1017, the order came from Admiral Mitscher: assemble all available fighters. Moments later, Hellcats began streaming off the decks of fifteen carriers, each succeeding launch mere seconds after the one before.

A scramble under combat conditions represented a state of ordered frenzy. With briefing data hastily written on leg pads, or clip boards, and flight gear donned in record time, the pilots dashed for their planes. Flight deck crews worked under terrific strain to help fasten seat belts and to hold wing tips as the revved-up engines sent blasts of prop wash across the deck.

As one plane shot off the catapult, the launch crew moved in fast to secure the cable yoke to the next aircraft in line. The pilot was given the signal to increase engine speed, and in turn gave back the ready sign when his instruments indicated proper RPMs had been achieved. As the catapult was "fired," the plane moved forward, seemingly without enough speed to become airborne, dipped toward the sea for an instant, then began climbing toward the sky.

Sent off the *Princeton* during the scramble were two four-plane divisions led by Bardshar and Stambook. One of these eight Hellcats limped back to the carrier with engine trouble, leaving a total of eighteen VF-27 aircraft in the air.

Flying with Wood were Red Shirley and Howie Gregg. For the air group commander, the moment he had been awaiting impatiently was about to arrive. It was Wood who gave the "tallyho."

Under the guidance of the *Princeton*'s fighter director, the Hellcats had climbed to twenty-seven thousand feet. The incoming Japanese Zekes, Tonys, and Judys were two to three thousand feet below them — the ideal situation for a successful interception.

As he gave a jubilant tallyho, Wood pushed the throttle "past the firewall" and rolled over for the attack. In seconds, he pulled away from his wingman as he hurtled down at incredible speed. Suddenly his Hellcat plunged into a huge cloud mass. He was lost from sight momentarily. When the plane reappeared, a portion of the tail was missing, and fragments of fabric and metal floated through the air.

It was not clear what had happened — a mid-air collision in that great cloud, too much speed, or too much turbulence for the plane to bear? Whatever the cause, Wood's F6F continued its frightening course toward the sea, and his fellow fliers could spot no hoped-for burst of white parachute silk.

Shirley and Gregg stayed together briefly, but were separated in the wild melee that developed. Shirley shot down two enemy fighter planes and started another smoking with his wing guns, but wasn't able to confirm the third "kill." Gregg also scored a number of hits but, in the confusion and fast-happening action, didn't have time to observe any of his targets crash.

On the decks of the task force ships, anxious observers watched for indications of what was taking place twenty to thirty thousand feet overhead. As the horizon-to-horizon aerial battle took shape, the blue Pacific sky was laced with a crazy pattern of vapor trails. Plane pursued plane in deadly individual duels. Periodically, one of the white streamers curved earthward, and became a plume of black smoke that finally disappeared in the sea.

In the wild scramble, Lamb's division became separated. Lamb found himself on the tail of a Zeke and poured 50-caliber slugs into the enemy with his wing guns. The Zeke refused to go down until nearly two-thirds of Bill's ammunition was exhausted. Finally, a smoke trail pointed to the end of the Zeke, as it spiraled down in flames and crashed.

Lamb pulled up and flew into a formation of scattered clouds to assess his situation. When he came out of the clouds, he suddenly was flying close beside a group of seven enemy torpedo planes, each armed with a "tin fish" for launch against the ships of Task Force 58.

Bill radioed a report of the approaching danger and asked for help. The enemy pilots were making no move in his direction, but his guns were jammed after the encounter with the Zeke. Working feverishly, he got all his six wing weapons operative again and turned them on the Japanese.

One by one, Lamb picked off his quarry until four of the seven had been destroyed. As he ran out of ammunition, other Hellcats put in an appearance and shot down the remaining three enemy planes. Later, Lamb was to be awarded the Navy Cross for the day's action.

Flying with him had been Hank Brotherton, Hugh Loveland, and Van Carter — Castaway Carter. Brotherton shot down two enemy aircraft, and was chasing a third, when forced to return to the *Princeton* for fuel. Loveland destroyed one and damaged several others. Carter was not seen again after the initial frantic moments of the air battle.

Bardshar and his division mates meanwhile encountered part of the second wave of Japanese bogeys headed toward the task force from another direction. Bardshar and his wingman, Art Munson, plowed into the enemy bomber formation, while Gordon Stanley and Leif Erickson, the other two members of the division, attacked their fighter cover.

In minutes, Bardshar shot down two enemy aircraft, Stanley four, Erickson two, and Munson one. Stanley accounted for two of his "kills" on a single run, turning to a second target as his first exploded under a hail of 50-caliber bullets.

Carl Brown's division was vectored to the Rota airfield, and shot down a lone Japanese plane attempting to land there.

Not all members of VF-27 got in on the actions. Les Blyth had a "sad story" to tell.

"I missed the fight in the Marianas turkey shoot," he said. "There were myself, Robert Hill, and about six or eight of us in the fighter squadron ready room when they first sounded general quarters. Then they told us to man our planes, but the launch was delayed for some reason.

"By then the rest of our squadron members had gotten to the ready room," Blyth said. "Our executive officer got his division together, came up on the flight deck and relieved us in the planes. They took off on the turkey shoot. We did fly in the afternoon but things were pretty well quieted down by then."

One of the torpedo squadron's planes did become involved in the turkey shoot scene. Two VT-27 Avengers were launched to fly Anti-Submarine Patrol (ASP) around the task force, one piloted by Tom Mooney, and the other by Warren "Pete" Burgess.

In their ASP assignment, the two planes covered pie-shaped areas fanning out some thirty to forty miles from the formation of surface vessels. Their specific task was to fly low — between 1,000 feet down to almost on the water — looking for any signs of enemy submarine presence or activity.

"We were armed with depth charges," Mooney said, "and were directed to attack any sub sighted without asking questions first. We were to remain in complete radio silence unless some major event occurred that the task force should know about at once. The hops usually were for three or more hours and generally were pretty boring."

To his surprise, Burgess sighted a Japanese plane low on the water, headed for the task force. He identified it as a twin-engine Betty, which was not a Japanese carrier-type plane and apparently came from either Saipan or Tinian.

"Burgess went after it with his forward-firing 50-caliber machine guns mounted in the wings of the TBM," Mooney said. "He either used up all his ammunition or jammed the guns. Whatever, he observed the Jap was not firing back at him, so he pulled up alongside. He told his turret gunner to fire everything he had, but the Betty remained in the air."

What happened next later became the topic of considerable discussion throughout the task force.

After Burgess' two crewmen, Aviation Machinist's Mate Robert A. Bullock and Aviation Radioman George A. Hodgins, had fired repeatedly at the Betty, which refused to go down, the pilot decided to employ a new technique. A Navy Department release shortly thereafter stated in part:

> "Burgess gradually overtook the Betty and tried to chew up one of its wings with his propeller. After the Avenger's propeller had come to within inches of the Betty's wing, the Jap's frantic work at the controls managed to get the Betty out of the way.
>
> "Determined not to let the Betty escape before he got his guns back in commission, Burgess flew in close formation with the Betty, with only about two feet between the wing tips. He looked over at the Jap pilot and waved. The Jap pilot was not amused and did not wave back. At this point, Bullock, the turret gunner, became mildly frantic. Unable to get his machine gun on the enemy, he opened the escape hatch and emptied all six rounds of his .38 revolver into the Betty. This did not destroy the enemy plane but Bullock said later it gave him great personal satisfaction.
>
> "Burgess got one of his wing guns in operation. He dropped back a quarter of a mile behind the Betty and then began his final attack. The Betty's starboard engine suddenly flamed and the fire spread in the wing. The blazing wing dipped against the waves and the Betty instantly did a cartwheel into the water. End of flight."

As squadron de-briefing reports were completed and details relayed to the admiral's staff on the flagship, full significance of the results emerged. It had been one of the most one-sided aerial victories ever, a telling blow to Japan's steadily dwindling air strength. Four hundred and two enemy planes had been shot down with the loss of two score Task Force 58 fighters.

Few planes from the Land of the Rising Sun had penetrated the task force perimeter, and little damage had resulted. Stripped of their sting, the Japanese carriers and escorts turned back toward the southwest.

In Fighting 27's ready room on the *Princeton*, the exhilaration of victory was coupled with an acute awareness of loss. Wood had been a well-liked and respected leader. Van Carter was a friend, a companion, and a fellow participant in a most dangerous business.

VF-27 pilots had shot down thirty enemy planes in the air battle just ended. Their number now included a half dozen aces, each with five or more "kills" to his credit.

With the loss of Wood, Bardshar became commanding officer of both the fighter squadron and the air group. In the months of training, and more especially in the days of combat, he had earned the respect of those with whom he flew — a respect he hadn't had initially.

Kleffner was among those who acquired an admiration for Bardshar.

"When he started out with the squadron, he was the meanest naval aviator that ever came down the road," Kleffner said. "He was a senior lieutenant when I joined the squadron. He'd been through the naval academy and that allegedly taught him a whole lot. He had 235 flying hours and I think I had 238.

"There wasn't all that much difference except I was a reserve ensign and he was a naval academy graduate. I thought he couldn't fly worth a damn and had everybody so mad there were some real threats. He got the message, finally, that he had to work with us dumb reserves or he was going to have trouble. He turned out to be one of the finest officers in the whole damn navy."

As Lt. Comdr. Frederic A. Bardshar, Annapolis-trained gunnery officer turned fighter pilot, assumed command, Air Group 27 was among the navy's elite — hungry to fly against the enemy from cruiser-become-carrier with a well-deserved reputation of her own.

CHAPTER XII

The Great Chase

ALTHOUGH THE JAPANESE HAD BEEN dealt a devastating blow in the loss of more than 400 carrier planes and — far more significantly — an equal number of hard to replace pilots, their ships had sustained no damage from air attack during the Marianas naval thrust.

This factor was not overlooked by U.S. strategists. Satisfied the combined marine and army position on Saipan was under control, Task Force 58 steamed in pursuit of the enemy carriers.

Through the long night of 19 June and well into the following day, the U.S. carriers, battle wagons, cruisers, and destroyers plowed through the waves with their engines gulping fuel to maintain high speed. During the daylight hours, patrol missions were launched to probe for the enemy.

A frustrating factor was the scouting range of the search planes. The pilots and the air plot crews on the carriers knew their quarry was just ahead; but time and again the hunters had to turn back with dwindling gasoline. In the late afternoon of 20 June after a reported sighting, the decision was made to launch a strike mission — and hope the attackers could inflict maximum damage on the Japanese force and nurse their fuel supply sufficiently to get back aboard. Despite the tremendous risks involved, the enemy warships could not be allowed to slip away unscathed. It was an opportunity that might be a very long time coming again.

Launch came shortly after 1600 hours. The carrier planes, bearing brim-full loads of fuel and munitions, needed two hours to reach the Japanese formation. Through intense anti-aircraft fire, the U.S. fighters and bombers blasted their prey. Four planes from the *Princeton*'s sister ship, the *Belleau Wood*, succeeded in sinking the carrier *Hiyo*. Sixty-five Japanese planes were shot down, and hits were scored on other ships, but the crippled enemy vessels remained afloat.

Running dangerously low on fuel, the U.S. planes turned back toward Task Force 58. While the U.S. Navy had some trained night-fighter squadrons, the pilots making the 20 June assault were not qualified in after-dark carrier operations.

Fading daylight gave way to night as the fighters, torpedo planes, and dive bombers struggled to return to their carriers. One by one, pilots used up their last ounce of gasoline and were forced to land in the sea, some as they came within minutes of making it all the way.

As the sea became dotted with bobbing signal flares and blinking flashlights, a remarkable order was given by Admiral Mitscher — turn on all the lights! Forget the danger of enemy submarines or aerial snoopers. Give the returning fliers every possible chance to bring their planes in.

In a combat setting, where total blackness was the absolute rule for survival, a vast stretch of sea suddenly became a lighted stage, on which the drama was one life and death act after another. Masts carried truck lights, flight decks were outlined by glow lights. Red and green running lights were everywhere.

Planes with engines coughing on gasoline fumes, and little else, ignored normal approach patterns and went straight for the nearest flight deck — sometimes two planes at the same time. Crashes were frequent. Surprisingly, the majority of those who got that far were able to land.

Signal officers gave wave-offs only in those several weird instances when lost and confused Japanese pilots attempted to land on one of the U.S. carriers, mistaking it for their own.

For the members of Air Group 27, the day was a disappointment. They had been confined to the chore of flying routine patrols over the task force and did not take part in the strike against the Japanese ships.

For the navy's high command, the day was an even greater disappointment, in which it was felt a tremendous opportunity to strike the enemy a mortal blow had been missed, with a sizable force of Japanese warships escaping what might well have proven their graveyard.

In his official action report, Admiral Mitscher stated: "The enemy escaped. He had been badly hurt by one aggressive carrier strike, at one time he was within range. His fleet was not sunk."

When it became apparent that no more task force planes would be struggling in, the lights were turned off. Carrier crews worked through the night to clear the flight decks of debris and to salvage any planes still worth saving. With the coming of dawn, a massive rescue effort got underway.

For three days, the ships of the force and the carrier planes scoured thousands of square miles of ocean for downed pilots and air crewmen. Life raft after life raft, and dye marker after dye marker were spotted. Each radio report brought a ray of hope that a friend, a shipmate, had managed to make it. Miraculously, most of those who had gone down in the sea were rescued. Finally, it had to be admitted further search would be fruitless.

As the month of June drew to a close, the task force turned back to the Marianas. The flattops provided air support for the combined marine-army force on Saipan and flew strikes against Tinian, Rota, and Guam, taking time out only for refueling and to take aboard replacement planes which had been ferried out from Eniwetok by escort carriers. These baby flattops took over the task of air support at Saipan as the fast carriers and their screening ships pulled away, low on bombs and stores. On 9 July the most breathtaking naval force ever assembled at one point dropped the hook at Eniwetok.

At every point of the compass there were anchored warships of Task Force 58 — four task groups, each consisting of four carriers, one or two battleships, and an assortment of cruisers and destroyers.

Meanwhile, as the ships were being resupplied and rearmed, their crews were given an opportunity to go ashore for recreation. This proved a mixed blessing. The sun in the southern Pacific areas can be intense, indeed, brutal. Any swimmer unaccustomed to the perils of even the briefest nap on the beach at such spots as

Eniwetok could arrive back at the ship a basket-case — with a dose of sunburn worthy of discussion in the *Journal of the American Medical Association*.

The agony of surviving such a "tanning" was a lesson learned permanently. The mere touch of a bed sheet to any flaming-red portion of the body was excruciatingly painful. Virtually every sickbay on the ships of the task force did a land office business in sunburn treatment.

But the tropical sun was not the only recreational hazard awaiting the task force's crew members. The varieties of fish were endless and fascinating, and servicemen turned loose on the beaches of the South Pacific found these too inviting to ignore. If the fisherman was lucky, he had been briefed as to the differences between the safe species and those to avoid like the plague. Some were edible part of the year, but fatal if eaten in the wrong season.

Sea shells also were a welcome source of diversion. Among those most sought after were cateyes, which were named from the colored pattern on the shell. When cleaned and polished, these could be made into attractive necklaces and bracelets, highly desirable for establishing social contacts in port or for taking home.

Surprisingly varied recreation programs were available during task force stays at Majuro, Eniwetok, Ulithi, and other atolls or islands seized from the Japanese and turned into fleet supply points.

"When we got liberty, we'd go ashore for a bottle of beer, a swim, and to hunt shells," said Aviation Machinist Mate Lyle Giddle. "At Eniwetok, they had one place fixed up pretty good for liberty parties. There was an old Japanese ammunition ship that had sunk there. Part of it stuck up above water, and guys would swim out to it, although they weren't suppose to. There was some swimming off the side of the ships, too, as well as movies on the hangar deck at night sometimes."

Organized sports took the form of volleyball and boxing. Even the rankest amateurs could become involved in the former, but the latter was confined generally to those with some experience.

Star of the *Princeton* volleyball team was Sam Jaskilka, who commanded the carrier's marine unit. Jaskilka, in his service career, went from second lieutenant to the four stars of a full general, serving as deputy commandant of the Marine Corps before he retired.

"Crew members from the *San Jacinto* [a sister ship of the *Prince-*

ton] were invited over for the first competition outside our own property," Giddle said. "They brought their volleyball teams, their boxers, and also their orchestra. They had better volleyball teams, but our boys won five of the nine boxing bouts. There was a turkey dinner that day with all the fixings, and the *San Jacinto* orchestra played.

"Later, we went over to the *Cabot* [another CVL], won the boxing card, and broke even in volleyball. Another time, our boxing team beat the guys from the *Langley*. We had in our crew one fighter who, before his induction in the navy, had a chance at the middleweight title back home. His name was Buddy O'Dell."

One would-be boxer was held in considerable awe by his crewmates because of his impressive physique and his predictions of what he planned to do to the opposition — that is, until he actually climbed into the ring for the first time. His opponent landed a flurry of telling blows in the opening round, to the obvious surprise and pain of Mr. Big. Before the bell sounded the end of the round, he climbed back through the ropes and let it be known he wanted no more part of boxing. His "pecking order" among his fellows went downhill dramatically, particularly with those who had made a bet on the bout's outcome.

Some of the pilots whose survival in the air depended on their own machine-gun accuracy, or that of their crewmen, got their "kicks" on the beach by impromptu target shooting with the 38-caliber hand guns issued to them by the navy. Their targets normally were empty beer bottles, or coconuts from the nearest tree.

One group from Air Group 27, tiring of such a target shoot, became involved with an Eniwetok octopus. Torpedo pilot Tom Mooney tells the tale:

"When our ammunition was gone, we got some cans of beer and went back to the beach, where somehow we came across a large metal wash tub several feet in diameter and maybe ten or twelve inches high. We filled it with ice for the beer and started wading around in the surf.

"Octopuses were common in the lagoon, and we were careful around any coral outcroppings where we might come on one. I'm not sure where we found the damn thing but it was my idea to unload the wash tub and try to scoop him up in the knee-deep water, which was so clear you could see for fifty feet.

"He wasn't very big, maybe ten to twenty inches across his

body when the tentacles weren't extended. He was pretty docile, and it seemed fairly easy just to slip the tub under him, lift it up, and carry tub and octopus thirty feet or so above the high water line.

"It was really exciting just to watch him lobbing up and down for awhile, not doing much of anything. It occurred to us that he needed a change of water periodically so we'd carry the tub into the surf, let a wave break over it, and carry him back. He attracted a lot of attention from other guys in the area; and I'm sure we had pretty good stories about how we had been deep-diving when we caught him in twenty or thirty feet of reef water.

"As the afternoon wore on it got to be a drag to carry the tub back and forth to the surf to refresh the creature's water supply. The beer we had been issued wasn't the greatest. I decided to empty the last several cans into the wash tub. I wasn't even looking at him. With no warning at all, that little devil went crazy. Two or more tentacles were wrapped around my left arm.

"In one millisecond all the grade 'B' movies I had ever seen about divers being dragged to their deaths by an eight-foot-in-diameter octopus flashed before my eyes. I have no clear recollection as to how I got rid of him, but do know that he had me flailing and pulling with my free hand, using all the strength I had.

"Somehow I pulled the tentacles off. There was a hunting knife in my belt, but I knew I couldn't use it without cutting my own arm. Once out of his grip, I made an instant decision — get rid of that octopus. We carried the tub carefully down to the surf and threw him out of it. Moral — never give an octopus cheap beer."

CHAPTER XIII

On to the Philippines

RESUPPLIED, THE FAST CARRIERS returned to the Marianas in mid-July to lead air support as U.S. Marine assault forces scrambled ashore, initially at Guam, and then at Tinian.

A coordinated team effort, involving ground forces and carrier squadrons, was being perfected at this stage of the Pacific war as an extremely valuable attack element. The capability of 250–300-mile-an-hour planes with blazing machine guns or wing-mounted rockets to lay a path of fire, to neutralize troublesome enemy gun positions in front of advancing troops, was just being fully realized.

This tactic involved a ground coordinator, working with the troops, to pinpoint desired target areas; and an air coordinator to relay constantly changing target information to incoming attack planes.

Because of speeds at which the Hellcats flew, the variety of terrain involved, and the broad impact area covered by airborne machine-gun fire, this was a very tricky maneuver at best. Early results were spotty, but the concept paid off with increasing success.

Japanese air capability in the area had been eliminated; and when the carriers ran low on bombs and ammunition during the marine landings on Tinian, the flattops anchored in the mile-wide channel between that island and Saipan. Within sight of the enemy forces still occupying much of Tinian, munitions were ferried out from Saipan by barge and loaded on the carrier. During the day-long supplying operation, ship crew members and air group personnel were given a spectator's view of the fierce fighting going on ashore.

A warship such as the *Princeton* — engaged in prolonged operations at sea — had to depend on its evaporators to remove the salt from seawater, and providing a continuous supply of fresh water. Because the *Princeton*'s evaporators needed considerable work to put them in good shape for future campaigns, the ship went back to Eniwetok.

When the necessary repairs were completed, the carrier returned to sea, joining in an attack against the Palau Islands — the last major roadblock before the inevitable assault on the Philippines.

Primary target was Peleliu Island, destined to be the next site of an amphibious push. After a series of bombing and strafing missions, the fast carriers pulled away and turned the task of air and bombardment support during the landing operation over to a force of baby flattops and older battleships. The fast carriers steamed toward the Philippines to neutralize the enemy's air power there and prevent the Japanese from launching air missions against the U.S. ships and troops at Peleliu.

For the first time since the flag of the Rising Sun had replaced the Stars and Stripes in the archipelago, U.S. Navy planes on 10 September attacked installations in the Philippines. That day, guerrillas, in their jungle hideouts, were able to see friendly forces attacking the enemy they had been resisting for two years.

Del Monte, on the southernmost island of Mindanao, was attacked by planes from the *Princeton*, *Lexington* and *Enterprise*. Three days later, air missions were flown against Cebu in the Central Philippines — close to Leyte, where landing craft soon were to carry U.S. troops back to the islands they had been forced to relinquish.

On 21 September the *Princeton*'s fighter planes joined the Hellcat squadrons from the other fast carriers in initial sweeps over Manila and the nearby Japanese airfields.

Under Air Group 27's commander, Bardshar, forty-eight Hellcats from the *Princeton* and two other CVLs struck the principal Japanese air installation, Nichols Field. The enemy launched every plane they had available. In the ensuing melee, the *Princeton*'s sixteen fighters accounted for thirty-eight of the enemy aircraft, a score that made VF-27 the top CVL fighter squadron.

Two of the *Princeton*'s pilots were shot down. One of these, Ens. Oliver Scott, made a forced landing near the island of Masbate. His plight was observed by guerrillas ashore. They went to his rescue in a canoe, took him to their headquarters, and were able to radio word to the carrier force. Later that same day, a seaplane from the battleship *Massachusetts* went to the area under fighter escort, picked up Scott, and returned him to the *Princeton* in time for dinner.

Lamb, another *Princeton* pilot and VF-27's executive officer, also made a forced landing in a lake near Manila. He, too, was retrieved by friendly guerrillas — literally under the noses of Japanese search parties, who had seen Lamb's plane go down. Lamb was spirited out of the Manila area and hidden by the guerrilla band until they were able to establish radio contact with U.S. Navy forces. A submarine moved in close to shore and took Lamb aboard. He was sent back to Pearl Harbor to await an opportunity to rejoin the *Princeton*.

A third VF-27 pilot made it back to a friendly carrier, but not his own, after a terrifying ordeal over the Philippines. Ens. Frederick "Fritz" Hautop was among those making the first fighter sweep over Manila since that city had been occupied by the Japanese.

"It was a pre-dawn hop," he said. "The weather was bad. When we got about half way to the target, they started jamming our radios. By the time we got to the target it was daybreak, and the weather had cleared.

"The only thing we encountered, besides enemy flak, was one enemy twin-engine bomber in the traffic pattern at Nichols Field. Our skipper [Fred Bardshar] and his wingman left the formation, went in to shoot it down, then rejoined, and we circled Nichols Field for half an hour at 10,000 feet.

"There were many planes on the field, so the skipper had us go down and strafe the field, which is exactly what they were waiting for us to do. When we came up, there they were, and we were engaged in one of the biggest dogfights I've ever seen in my life."

Hautop got a Japanese Zeke fighter in his sights.

"All I had to do was give him a few bursts and that blew him out of the air," he said. "Immediately after that I had a Tony on my tail, and to this day I don't know what type of maneuver I made, but when I came out I was on his. The only thing was, I was slow and it took a long time to close. I had to chase him all the way across Manila Bay before I could hit him right, have him roll over and go in."

Hautop realized that the air seemed clear of enemy planes, and that it was time to rendezvous for the return flight to the carriers.

"Heading in the direction of the task group, all of a sudden we were jumped by a couple of dozen Tonys. One Tony got on me as I started to turn into my division leader and blew my guns right out of the wings. I expected my division leader to turn into me to get him off my tail, but he had left to shoot another Tony off the skipper's tail. I had no alternative but to dive down toward the earth."

The Japanese Tony was armed with a pair of 20-millimeter guns in each wing and two 12.7 machine guns in the plane's nose. Hautop knew full well his attacker was making optimum use of all his weapons.

"During the entire time of his pursuit," he said, "I could feel the force of bullets hitting the armor plate behind me. As I dove toward the earth I grabbed my microphone, which was made of a type of plastic, and screamed 'get this bastard off my tail.' My fear was so intense that my microphone crumbled right in my hand."

The beleaguered pilot continued his dive wide open "damn near into Lake Taal."

"When I leveled off, there was a hill ahead of me, and as I went over the hill my prop pitch went out and dropped back to 1,700 RPM. This guy was on me all the way. Fortunately, there was ground fog, which I went in and out of three times. He was on my tail all the way, blowing me apart every time I came out."

After what seemed to be an eternity, Hautop reached the sea where the weather had again turned foul.

"I went into a black, mean-looking cloud hanging right over the water," he said, "and when I came out he was gone — apparently into the sea."

He turned on his emergency IFF (identification device), hoping to receive word by radio as to his location.

"One of the carriers sent three planes out to pick me up and I followed them in. I couldn't slow the plane down below 120 knots or it would stall out on me. I couldn't land aboard the *Princeton* at that speed because it was too small, so I had to land on the *Hornet*."

His landing was hair-raising. He approached the *Hornet*'s flight deck straight in and low on the water.

"I almost got into position, but an SB2C [dive bomber] was coming in at the same time and I had to get out of there. I called the *Hornet* and told them I couldn't slow it down — I had no prop control, 1,700 RPM and I was very low on fuel."

He knew he could not make another pass at landing on the carrier and asked if he could make a water landing beside the *Hornet*.

"They said 'No, come aboard.' Fortunately, everything went well and I got aboard."

As soon as the deck crew had loosed Hautop's landing hook from the arresting cable, the plane's wings were folded, and he taxied forward on the flight deck. "After I jumped off the wing," he said, "I collapsed and sat there looking at the plane. I couldn't believe how badly it was shot up. They just removed the radio equipment and things like that, then shoved it overboard."

The following morning, Hautop was provided with a *Hornet* Hellcat and flew back to the *Princeton* to rejoin his squadron.

The carrier ammunition "larders" had been depleted by the softening-up sweeps through the central and southern Philippines. The fleet turned back to the northeast and, in a calculated gamble, anchored in the Koror Passage, hugging the north shore of Babelthuap, in the Palau Island group.

Babelthuap remained in the hands of over 20,000 Japanese troops. Well within eyesight of that enemy force, the carriers were replenished with bombs, ammunition, and supplies. The resupply operation continued until late in the day. The U.S. ships remained at anchor until their departure the following morning, to the great relief of the command strategists, who had opted to go with the risks involved.

That incident turned out to be a unique supply-by-night operation in the drive across the Pacific. Bombs and stores had been loaded on the task force ships right under the noses of enemy troops ashore, totally unlike the scene at such points as Ulithi. There, the island had been seized from the Japanese, and all the necessary supply facilities had been installed in a near-miraculous manner, creating a bustling port scene on a spit of land in the middle of nowhere.

Where there had been little else but the wind and the lapping of waves on a reef-protected beach, there suddenly were ships, piers, forklifts, and mountains of crates containing high explosives, medical supplies, and foodstuffs.

It was while the task force ships were moored at Ulithi, in early October, that word was received of an approaching typhoon of massive force. Hurriedly, the carriers, battleships, cruisers, and destroyers weighed anchor and headed for the open sea, where they would have a better chance of riding out the raging storm. A ship caught in harbor could be washed ashore and destroyed.

The next two days were brutal, especially for the crews of the destroyers. The ships rose and plunged with every wave, and even biggest among them took "green water" over their decks. Sailors who had been at sea for months, even years, were violently sick for the first time. Trying to maintain any semblance of cruising formation was almost impossible, as the tip of a battleship's superstructure would disappear in the trough between mountainous waves — momentarily lost from view to those on the bridge of any carrier, or other ship, nearby.

On the destroyers, it was a matter of holding onto something at all times. Hot food was out of the question for those who still had the stomach for eating. Sleeping involved bruising contact with one side of the bunk, then the other. Any object not firmly lashed in place was in constant motion.

The *Princeton* and her sister CVLs demonstrated their flair for extreme rolls, as much as thirty degrees from dead level, with seawater crashing across their forecastles, and even washing over the flight decks.

During this period of violent weather, a strange event took place on the *Princeton* — a court-martial proceeding in the middle of a typhoon.

Lt. Comdr. (later Commander) Jim Large was named president of the summary court-martial to hear evidence and preside over the trial.

"Some of the shipfitters, usually a rough and ready rating, had broken into a supply of aviation alcohol," Large said. "The resulting midnight party developed into a near riot as the shipfitters became embroiled and used the heavy tools of their trade as weapons. It was a real donnybrook, and our medics had a busy night."

Charges were brought, and the court-martial convened despite the typhoon.

"What a trial it was," Large said. "Members of the court, witnesses, and the accused were seated in chairs lashed to a table. There was some slack in the president's line [Large himself] and, as the ship rolled heavily, he occasionally slithered right out of the proceedings, to return majestically with the counterroll. Somehow we reached a tortured verdict, which later was lost with the ship, to the delight of the defendants."

Through the first two weeks of October, the fast carriers roamed the western Pacific at will. Bold attack missions were carried out against Okinawa, principal island in the Nansei Shoto, or Ryukyu group, bringing the U.S. naval units closer to the Japanese homeland than at any point since the start of the war.

Air Group 27 Hellcats and Avengers were part of four strikes on Okinawa, catching the Japanese by surprise and wreaking major damage on enemy installations and planes caught on the ground.

As Task Force 38 moved on to Formosa (the old Portugese name for Taiwan), the element of surprise was gone. Japanese aircraft attacked both by day and by night. A chilling new weapon — the kamikaze or "Divine Wind" — was introduced. Japanese kamikaze deliberately sacrificed themselves by piloting their planes into the U.S. ships, insuring direct hits.

The cruiser *Reno*, in formation beside the *Princeton*, was struck by a kamikaze and sustained serious damage to the ship's after tow gear — a result destined to have an effect on efforts to save the *Princeton* a short time later.

As the task force left Formosa, the cruisers *Houston* and *Canberra* were hit by aerial torpedoes. The *Princeton*'s fighter planes provided air protection as the crippled vessels limped away at a four-knot pace. For days, the Hellcats battled back enemy planes trying to finish off the damaged cruisers. Both the *Houston* and *Canberra* made it back to Ulithi.

By 21 October photo missions were being flown over Luzon to help plot the invasion of the Philippines. The fast carriers and their screening vessels hastily refueled at sea, preparing for a show-down with the Japanese naval force that U.S. submarine reports indicated was moving down from the north.

On to the Philippines

CHAPTER XIV

Fighter Pilots' Day

BY 24 OCTOBER 1944 THE global conflict had moved into its sixth year. In Europe, the Soviet army was invading Hitler's Reich along an eighty-seven-mile front.

With the Pacific war nearing the end of its third year, the Japanese tide of conquest was receding under the mounting pressure of Allied land, sea, and air power. Although the future appeared certain to include a fierce and bloody invasion of the Japanese homeland, the end could be anticipated.

In the pre-dawn hours of that squally October day, Adm. William F. "Bull" Halsey's Third Fleet was steaming in the waters east of the Philippine Islands with a dual purpose — to lend backup support to the U.S. invasion of the central Philippines and, hopefully, to deliver a crippling blow to the Imperial Navy.

Halsey's naval force was awesome — eight large carriers; eight smaller fast carriers, including *Princeton;* a half dozen new battleships; fifteen cruisers; and fifty-eight destroyers.

They were divided into four task groups. The *Princeton* was teamed with the bigger carriers *Essex* and *Lexington,* and her sister CVL, the *Langley*; the battleships *South Dakota* and *Massachusetts*; the cruisers *Mobile, Birmingham, Santa Fe* and *Reno*; and a screen of thirteen destroyers.

The first hint of sunrise was not yet evident when the *Essex* and *Lexington* launched a flight of fighters and torpedo planes to carry out a 300-mile search of the Sibuyan Sea and the waters off Mindoro, where it was believed some units of the Japanese fleet were lurking.

In other pre-dawn launchings, the *Langley* sent up Anti-Submarine and Anti-Snooper Patrols, the *Essex* dispatched a twenty-plane fighter sweep to cover the airfields around Manila, and the *Princeton* provided an eight-plane combat air patrol to give air protection for the task group.

Air plot had reported bogeys in the area even before the carrier launchings. In their first hour of patrolling, *Langley* pilots shot down two Japanese snoopers and *Princeton* fighters accounted for four more.

The relative quiet didn't last long. Shortly after the last of the six snoopers had been destroyed, a large group of enemy planes, estimated to be between forty and fifty in number, was detected by radar about seventy-five miles west of the task group. Another flight of thirty or more soon joined the first. The bogeys were stacked at various altitudes up to 25,000 feet.

The eight *Princeton* fighters on combat air patrol were vectored to intercept the approaching enemy force, and all the carriers were ordered by the task group commander to launch additional fighters to join the attack. The *Princeton* sent up three more four-plane divisions, twelve Hellcats to join her eight fighters already committed.

The *Princeton* combat air patrol intercepted the enemy about fifty miles from the task group. Before other U.S. planes reached the tallyho point, a wild aerial melee developed.

One of the *Princeton*'s four-plane combat air patrol divisions was led by Carl Brown, a truly remarkable aviator whose proud boast was that he came from Texas. The second division was led by "Red" Shirley, who was to become the top ace in the squadron.

"That day had begun about 3 A.M. for the pre-dawn combat air patrol," Shirley said. "I led Division Four off the ship about 4 A.M. and during joinup was given a vector toward a low target. After a few steers, I sighted the bogey and we closed to splash a Judy.

"More single targets were given to us, and in the next forty-five minutes we sighted and downed three more bogeys at low- and mid-altitudes near the perimeter of our operating area."

Fighter Pilots' Day

Shirley then was instructed by radio to climb to maximum altitude and speed toward a large bogey group sixty to seventy miles to the west.

"Just after daylight," Shirley said, "we began to make out an unusually large formation of planes of every Japanese make stacked in altitudes from six to twenty-five thousand feet and headed toward our fleet."

He reported the sighting by radio. He said he would start an attack and continue until out of ammunition or fuel.

"We started in head-on," Shirley said, "at our altitude of about twenty-three thousand feet and worked our way down as we had to. First, we reversed course with an overhead run, and each of us took out one or more planes on the first pass. Our speed advantage was about fifty knots, so we repeatedly made runs in and through their formation, bringing down planes each time."

With all ammunition expended, Shirley and his companions returned to the *Princeton*.

"On final debriefing," he said, "as best we could account, Division Four splashed four Jap planes before the large contact, and fifteen of the large group, for a total of nineteen planes during that one flight."

Brown, who after twenty-four years in naval aviation became dean of aviation technology at Embry-Riddle University and wrote several aviation textbooks, recalls the pre-dawn launch that started "one of the most exciting days of my life." An understatement if there ever was one.

"We had been briefed that we could expect some snoopers," Brown said. "At that time, I had a replacement pilot assigned to me for training. Because snoopers were likely, I put the new man on the number four spot in our division, figuring he'd learn more by following the example of the three pilots ahead of him."

In the world of naval combat aviation, a lead pilot and his wingman — who flew formation beside and slightly behind his leader — formed a team that survived for any length of time only if one protected the other.

"In the blackness of that pre-dawn launch, my regular wingman wound up on the other division leader's wing and I had the new man on mine. My division was assigned high patrol at 20,000 feet and the other division was given low patrol at 10,000. We usually swapped altitudes halfway through the patrol. I figured when we did we'd reorganize and I could get my wingman back. As it worked out I never again flew combat with my wingman on that flight or any other."

Brown's introduction to the air battle that followed came in the form of a radio message from Hatchet Base (the *Princeton*'s code name during this operation): "Hatchet Three-One [Brown's division] and Hatchet Six-One [Shirley's], vector 240. Gate!" The *Princeton*'s pilots were being told to head in the indicated compass direction using all possible speed. If air command wanted its planes to get somewhere in a hurry, the code was "Buster." Gate was reserved for *emergency* emergencies.

As Brown's division went to gate speed, and at the same time began gaining altitude, the pilots shifted into a wide combat formation. By radio, they heard Shirley's "Tallyho. Three bogeys." Then, moments later, three plumes of smoke trailed down in the sky and another radio transmission: "This is Hatchet Six-One. Grand Slam. Three bogeys."

"I was cussing a little to myself," Brown said. "I thought the three bogeys were all there were — but all of a sudden there they were. I let Hatchet Base and the other division know the enemy force was high at 240 and added, 'the sky's black with them'."

Figuring his group's best bet was to gain as much speed as possible and pull right up into the Japanese formation, Brown tried to estimate the enemy's strength. His quick count — sixty-five fighters and fifteen dive bombers. In the initial moments of the fight there were only eight U.S. planes present.

Due in large part to his abiding interest in air tactics, Brown's recollections of the air battle are vivid.

"Shortly we were into them. I pulled up, carefully keeping my speed above 160 knots indicated, for the Zero liked to get us when we were slow. We were at about 21,000 feet, maybe a little higher. Some Zeroes came at me from two o'clock. I turned hard into them and fired. As they flashed by I reversed my turn.

"I made some violent reversals, firing at a minimum of six aircraft while the new man, Hatchet Three-Two, was on my wing. The next thing I remember is weaving a couple of times with my wing man and shooting at planes coming in on his tail. I remember, too, that as we came at each other in the weave, Three-Two's guns were going, so I knew he was firing at enemy coming in at me.

"Then I couldn't find Three-Two and couldn't see any of our

Fighter Pilots' Day

planes. In fact, all I saw was aircraft with meat balls on them, and they were everywhere. The thought came to me, as I saw no other friendlies, that I was the only American left in the fight. I didn't believe I could get away with all those enemy planes around. From that point my memory of what happened is quite clear."

As Brown whipped out of a turn a Zero appeared dead ahead. Brown pulled up closer and opened fire with his 50-caliber wing guns. He saw bits and pieces fly from the enemy plane, which came out of its gradual turn and flew straight.

"I knew better than to fly a straight line in combat," Brown said, "That's deadly, but I got stubborn and followed the Zero. Just as he burst into flames, all hell broke loose in my cockpit. Bullets were flying into it and, fortunately, I reacted fast, jamming my stick all the way forward.

"I was thrown against my safety belt as dirt, pencils, and whatever came flying against the top of my canopy. I was pointing straight down at the sea and the hail of bullets stopped. No one can follow that maneuver and track for accurate shooting. I always kept it for last ditch use."

Using the moment's respite he had gained, Brown looked back. There were four Zeroes coming down on him for another attack. Still in a vertical dive, he turned sharply to the right and lost the Japanese fighters, which couldn't turn well to the right at higher speeds.

Emerging from large cumulus clouds, Brown found himself alone. He called Hatchet Base and requested a vector to any enemy aircraft in the area. As he began to follow the directions provided, he assessed the damage to himself and his Hellcat.

"They had hit me pretty well," he said. "Two 20-millimeters came into the cockpit, exploding on the instrument panel. I didn't have many instruments in working condition. My air speed indicator was okay.

"One piece of shrapnel went out of the cockpit just above the throttle, grazing my thumb. Another cut a fuel line leading to the transfer valve. Fuel was all over the cockpit deck and even though I wanted a cigarette, I didn't dare light one."

Twenty-millimeter shells had ripped through his port wing and gone into the port wheel well. Brown could see torn rubber and so he knew that tire was flat. Then he realized the inside of his left thigh was numb. He was bleeding.

"I cut my coveralls with my hunting knife and saw two small pieces of shrapnel in my leg, about an eighth of an inch in diameter and three-quarters of an inch long. I pulled them out and bled like a stuck hog, so I got a compress bandage out of my first aid kit to stop the bleeding."

Meanwhile, he was following the vector given him toward the enemy planes still in the air, hoping to rejoin the fight. Another *Princeton* Hellcat joined Brown, and together they headed for their carrier — a carrier they were shocked to find on fire. Brown was told the *Princeton* couldn't take him aboard. And the presence of gasoline in his cockpit, coupled with other damage to his plane, posed a landing hazard to other carriers about to receive their own aircraft. Brown radioed he would make a water landing near the lead destroyer of the formation.

As he was preparing to let down, he was given a go-ahead to land on the *Essex*. "Here she was," Brown recalled, "volunteering to take me aboard when it was almost certain that I'd foul her deck. To say I was grateful was to put it mildly. The captain had to have great confidence in the ability of his deck crew to clear wreckage quickly."

The *Essex*'s landing signal officer gave Brown a "roger" (everything is fine), although Brown knew he was coming in high and fast.

"I kept coming in a descending approach, not the standard type we flew. But there he stood, letting me make my own approach. I liked that. He knew my aircraft was shot up and was letting me fly the way I thought best, at the same time ready to signal me at any time I got dangerous."

Using an emergency carbon dioxide bottle, Brown managed to lower his wheels and the plane's flaps were working. The hook which normally catches one of the deck cables to bring the plane to a halt in landing, however, refused to come down. Brown solved that problem at the moment of impact by bouncing the tail on the deck and out popped the hook, just in time.

Lieutenant Commander Bardshar, who later was to rise to the rank of vice admiral, as Air Group 27 commander had been assigned strike leader for a planned attack against Japanese forces in the Sibuyan Sea, using torpedo planes and fighters from the *Princeton* and other carriers. On the *Princeton*, nine torpedo bombers were sitting armed and ready on the hangar deck as the oncoming Japanese air formation was detected.

"When the enemy sent out a number of planes to attack our ships, we countered in self-defense and put up increasingly more fighters. They'd call for a division from this carrier and then a division from that one and so forth," Bardshar said.

"I was sitting in the *Princeton*'s ready room, preparing to go on the big attack against the Japanese ships, when it became clear to me that the strike wasn't going to occur. There wasn't any point of me waiting in the ready room with most of our fighters already in the air, so my division went off with the last four fighters launched from the *Princeton* that morning."

Flying at 10,000 feet, Bardshar requested permission from the ship-based command to join the "Japanese circus going on out there about 10,000 feet above us," but at that point air command was "just too busy."

"The Japanese made a pass at us," Bardshar remembers, "and then disappeared in the overcast. We smoked two or three of them, but it was difficult to tell whether we scored any kills. Some of our planes had been hit, but nobody was hurt."

At that point, he was informed the *Princeton* had a "fouled deck" and couldn't take Bardshar's group back aboard. It wasn't until he approached the task group that he realized from the rising smoke and the disarray of the ship formation that his carrier had been hit. He was instructed to land on the *Essex*.

"In circumstances like that, when you land on another carrier and finally they have too many planes on board, the ones that were shot up are pushed over the side. There was a bit of folklore about that. The bluejackets always liked it. They'd put a badly damaged plane out on an elevator and then one-two-three, yell 'Buy Bonds!' You have to remember that fighter planes then cost somewhere around $65,000 to $70,000, while fighter planes later cost twenty million dollars or more."

Kleffner was among the *Princeton* pilots taking part in the wild aerial melee 20,000 feet above Task Group 38.3. After a series of dogfights, in which he "shot down a couple," he headed for home base low on ammunition and fuel. As he approached the *Princeton*, Kleffner was given a wave-off by the carrier landing signal officer.

"That upset me more than a little bit," he said, "because by then I was a fairly accomplished aviator and didn't like to get wave-offs. As I pulled up to go around, I noticed smoke was coming out where it wasn't supposed to. I radioed with a little touch of sarcasm 'it looks like you've got something wrong down there.' The landing signal officer responded 'We've just taken a bomb. Land on Buick Base [the *Essex*]. I did that, and compared to the *Princeton* it was like landing on a runway at Alameda Naval Air Station.''

Ens. Paul Drury and Lt. Ralph Taylor were two *Princeton* pilots who managed to land before the bomb hit, but under considerably different circumstances. Drury was a member of a division of four fighters involved in the interception of the Japanese planes, along with Shirley's group.

"After we took off in the dark, radar vectored us out to a couple of Japanese observation planes. That was easy, because they were just singles and there were four of us.

"Then radar said there was a huge bunch of bogeys out there and they sent us after them. We had the advantage by getting up into the sun and coming down on the Japanese. Things happened so fast, but I do recall thinking this is exactly like they said we ought to do it," Drury said.

After helping to break up the initial Japanese formation, and a second one intercepted by *Lexington* fighter pilots, Drury returned to the *Princeton*. He was in the ready room being debriefed when the *Princeton* was struck.

Taylor had been wounded during the giant battle in the skies, but managed to land on the *Princeton*. He had to be helped from his plane on the carrier's flight deck. Taylor was having shrapnel wounds in his leg treated when the enemy dive bomber came down.

It had been a fighter pilots' day. Two Japanese flights of more than one hundred planes attempting to strike Task Force 38 had been turned back with heavy losses. The *Princeton*'s fighters alone had accounted for thirty-four enemy planes, with the loss of one of their own.

CHAPTER XV

One Plane, One Bomb

ABOARD SHIP, EXCEPT FOR THOSE who had turned in after their midnight–0400 watch, the day had gotten off to an early start.

Captain Buracker was on the bridge along with his designated successor, Captain Hoskins, who was getting on-the-job experience before assuming command of the carrier. Lieutenant Moitoret, the ship's navigation officer, was at his general quarters station on the bridge.

In air plot, former Philadelphia banker Lt. Comdr. James Large and members of his staff were continuing their radar surveillance of the skies and waters around the *Princeton*. In the forward and after ready rooms, just under the port side of the carrier's flight deck, the squadron air combat intelligence officers, Bill Kerr and the author, were sorting through the logistics, weather, and other information they would need shortly to brief the torpedo and fighter pilots.

On the flight and hangar decks, fire hoses had been strung as the ship went to general quarters at 0520.

In the bake shop, three levels below the flight deck, the bakers were turning out bread and pies under the critical-eye of Chief Commissary Steward Frederick Plath, who came to the *Princeton* after surviving the sinking of the aircraft carrier *Hornet* at the Battle of Santa Cruz.

Under the promise of enemy engagement, the ship was prepared for a long stretch at the alert, and plans called for bringing food to the gun crews, bridge personnel, and plane handlers at their stations.

Flight deck crews were kept hopping as the combat air patrol planes were armed, fueled, and launched, immediately followed by more fighters scrambling to join the battle that had developed.

The enemy attack was broken up by 0845 and the carriers were ordered to recall enough fighters to provide an escort for the planned torpedo assault against the Japanese fleet.

To make room on the *Princeton*'s flight deck, six armed torpedo bombers had to be moved to the hangar deck. With them out of the way, ten fighters were taken back aboard and two others were headed home. Although some of the F6Fs had been shot up and damaged, the twelve planes were expected to include eight sufficiently airworthy to accompany the strike mission.

But the pilots of VT-27 never got the chance to carry out their scheduled torpedo attack against the Japanese fleet. And the waiting had not been easy.

"It was a pretty exciting prospect," said Tom Mooney. "Our squadron never had dropped live torpedoes against the enemy. There just weren't too many experienced torpedo pilots because they were a little like the Japanese kamikazes. You get one chance. Because of the nature of the attack you come in very low and slow — the TBM did only about 180 knots — and you had to have the airplane well-stabilized in a proper position above the water to make a successful drop. You had to do a lot of things that made it all the easier to shoot you down.

"The prospects were rather stimulating. In fact, some of our people were shaking with patriotism."

At 0912 the *Essex* reported a possible bogey, along with a friendly plane, about six miles northwest of the task group. No other unidentified aircraft were reported within twenty-five miles of the formation.

Less than a half-hour later — at 0938 while the gasoline detail was fueling Hellcats on the flight deck, a lone Japanese dive bomber plunged out of the low cloud cover ahead of the *Princeton*. The intruder — identified as a type known as "Judy" — was spotted by *Princeton* lookouts. The carrier's rudder was put twenty degrees to the left in an effort to avoid the attack. Although gun crews on the *Princeton* and other ships opened fire, the Judy's pilot dropped a single 550-pound bomb, which scored a direct hit slightly to the port side of the flight deck center line and about seventy-five feet forward of the after elevator.

While 20-millimeter gunners on the *Princeton* believed they registered hits, the Judy pulled out of its dive at 1,000 feet, directly over the carrier, and disappeared aft. The *Princeton*'s rudder was reversed and the ship rejoined the task group formation, maintaining a twenty-four-knot speed. A radio report was made to the task group commander: "I have taken a bomb. Will keep you informed."

In penetrating the flight deck, the bomb made a hole less than a foot-and-a-half in diameter. On the hangar deck and the second deck where the bomb exploded, the results were devastating. Among the eventual survivors there were nearly as many accounts of what happened "when the bomb hit" as there were individuals to relate them.

On the bridge, Captain Buracker had only a brief warning when a *Princeton* lookout detected the Japanese plane diving on the ship.

"Our guns and those of the ships in company, took the plane under fire," Buracker said. "I started to maneuver, but there wasn't sufficient time. The bomb was dropped from 1,200 feet, hitting the *Princeton* forward of the after elevator.

"From where I stood on the bridge, the hole in the flight deck appeared so small it seemed hardly possible major damage had been done. I visualized slapping on a patch in a hurry and resuming operations, but the bomb put out of commission the after firefighting system. It also passed right through the gas tank of a torpedo plane, spreading the fire instantly to others.

"The bomb exploded below the hangar deck. Flames shot through the engineering spaces aft and back into the hangar. Smoke was intense from the start, and soon was billowing up from the sides of the ship, flowing aft and making the stern untenable for personnel there. Because of the heat and smoke, men were forced to jump overboard. Circling destroyers picked them up."

Lt. Frank Bell, the ship's assistant navigator, had been a prep school teacher and coach. He was one who volunteered under a special naval reserve program for men with a coaching background, and as such served as athletic officer on the *Princeton*. When the ship went to general quarters, he was stationed at a 20-millimeter battery near the forward port corner of the flight deck.

"I just happened to be looking up from my vantage point, and I spotted the enemy plane diving on the carrier. It was too late to take evasive action, for the clouds were low. Following the plane with my eyes, I could plainly see the bomb under the fuselage. I saw the bomb released and the plane pull out of its dive. You wouldn't think one bomb could do so much damage to an aircraft carrier."

Americo Mazziotti, an aviation ordnanceman, was on the wing of a fighter plane, reloading the F6F with ammunition after its return aboard.

"I told my helper I needed boxes of right-hand feed and he had to go to the port side of the flight deck where we had the ammunition stored. When he came back, he brought left-hand feed boxes and I had to send him back again. While he was gone, I kept an eye on the aft part of the flight deck and the barrier, the cables which were stretched across the deck to form a sort of fence to stop planes when they had to.

"I had seen planes miss the arresting cables and hit the barrier, sometimes plowing right into planes forward. Anyway, while I was looking down the flight deck I saw splinters fly up from the flight deck and I just knew it was a bomb.

"There were explosions on the hangar deck while I was still loading ammunition in the fighter plane. Then after awhile the word came to abandon ship."

When the bomb hit, Lt. Comdr. Louis Levy, the air group flight surgeon, was at his battle station on the flight deck at the base of the island structure.

"Thinking the PA [public address] system might have been damaged," he said, "I began wandering around the flight deck to make myself fully visible in the event medical aid was needed. Shortly afterwards, I heard explosions below and machine-gun firing. I felt the deck, and it was quite hot. Then I decided I had better return to my battle station. I am happy I did because the elevator I had been standing on a few seconds earlier blew up.

"The order to abandon ship was given. As always at general quarters, I had my flight gloves tucked under my belt and my knife, in its scabbard, hooked onto my belt. Wearing this equipment had been the source of ribbing by the aviators frequently. This time they came in very handy. I was able to cut loose two life rafts on the port side with the knife, and I went down a line, using my gloves to prevent rope burns. I landed on the deck of the destroyer *Irwin* alongside the *Princeton*, and went to the sick bay where there were a number of casualties needing help."

Marine First Sgt. Adrian Chisholm had taken a coffee break away from his 40-millimeter mount when he heard gunfire from nearby ships, then from the *Princeton* itself.

"I had my foot out to go on the walkway to take my post when all hell broke loose," he said. "The bomb had hit just ahead of midship. Flames spread rapidly, and the smoke drove us back, so we couldn't return to our gun stations.

"When the bomb hit, I was spun around and cut my leg on an anchor chain. I was bleeding, and I figured 'I've got to get this fixed,' so I went aft to a battle dressing station where a corpsman put sulfa or something on my leg and wrapped it up. There was a life jacket behind some oxygen tanks, and I put it on. It may have saved my life."

Chisholm found himself in charge of a group of ten or twelve sailors and marines, some of whom urged him to lead the way off the ship.

"You're not going to abandon ship," he told them. "I hadn't had any order and I was a stickler for that sort of thing. I was trying to keep the guys together. I was too excited to think how really scared I was. All of a sudden the ship shuddered. I looked around and the after elevator blew up. I put my hands up to protect my face and got burns on both hands. I don't know whether I jumped or was blown off the ship, but the next thing I knew I was flying through the air in a fetal position, and that's how I went into the water."

George Green was topside serving as director-operator on a 40-millimeter quad (4-barrel) anti-aircraft gun mount on the forecastle.

"That morning we were told to remain on our guns and that food would be brought to us. We had to remain on general quarters, and we grumbled a lot. Along about 8:30 or so, we got some ham sandwiches and coffee. As I was eating, my phone talker said 'bogey at eight miles'. I turned to him with a sarcastic note and said 'just one?' and he replied 'uh huh.'

"At that stage of the war we paid little attention to just one bogey, with all the guns we had in the fleet. I finished my sandwich and took my coffee along when I strapped myself in the director's chair, just in case we did see this little old bogey.

"I couldn't figure out why that plane was not detected and followed all the way in, but no one reported that plane at all as it got closer to the fleet.

"The first inkling of trouble I had was when the carrier next to us, I believe it was the *Lexington,* started firing at something above the broken clouds. Then I saw this plane coming down right directly in front of the ship. When the plane released the bomb, it seemed to jump in the air, so I knew it had to be a pretty heavy bomb.

"The bomb seemed to come down in a low arch, and I thought it was going to land right in my cup of coffee. I was transfixed for a second, then I got rid of the coffee by slamming the cup down on the deck where it broke in a thousand pieces.

"I tried to elevate the gun to get a shot off. The gun elevated all right, but didn't move otherwise and I couldn't fire. The bomb went over our heads. I heard a piercing crack and the ship trembled. I turned to the phone talker and asked 'are we hit?' He finally said 'uh huh' and his eyes were as big as saucers. I said 'boy, we're going back to the states for repairs.' The fire controlman beside me looked at me and said 'we're not out of this yet.' He was a survivor of the carrier *Hornet* sinking, and he knew what he was talking about, as I was to find out later."

Lt. John C. Beckett was aboard the *Princeton* partly because he needed a tour of sea duty to gain a promotion to lieutenant commander. Planning to make the navy his career, he had an engineering degree from Stanford University and was assigned to the *Princeton* as electrical officer because of his familiarity with cruiser hulls.

"On the morning of October 24 we were called to general quarters at dawn, which was normal for a planned day of combat strikes," he said. "My duty station, repair five, was cramped, really just a passageway selected for its location slightly forward and above the two firerooms and enginerooms. Routinely, men were bored and would have preferred to go back to their bunks or to breakfast. Repair station duty was not an exciting place until the bomb hit.

"There was no warning. We were shaken and deafened by an explosion in what sounded to be the hangar deck just above us. My first thought was that one of our planes or its armament had let go by accident. There was a small door in the hatch from repair five to the hangar deck. I opened this, stuck my head through to take a quick look and saw what appeared to be a large fire aft.

"Assuming the hangar deck repair party was in control, I awaited orders and began checking by phone all the engineering substations. It was then I learned we had been hit by a bomb and there was trouble in the engineering spaces as well as the hangar deck, at that point largely smoke."

Beckett tried to contact the ship's chief engineer, but without success.

"It was only a matter of minutes before we, too, were in trouble," he said. "The automatic sprinkler system in the hangar deck was working forward, over our heads, and pouring tons of water onto the raging fire. Successive explosions from gasoline and ammunition opened up the hangar deck above us, and scalding water began pouring into our area."

Beckett said he had attended the navy's firefighter school at Treasure Island, San Francisco, and knew how to contend with smoke and fire, but "I was totally unprepared for scalding water on the deck, which burned our feet and made any kind of work impossible.

"I gave the order to move forward away from the fire amidships. I knew the major gasoline storage was forward and below us, but I thought it was far enough forward to be safe. Leaving repair five wasn't easy. We got out by climbing on bulkhead boxes and fittings which were above the scalding water and by hanging onto fittings on the overhead. I was tall and could hang from cable racks to keep my feet clear. Some of the shorter men suffered severe burns."

Peter Callan had gone on duty at 0200 when he and other members of the ordnance crew were awakened and sent to the hangar deck to rig the TBMs with torpedoes. This was a tough job at best.

"The bomb bays had to be rigged to carry each type of ordnance," Callan said. "We worked for hours rigging the planes, and then started to load the torpedoes. Torpedoes are stored in a peculiar manner. The warheads were kept in the magazines and the bodies were stored in racks on the hangar deck. This meant the warheads had to be brought up and the torpedoes assembled before we could load them on the planes."

The task was barely completed just before dawn when word came from the bridge to substitute 2,000-pound bombs for the torpedoes. While the ordnancemen were voicing their unhappiness over this turn of events, a second order came from topside — leave the torpedoes in the planes.

"In view of what happened later in the day," Callan said, "this was fortunate for the ordnance crewmen. A torpedo has great impact when it explodes under water. Out of water it's about as powerful as a 500-pound bomb. If we had loaded those planes with 2,000-pound bombs, I don't think any of us would have survived that day."

Because of the combat conditions, the *Princeton*'s cooks had made sandwiches and prepared stainless steel pitchers of coffee. Each crew or work unit designated "go-fers" to get the food for those they worked with.

"Our chow was brought to the forward end of the hangar deck," Callan said, "I remember the coffee was unusually good that morning. I was just about to have a second cup when flight quarters was sounded, meaning our fighters were about to land. I forgot about the coffee and followed the rest of the ordnancemen to the flight deck."

Callan remembered he hadn't had his after-coffee cigarette. He ducked into a small armory compartment just off the catwalk.

"I found there another ordnanceman with the same idea. We lit our cigarettes and were walking away when I heard a long burst of machinegun fire. It didn't sound like any of ours. Then one of our 20-millimeter guns opened fire, followed by one of our forties. That's when the bomb hit the ship.

"By the time I reached the flight deck there was no sign of the Japanese plane. The damage to the ship didn't appear to be bad. There was this hole in the deck with a small amount of smoke coming from it. In a few minutes the smoke grew heavier and blacker. I got a firehose from the foamite station on the port catwalk, but when it was turned on nothing happened. No water.

"Under the flight deck, and overhanging the hangar deck, was a small compartment called the conflagration station. It was occupied by three men whose job it was to open certain valves in case of fire. The hangar deck had a system of sprinklers that sent down curtains of water every few feet. I heard later the bomb passed through this compartment, killing two of the three men in there."

Lyle Giddle was attached to the *Princeton*'s aviation crew assigned to maintenance of the torpedo bombers. Before coming to the *Princeton*, he had seen Atlantic duty on the carrier *Sangamon*, including D-day support of Allied landings on the coast of French Morocco. When the bomb struck the *Princeton*, Giddle was in the metal shop, just off the hangar deck.

"A fighter had just landed, and I heard firing," he said. "There were about six of us in the shop. We started out when there was an explosion from the hangar deck. A couple of fellows were thrown down the ladder, and I got a bunch of dirt in my face. When I managed to get up and take a look, there was a large blaze under one of the TBMs. We slammed shut the hatch between us and the fire and went aft. By then we figured the ship had been hit by a bomb."

Giddle said as the small party got closer to the stern of the ship, the smoke became thicker and thicker.

"I stepped into a small compartment filled with oxygen containers. There were three other men already there. It was fairly clear of smoke in the compartment and quiet — too quiet for me. We found a clean undershirt and cut it up, then wet spots to put over our faces."

Giddle announced his intention of trying to get topside, and another sailor said he would accompany him.

"The smoke was so thick in the passageway I couldn't see and I had to feel my way, relying a lot on my memory of the ship's layout. When I found a ladder, I just about ran up to the compartment above. When I got topside, there were a lot of men on the catwalk and flight deck.

"Smoke was pouring out of the middle of the flight deck, and we couldn't get forward. Ammunition was going off on the hangar deck. Then there was a large explosion as one of the elevators blew out. Another explosion came and pieces of the after elevator flew up. I climbed up from the catwalk, and joined about twenty others on one corner of the flight deck. We could see a lot of men in the water.

"A really big explosion came up from the hangar deck, and hot air, burning particles, and flames shot over us. I could feel the heat like a blanket, and a finger of flame touched the back of my hands. I wondered for a second if my clothes were on fire or whether a hole had been burned in my life belt. I decided right then and there it was no place for me to stick around. I jumped to the catwalk and climbed down a line."

In the after radio shack, Joseph Christie was on duty with four others.

"The bomb sounded like it was right over our heads," Christie said. "It punched down some of the overhead and smoke started to pour in. When we got word to leave, we formed a line, with me leading, because we couldn't see anything.

"When we reached topside, we were near the after elevator when it went up. We were all thrown back several feet, and I got burns on the hands, neck, and back, but I didn't even realize that until I was in the water later.

"We heard someone say to abandon ship, so we all went over the side. I was halfway down a line when some of the ammunition from the hangar deck exploded and went whizzing by. I just let go and dropped. It was a long way to the water."

For Seaman Roman Kiefer, the day was like many others until he felt an urgent need to visit the head.

"Where I was I would have to go down two decks and wind up below the bake shop. It took time to open and close hatches under general quarters conditions. Something told me not to get permission to go down."

Kiefer decided to go aft a short distance and solve his problem off the side of the ship.

"I couldn't wait any longer, and I was sure I could slip down and be back in a couple of minutes. On the way down, I heard a different kind of sound and the ship started bucking. On the way back up, I did my business in my pants."

When he returned to his gun mount, he felt the steel deck getting hot and paint near him started to blister.

"The gun captain said 'Let's get out of here.' The ship had slowed down. As I got up on the flight deck, the forward elevator blew and a man in front of me had his legs torn off by a big piece of flying steel. I couldn't help him, and I didn't know what to do but follow the others. As I got to the bow and started to go over the side, there was a loud noise and something or somebody fell on me. Over the side I went, into the water."

Luciano "Lou" Shaffer, an ordnanceman third class, was checking the ammunition in the Hellcats as they landed back aboard because some of these planes were due to go back up when ready.

"We were in a rain squall," Shaffer recalled, "and the planes as well as their tires were wet. As I stood up on a tire, I slipped and my hand was cut right to the bone on the wing edge. I was bleeding like a stuck pig, and I had to go below to an aid station just under the flight deck. As the doctor was putting on some sulfa powder and a bandage, the 40-millimeters, and then the twenties, began going off, and seconds later the bomb hit.

"The whole ship shook. The dirt from the beams above us came down, and the doctor said 'what the hell happened?' I said, 'it looks like we were hit by a bomb.' The doctor kept wrapping my finger, and I think he thought he had to wrap the whole world in there, because I wound up with a big fat bandage."

Shaffer worked his way up to the flight deck where, despite his "big fat bandage" he helped push planes over the side.

"Meantime, the destroyers *Irwin* and *Morrison* came alongside and began fighting the fires with their hoses. Some of the fellows on the hangar deck began jumping across to the *Irwin*. I could see them from where I was on the flight deck and I could hear them screaming when they missed as the ships banged back and forth."

When the abandon ship order reached him by word of mouth, Shaffer said he recalled his survival training at the Great Lakes Naval Training Center.

"When I got to the bow of the *Princeton,* just below the flight deck, I took off my shoes, and laid them up against the side of the bulkhead neatly. I had a waist-type life preserver, which used CO_2 bottles. I finally managed to blow it up by mouth, went down a line, and started swimming away from the ship."

A native Californian and the son of Greek immigrants, George Pantages came to the *Princeton* with a deep-rooted desire to go to sea and eventually to follow a career in pharmacy. He graduated from college, took the state pharmacy examination, and joined the U.S. Navy — all in the same month, July 1942.

As a "plank owner," or member of the crew from the ship's commissioning, Pantages had spent his early days aboard ship readying the pharmacy for the shakedown cruise and eventual departure for the Pacific war theater.

Pantages still has a reminder of the *Princeton* sinking, a life belt which hangs in his garage.

"We were issued life belts when we first came aboard the *Princeton* and, all the time we were at sea, I never once tested my life belt to make sure it worked properly. As we encountered more and more enemy action, I felt it was about time to check it out."

Pantages found it was impossible to manually activate the preserver — a pair of pliers was needed to turn the valve.

"I thank God to this day I took a few moments then to check it out, since the preserver did play a significant part in my eventual rescue," he said.

When the Japanese bomb hit, Pantages remembers "sitting along the starboard catwalk, with my feet propped up on the rail, and daydreaming.

"I remember eating a sandwich," he said, "which suddenly disappeared from my hand. A column of smoke began to rise from amidships, and I knew we had been hit. I headed for my battle station, the farthest compartment aft on the ship. Three or four casualties were treated quickly, and then the intense black smoke from the flight deck made our position untenable."

Pantages tried using a gas mask, but that only made matters worse. Because he was alone, he made the decision to head for the hangar deck, believing there probably were casualties to be treated there.

"That was a mistake," he said. "As I opened the hatch to enter the hangar deck, it appeared the place was a solid inferno. I headed back to the flight deck and my battle station, again. The smoke was still so thick that I crawled along the catwalk to the port side of the ship to fresh air. Then the abandon ship order was given."

Chief Commissary Steward Plath was relaxing after a busy morning.

"We had baked 240 pies," he said. "I remember we baked 400 mince pies on the *Hornet* the night before that carrier was sunk."

On 24 October he was in the provisions issue room of the *Princeton*, amidships on the starboard side of the second deck, sitting on a case of canned beans reading *The Last Flight of Butch O'Hare*, an account of the navy ace's exploits.

"I had taken off my flashproof clothing just before the bomb explosion. A pay clerk hit the deck in front of me. An ash tray and other things were thrown down and all the light bulbs smashed. There was another explosion and the smoke got so thick a flashlight was no help at all."

Plath groped through the darkness to a ladder and worked his way to the forward end of the flight deck.

Two of the first to leave the carrier after the bomb hit did so unintentionally. Edward C. Montani and Leo P. Kieri both were stationed on the hangar deck when they were blown off the ship through a bay that was kept open during daylight hours for ventilation and light. At night and during storms, a steel rolldown curtain was lowered.

"I landed in the water without a life jacket," Kieri said. "The mechanics didn't usually wear their life preservers while working because they were bulky and subject to getting snagged."

Kieri realized he was alone and the task group appeared to be steaming away. He experienced panic, then nausea. He vomited up the water he had swallowed on entering the sea, easing his nausea.

"I took off my shoes. I thought about taking off my pants and making water wings out of them as we had been taught in survival school. Then it occurred to me sharks might be attracted by my white legs and even whiter bottom. I kept my pants on."

Like Kieri, Montani was certain he had been the first one off the carrier.

"When I heard our 40-millimeters open up," Montani said, "I reached down to pick up my helmet; but I was immediately blown out the hangar deck opening, hitting my head on the safety chain. I spread-eagled myself so as not to go under when I hit the water, because I was aware of the starboard twin screw directly below me."

He escaped the propeller, but the ship's wake dragged him under. When he got back to the surface, all he could see was the disappearing *Princeton*, with smoke bellowing from the starboard side.

"I was minus my life jacket and got rid of my heavy work shoes to make treading water easier. I knew I was about forty miles from the nearest land. As I prayed silently for help, I thought I was all alone. Little did I realize that Leo was so close. The waves seemed mountainous, and there was no chance of seeing one another."

Kieri couldn't see Montani, but he "heard someone hollering and thought they picked him up and passed me by." However, the destroyer *Cassin Young* retrieved not only Montani, but Kieri as well. They had no opportunity to compare notes in those hectic hours, but later when the two men both spoke of being first off the *Princeton,* Montani said, "We'll have to settle for a tie."

CHAPTER XVI

Fire and Water

IN ADDITION TO PROVIDING living quarters for the 1,570 individuals aboard, the *Princeton* was a floating airfield. The ship carried nearly three dozen aircraft and an arsenal of weapons, as well as vast quantities of highly combustible fuel for the air squadrons and the carrier itself.

The ship's 600-foot-plus hull was divided into a maze of compartments on five decks. Crew berthing, gasoline storage, munitions magazines, galleys, mess areas, engine rooms, and fire rooms were all located beneath the hangar deck — a huge "garage" and service area running half the distance from the bow to the stern, directly under the flight deck.

The ready rooms, where the pilots prepared for their flights and reported back the results, were compartments suspended under the flight deck on the ship's port side.

Control tower for this airdrome at sea was the island, a superstructure rising from the starboard side just forward of the four offset stacks that served as exhaust outlets for the carrier's engines. From the island were issued all necessary operating orders. There also were "talkers" manning communication lines to the various parts of the ship, and the log keepers.

One of the intriguing facets of modern naval warfare is the

wealth of on-the-scene documentation — often more than is normally feasible in land battles.

On every naval vessel, certain crew members are assigned to the task of keeping a variety of logs — making continuing entries on the weather, sea conditions, times of various events, radio transmissions, orders given, and orders executed.

No matter that minor differences crop up between one log and another, they rarely vary more than a minute. The fact is these reports do exist and they were made by ordinary individuals under the very trying pressures of combat.

Thus, it is possible to note that at 1002 or 1003 there occurred the first of a series of major explosions on the *Princeton*'s hangar deck.

These extremely heavy blasts exerted incredible force against the flight deck and the sides of the carrier. The steel-and-timber landing surface of the flight deck between the forward and after elevators bulged upward. The after elevator — capable of raising or lowering a fully armed plane with its 2,000-pound bomb or torpedo — was lifted clear of its opening, flipped over, and landed upside down.

Gun crews manning the 20- and 40-millimeter mounts along the port side were hit hard. There were many casualties with burns and shrapnel wounds. Men were blown from the carrier's catwalk to the water fifty feet below.

Gunnery Officer Jim Kelleher lost contact with the three gun crews on the fantail, but those men received word, along with others crowding the stern, to abandon ship. Conditions had become too hazardous to remain, and there was no apparent path forward out of the engulfing cloud of acrid smoke. The gunners joined their fellow crewmen in going down hoses or lines to the water. Most were picked up by the destroyers circling the *Princeton*.

Minutes after the after elevator blast, there was an even heavier explosion forward in the hangar deck. Again the flight deck was bulged upward and a large section burst open near the stacks. The forward elevator was blown free, then landed cocked up with one corner in the elevator well.

As word was passed on the *Princeton* for all hands to come topside, the commander of Task Group 38.3 instructed the *Birmingham* to join the rescue flotilla and assume command of the firefighting and lifesaving operations.

At 1010, the order was given to exercise "salvage control phase one." All but 490 key personnel were to leave the stricken carrier. The destroyer *Irwin* moved in against the *Princeton*'s forward port side. Hoses were passed from destroyer to carrier. Some men on the *Princeton* jumped onto the *Irwin*'s deck, and others went down lines into the sea.

While they represented the carrier's striking power in normal operation, members of the air group, under the conditions created by the bomb hit, assumed a strictly non-essential role.

In the torpedo squadron ready room, where air group members were being briefed at the time of the bomb blast, pilot Tom Mooney recalls the hit as "just sort of a jolt." He thought perhaps the carrier might sustain enough damage to require a trip back to the United States and home, but in those initial seconds the "jolt" didn't seem that significant.

"Then I happened to be looking at the open ready room door," Mooney said, "and this gigantic fire ball went by, sailing down the passageway. It apparently was explosive gases that were caused by the bomb blast. They may have been picked up by the ventilation system and moved through the ship, causing fires in many places."

Mooney learned later that in passing through the hangar deck, the bomb struck his own plane, which he had named "Sweet Sue" after his wife. All the TBMs there still carried torpedoes and full auxiliary wing gas tanks. There hadn't been enough time to remove them when the planes were shifted back down from the flight deck.

"My plane captain was standing on the plane's wing when the bomb came down," he said. "It torched the fuel and covered him with flames. He was just like a marshmallow, seared. Later, when we had been picked up, I saw him, like a mummy, and I thought 'He's going to die,' but he lived."

With other air group members, Mooney went to the port catwalk, then onto the flight deck. He helped push planes over the side, and wound up helping man a hose line near the forward elevator.

"Then there was an enormous sound. It wasn't like an explosion. It was an incredible rush of air and the elevator, which was down on the hangar deck level, came in front of me and went straight on up as high as the ship's radar mast.

"I can't remember any shock," he said. "I don't recall being knocked out or anything. I just thought, 'Jesus, the number one elevator just flew out,' and I decided there wasn't any more point in pouring water at that spot."

Word was passed for all non-essential personnel to abandon ship.

"I caught the term non-essential, and I was offended by it because I considered myself pretty damned essential. However, when you saw all the ship's officers and men who had duty stations being so collected, you realized us air group types were really useless under the circumstances."

Mooney was wearing a shoulder holster containing a .45 Colt automatic, which his father had "acquired" while in the U.S. Army in World War I.

"That forty-five was my prized possession, and I knew the old man wasn't going to like what I was about to do. But I knew I was going into the water and had no idea how long I would be swimming."

He laid the gun and holster on the deck and, with fellow torpedo pilot Doc Manget, started down a fire hose.

"They threw gas hoses down the side because they were handy and they didn't have a lot of things to use. The hoses were thick, and it was tough going hand-over-hand down fifty feet from the flight deck to the water.

"I went first, and Manget was right behind me. He was in as big a hurry to reach the water as I was, and on the way down he stepped on my hands several times. I remember remonstrating with him, which is a nice way of saying I wish you hadn't done that."

Mooney had no fear of entering the water, because he was an experienced swimmer.

"I'll tell you, though, fifteen knots of wind in the middle of the ocean is a lot of wind. You go down in a trough and can't see anything. Then you come up top on a crest and there is the ship and some people. Again you go down and the world goes away. I had figured it would be like swimming off Hawaii, but it was not like that at all."

He and Manget were taken aboard the *Irwin*.

Fred Hautop was among the fighter pilots who had taken part in the morning's combat air patrol mission and was in the forward ready room being briefed for another flight when the bomb hit.

"The initial explosion knocked us right out of our seats," Hautop said. "I got up and headed for the wardroom, which is the officers' dining area, but at that point was being used as an aid station. One of my friends, Swish Taylor, had landed aboard with a bullet hole in the leg. A couple of us helped him and saw that they got him off the ship.

"By then the lights were dimming. People were panicking, coming up from down below hurt badly — scalded, screaming. We heard the captain had ordered 'abandon ship,' and I went to the forecastle where there were many people, with the *Irwin* rammed up against our bow to take aboard survivors.

"The ships didn't meet too well, so you couldn't jump from one to the other. Some tried it and were crushed in the attempt. Hoses and lines were put down the *Princeton*'s side, and I used one to go into the water."

Although he was an excellent swimmer, Hautop realized the fact the carrier and destroyer were so close together meant the surge of water between them probably would keep him under much of the time.

"There were bodies all over the place," he said, "plus some sharks that were kicking around. Someone on the *Irwin* dropped a line right next to me. I got it, wrapped it around my hand, and they started to pull me up. There was a man hanging on each of my feet. By the time I got ten feet out of the water I thought the rope would cut my hands off with all that weight, so I dropped back into the sea."

Another line with a loop was dropped from the *Irwin* and Hautop grabbed it.

"I still had people hanging on my feet, and with my last bit of strength I had to kick them off. They finally got me on deck."

Fighter Pilot Red Shirley, who had been on the flight deck and had seen the Japanese plane release the bomb, worked his way to the island structure and then on to the ready room. After a brief stay there, he decided there was a good chance the ship might be abandoned and went a deck below to retrieve his log book.

However, he was unable to reach his stateroom because of the smoke and the hatches that had been closed under damage control orders. He went next to the forecastle, but it occurred to him his log book might be in the ready room. He found that compartment smoke-filled. He also found Lt. (jg) John Fitzgerald and a sailor who was nearly overcome by smoke but still insisted on remaining by his phone set.

Fitzgerald, a non-flying officer attached to the fighter squadron, at first pleaded with the "talker" to turn his phone over to him and seek fresh air topside. He finally had to order him to accompany Shirley forward.

"That kid — I mean we were all kids — but he was not about to give up that phone," Fitzgerald said. "From the ready room the way you got to the flight deck was to go out on the port side up a ladder, which was open to the fresh air. So I had been able to check the action from time to time, and the poor kid on the phone couldn't. That's why he was suffocating. I wasn't suffocating, although later, when I took over the phone, it became difficult."

"Just as we got out on deck," Shirley said, "the word was given to abandon ship. There were about thirty of us there on the forecastle, some air group and some ship's company. We got the nets, lines, life rafts, and so forth over the side, and followed into the water ourselves. Some went down the lines, some jumped, but most went down the anchor chain, which had been paid out to water level."

Fitzgerald stayed behind in the ready room, manning the phone until the abandon ship order. The heat and smoke were increasing. He suffered burned hands from pressing against the bulkheads as he went forward to leave the carrier.

One of the ship's officers, Lt. Richard M. Jackson, was on the crowded forecastle deck in the moments following the bomb hit. He observed with interest as several pilots "lightened up for the swim they were expecting by dropping their 38-caliber pistols on the deck.

"I saw the same pistol surreptitiously picked up, stuffed inside a shirt, then removed and dropped again by three different sailors," Jackson said. "A naked display of the power of self-preservation."

Jackson also observed with shock the sight of men who jumped or went down lines and attempted to swim the gap between the *Princeton* and the *Irwin*.

"The eccentric wave action between the ships made this a nightmare for many," he said, "as they closed the gap only to be thrown back just as their fingers were clutching at the cargo nets, which had been dropped over the destroyer's sides.

"Equally disconcerting was the sight of nine or ten men

slopped together on a single wave, catching a net simultaneously, and then the stronger climbing over the weaker."

Jackson said some of the swimmers drifted aft of both ships "and with the help of machine-gun fire from the *Irwin*'s fantail eluded sharks and were picked up by small boats."

He decided to go to his cabin near the forecastle and pick up any of his "valuables" he might want to take off the ship with him. When he opened the safe in the pitch-dark cabin with the help of a flashlight, the contents "didn't look so valuable after all." He retrieved only a 32-caliber target pistol, which had been given to him as an usher at his brother-in-law's wedding.

Back on the forecastle, Jackson found badly burned members of the *Princeton*'s "black gang": the fire room crew.

"Several of us assisted in tossing them across to waiting hands on the *Irwin*. This was more difficult than it sounds, because the bows of the carrier and destroyer were rising and falling at different rates, creating a constantly changing vertical gap ranging of from three to ten feet. Also, the bow of the *Irwin* at that point was only about three feet wide."

In the middle of this life saving operation, Jackson noted "two strange incidents."

"One was our communications officer in the water caught on the destroyer's sharp bow and unable to go one way or another because of fatigue and continued water pressure. He was saved. The other was a warrant officer with thirty years experience in the navy. In descending, a line from the carrier's forecastle twisted around his leg, and he apparently drowned before he could get free. We pulled him back aboard and left him on the forecastle."

Marine Maurice Keilman almost was forced to remain aboard the *Princeton* involuntarily. He was helping man a twin 40-millimeter gun, wearing a headphone, when the bomb struck.

"I felt the jar of the bomb," he said, "and heard one of the marines say we had been hit. Without anyone telling me to, I went into the storage room near our gun mount, figuring I'd bring out some ammo.

"When the fellows outside began to smell smoke and realized there was a fire below, they shut the door to the ammunition compartment. They were locking me in! I kept trying to open the hatch locks and the guys outside kept shutting them on me. Luckily, they spotted the phone cord under the hatch and knew that I was inside.

I got out of there and someone told me the phones were dead anyway, so I finally put that headset down."

One of the frequent reactions of a man in combat is his tendency to cling to his duty assignment — almost a mental security blanket in a period of frightening confusion. He's very apt to feel that if he goes where he has been told to go and does what he has been told to do under such conditions, just maybe things will turn out all right.

Then there may come a time when the ordered reaction he's been taught to expect doesn't happen, and he's cast adrift with a lot of other confused individuals.

"Pretty soon people started getting up on deck," Keilman said. "We didn't have anything to shoot at, so we started leaving the gun. All of our life jackets were locked up in a tool box. We didn't have to have them on at battle station, just had to have them nearby.

"The thing was during our night watches some of the fellows would take naps using the life jackets as pillows, and in the morning you had to pick up all the jackets some other guys had left out. Soon they started locking them up under padlock. Ours were still locked up when the ship was hit. Later I had a chance to tell the guy with the key what he could do with it."

Keilman said he "wandered around the flight deck for an hour or so before another fellow and I decided to get into the water."

The second sailor confided he didn't know how to swim, and Keilman said "we were kind of chumming around trying to decide what to do.

"We didn't have any life jackets and this guy couldn't swim. He wanted to go forward and try to get on a destroyer that was alongside the carrier. I agreed to go with him, but the smoke got really thick, and I knew there were all those arresting cables across the flight deck right near a big hole I might fall into if I tripped over one of them. I chickened out. He went on and a short time later there was a big explosion, which burned me a bit and, I guess, killed him."

Keilman joined forces with a friend, and they decided to jump into the ocean, life jacket or not.

"A lot of guys, when they went into the service, got real nice knives to hang onto. In our little group, though, not one man had a knife like that. So instead of having a knife to cut loose a life raft, we went into the water without jacket or raft."

He found more company in the rolling sea.

"There were a couple of others that had jackets," Keilman said. "A life jacket will support three people if you're not crazy and don't panic, just hang on real nice and tread water."

Destroyer crewmen threw empty ammunition cans in the water, and Keilman used one to stay afloat until he was picked up.

In the after ready room, not far from the ship's fantail, Robert Charles Gibbon, who had made an assignment "swap" to get aboard the new *Princeton* early in the ship's career, didn't feel the actual bomb explosion — but did realize the *Princeton*'s sudden change in course was unusual.

He started forward, met some crew members coming the other way from the shipfitters shop and the aviation metal shop. They told him the carrier had been struck by a bomb.

Gibbon continued forward as far as the after elevator well. Sitting on one of the metal gear lockers was a sailor. Gibbon asked him why he was not moving to a better place of safety. The sailor replied he couldn't swim and didn't have a life jacket. Gibbon told him to wait and he'd bring him one.

"I went on but because of the dense smoke I never got back to that man and until this day that haunts me," Gibbon said.

The smoke became so dense that Gibbon was almost overcome. He was crawling on his knees when an air group crew member found him and suggested they try to reach the catwalk beside the flight deck.

"We made it to fresh air," Gibbon said, "and, boy, the air felt wonderful! About that time the internal explosions started, and I went down a ladder by the fantail. I was just partway down when the word was passed to abandon ship, so I jumped into the water, getting one heck of a jolt, because I still had on my steel helmet."

He was picked up by the *Gatling*.

Also in the carrier's stern was the after gasoline pump room. One entered the pump room through a hatch door from the third deck, and then climbed down a twelve-rung ladder to the fourth deck level.

The deck beneath was armor plated — a three-inch steel shell with a two-and-a-half-foot interval separating it from the aviation gas tank below.

Thomas Cusick and another crew member were in that space

when the bomb blast and subsequent heavy explosions occurred. Through their telephone lines, Cusick and his companion learned of the bomb hit and the fires on the hangar deck.

"We just sweated it out," he said. "Under those circumstances, with all that gas under us, it seemed like an eternity. We finally got word from the bridge to secure the pump room, which meant flooding the area as we left by means of a CO_2 bottle control on the third deck level.

"On the way topside, we passed through an area where a doctor had some wounded on a bench, and we were told to get out of there. Being good little sailors, we obeyed."

Cusick and his companion got to the area of the port catwalk platform, where the landing signal officer normally was stationed when he guided incoming planes to a flight deck landing.

"It was a hell of a long way down," Cusick said, "but we knew we had to leave as soon as we could, or else. My buddy went first and I followed, trying to land between the pieces of debris in the water. We made it okay. I don't know how my friend felt, but that was the highest jump I ever made into water or anything else."

Cusick hadn't been in the ocean long before he and his buddy encountered the *Princeton*'s landing signal officer.

"This Lt. Comdr. [W. L. Curtis] suggested we all stay together so we would have a better chance of being picked up. There were several of us, including one young boy who had been burned so bad he couldn't do anything but scream. I had been burned on the hands, too, and the salt water wasn't helping at all. I tried treading water to keep my hands out of the ocean, but this other sailor was hurting so much I couldn't think about my own problems."

Cusick said the landing signal officer "kept us together and helped put a dye marker in place, which was very visible from a distance."

"I just couldn't think of anything but the young fellow with the bad burns. Finally this destroyer came and took him aboard first. We had a very hard time. They threw cargo nets over the side of the destroyer and we tried to push him up by the buttocks, even using our shoulders to hold him in place while we treaded water, but the sailors on the destroyer would pull him by his hands and all they would get was raw burnt skin. We finally got him on board, but he died a few days later."

One of the quirks of naval combat in World War II was that many who suffered ship sinkings early on were reassigned to other ships and experienced the same trauma in their new assignments. Among these was Ray Arlequeeuw, who survived the sinking of the carrier *Hornet*, returned to the United States for a month-and-a-half leave, was assigned to the *Princeton*, and was on that carrier at the time the ship went down. He was a cook on both ships.

"I was between the galley and the butcher shop, in a store room on the starboard side, on the *Princeton* when the bomb landed," he said, "on a level right underneath the hangar deck. The bomb landed in a passageway between the bake shop, galley, and radio shack.

"I knew right away it was a bomb like from before — the way a ship acts, pulling back a little and then it stops."

He went into the water from the bow of the *Princeton* and found two five-inch shell cans. He put one under each arm for support. He knew from past experience he couldn't really swim. Arlequeeuw tried merely to keep afloat, staying as close to the ship as possible without running afoul of the debris or the rescue operations. He spotted a piece of scaffolding, a plank.

"I don't know how long I was in the water before I spotted that plank," he said. "You couldn't swim. You went where the swells took you. One minute you're down and couldn't see anything, and the next you're up on top and could see everything.

"I figured I was out there all by myself, and then I spotted this board with a guy sitting on it. I said something like 'I'll take the front and you take the back.' I took off my shoes and socks. Don't ask me why. I guess I didn't want to get my socks wet or something."

Arlequeeuw's companion proved to be shipmate George Green.

Larry Addison, who was stationed on the same quad 40-millimeter gun mount as Green, was among those who later reported there were probably sharks in the water — although he wasn't conscious of them at the time.

When the abandon ship order was passed, he went over the side from the starboard side, jumping to avoid the destroyer that was then alongside the *Princeton*.

"I was in the water about two hours, alone most of the time," he said. "I saw others occasionally, and we would try to get together, but the waves kept us apart. I lost all of the ships and couldn't see anything, then suddenly there was a whaleboat alongside. I heard some rifle shots and wasn't aware of what they were doing until I got aboard. Then I found out they had been shooting at sharks. I don't know what I would have done if I had been attacked by sharks, particularly because I had no shoes on."

An "airdale," or plane handler assigned to flight deck duty, Don Scheer helped man a hose line, then followed an officer's instructions to assist in pushing planes over the side, near the forward elevator.

"We backed up the ones we had just landed and spotted. We pushed them on the elevator, then turned them outboard and ran them off the edge of the flight deck. They plunged down and sank in the sea.

"We were on the elevator, which kept bouncing up and down a little bit every time we went over it, and I thought, 'Hey, we better get off this thing.' Well, we pushed one final, or maybe next-to-last, plane off the side when the elevator exploded."

Scheer said somehow he escaped injury. He looked at the elevator cocked up on a corner in its well.

"If I had been on that thing, I'd be down the hole."

He crawled to the port side and went down a line to the water, along with another sailor.

"We started swimming. My life jacket was one of those air jobs. When we hit the water, the thing just went whoosh and all the air went out of it. I started swimming and the other guy was behind me. He called my name, 'Don,' and I turned around, but he was gone. I don't know whether a shark got him or what, but from then on, until some ship picked me up, I was alone in the water."

Another "airdale," Percy Sherman, had the assigned task of manning a foamite station in the event of a flight deck fire.

A foamite station was a small compartment with a single entrance off the carrier's catwalk. It contained a fire hose and a large hopper in the center. Lined up on the walls were stacks of pails filled with powder. The powder was dumped into the hopper, which had a hoseline feeding water into its bottom. The mixture of powder and water became foam, which emerged from the hose to fight fires. The compartment was not high enough to stand up in, but five or six men could play cards in it if seated.

After the bomb impact, Sherman began pulling out a fire hose and opening the powder pails to pour into the hopper, which fed foam to the water line. He stayed at that station until the failure of water pressure.

"When I climbed out on the flight deck," he said, "I was amazed to see the *Princeton* all by itself where there had been so many other ships with us before the bomb hit. When the word was passed to abandon ship, I went over the side with a friend.

"We were swimming toward one of the destroyers," Sherman said, "and it seemed like we'd never get there. My friend had a long cut on his forearm that was wrapped up but bleeding badly. We were in the water only a short time when I saw a shark fin coming toward us on the surface. Then the fin turned under. My friend came high out of the water and shouted to me. Then he disappeared for the last time."

Sherman said he has had many thoughts of his friend.

"I wanted to visit his parents but always backed out at the last minute because I didn't know what to tell them. I never did go to see them."

Green, who had been at his anti-aircraft gun mount when the bomb struck the *Princeton*, helped a fellow sailor with a foot wound get down a chain to the water.

"He had a cut on one foot and the shoe was gone," Green said. "He must have been injured by one of the explosions. After I went down the chain, I swam into the wind to get away from the ship as fast as I could, the way we had been trained."

He spotted a destroyer, the *Irwin*, alongside the *Princeton* and tried to swim in that direction, but wind and current kept him from reaching his goal.

"They kept throwing me a line, but it was always just out of my reach. When I was just about exhausted, I gave up and floated. I floundered around in the waves, drifting past the *Princeton*, and then I came across this fellow face down in his life jacket. I swam over to him and raised his head to see if he was alive. There were no signs of life, and I realized he was the man I had helped down from the flight deck earlier."

Green pushed the dead man away and quickly became separated from him by the waves.

"Then," he said, "this fellow disappeared entirely. At the time it didn't really register, and I didn't pay much attention to what happened to him."

Green became aware of a man sitting in the water on one end of a piece of scaffolding used in painting the ship.

"He was sitting on the very end of the board with a life jacket on, wearing a helmet and with a five-inch ammunition can under each arm. He was in a state of fright because he couldn't swim. I got on the other end of the board, and we began teetering and tottering back and forth through the waves.

"I told him there was no sense in wearing the helmet because it weighed him down. He took it off and with a swoop of his arm flung it out into the sea. He had no more done this than a huge piece of metal landed in the water not more than twenty feet from us. Then another chunk of metal came down fifty to 100 feet on the other side."

Green said that for a moment he was at a loss as to the source of these aerial droppings because there were no explosions on the *Princeton* at the time.

Suddenly, the source became clear as a pilot emerged from the clouds suspended from a parachute with a rubber raft dangling beneath him. The main body of his plane hit the water shortly before he did.

"When he hit the water," Green said, "luckily he fell right into his raft, which was part of the pilots' standard survival gear. He was badly injured. The side of his face was bloody, and he seemed to be having difficulty staying in the rubber raft. The guy on the plank with me and I tried paddling hard to work our way to him, but he was a good 300 yards from us."

Just then a whale boat came up to Green and his companion. He pointed to the wounded airman and suggested he needed help more than Green and his new friend. The whale boat crew picked up the wounded man, sent up a flare and pulled away.

"The guy on the other end of the board I was riding was ready to kill me about then," Green said. "He thought we were doomed to spend a long time floating in the ocean."

Another rescue boat came out, however, and took Green with his companion to the destroyer *Cassin Young*. As Green got aboard, he became aware of small arms fire on the starboard side of the destroyer. He went over to investigate.

"I saw maybe a dozen people swimming off that side and what they were shooting at from the *Cassin Young* were sharks. Suddenly I realized the man I had helped off the *Princeton* and later was floating dead near me didn't just go under when he disappeared. He probably had been eaten by sharks. Why they didn't go after me I'll never know. The thought of those sharks made me a little faint, and I had to sit down for a while."

For those on the cruisers and destroyers, the early rescue operation was a nightmare to be long remembered.

CHAPTER XVII

Devastation Below Decks

THE BOMB HIT HAD BEEN felt as a "dull jar" below decks in central station. While no immediate report was received of exactly what had happened from any of the topside stations or repair parties, the alarm for the hangar sounded and Lt. Comdr. H. E. Stebbings, the first lieutenant, ordered the conflagration station to turn on the hangar sprinkler system.

That order was transmitted over two phone lines, damage control information and damage and stability control, and was acknowledged. However, there was no positive report made that the order had been carried out.

In a matter of seconds, personnel in the conflagration station requested permission to leave because of the stifling heat and smoke. Permission was granted, but once more a request was made to confirm that the sprinkler system had been turned on.

"Aye, aye, sir," the message came back. "We are abandoning."

The conflagration station was a compartment suspended over the hangar on the port side, nearly amidships, directly under the bomb's point of flight deck impact. There were three men stationed there — a "talker" manning the damage and stability control circuit, a second manning the air operations circuit, and a relief man.

The Japanese bomb landed just slightly aft, and a matter of feet inboard, of the station. When the bomb exploded, fragments were driven up through the deck at that location. The compartment was filled with dense smoke and became intensely hot.

The "talker" who was in contact with the first lieutenant through the damage control information circuit, was severely wounded by the bomb blast. His two companions were driven from the compartment. Despite repeated attempts to re-enter the area, they were unable to rescue their companion. They called for help. A sailor wearing an asbestos suit tried to effect the rescue from the port gallery walkway. He, also, was driven back by the intense heat, which turned his own perspiration to steam within his asbestos suit.

The initial fire, which started when the bomb struck Mooney's torpedo plane in passing below, instantly spread to the other TBM wing tanks on the hangar deck. Hangar deck personnel were forced to evacuate their stations almost immediately.

One man managed to reach the panel control box, at the after end of the hangar, and pushed the buttons to activate sprinklers in the fourth bay area and hangar curtains three and four. The indicator lights did not come on, and the sprinklers never worked.

The same man tried playing out a two-and-a-half-inch fire hose in the after section of the hangar, but there was no water pressure. Lt. (jg) Henry Auclair, the hangar deck officer, went to the fire station on the hangar's port side. He turned on pressure to two hose lines leading to the hangar sprinkler system. Then he dashed to the control box to turn on the sprinklers, but found switches smoking heavily from an electrical short circuit.

Because all the talkers in the area had been forced out by smoke, Auclair went to the starboard catwalk where he met the ship's executive officer, Comdr. John Murphy. Murphy was on his way from combat information center to assess at first hand the extent of the damage below decks.

Auclair reported to the executive officer that all hangar personnel had been forced to abandon their stations, and that no hose lines could be manned there. While the two officers were conferring, a messenger brought word that the conflagration station had been "blown out" and the central talker killed.

Repair one, the upper deck repair station, reported to central station they were unable to establish phone communications with their auxiliary unit located in the shipfitter shop on the port side aft of the hangar. Repair one officer, Lt. (jg) F. R. Carson, also reported fire hoses were being broken out, and that he would lead a party to the hangar deck.

Commander Murphy and the hangar deck officer worked their way to the executive officer's stateroom, just forward of the hangar, where they were able to phone a report that the hangar sprinklers were not operating.

Acting on this information, the first lieutenant called the repair two officer, Ens. A. A. Christie, and instructed him to go from his forward station down to the log room on the third deck, starboard side, to check the status of the valves serving the sprinkling system in the forward hangar.

Christie reported back a short time later that the valves apparently had not opened automatically when the main control buttons were pushed. He said he had opened the valves in the log room and barber shop. There were signs water was passing through the system.

Christie was told to lead a party to repair five (engineering repair), which had reported losing communications with its satellite stations.

In the after engine room, a flash of fire roared through the vent ducts and burned the chief of the watch. In main engine control, where the bomb had been felt only as a "thud" from an undetermined source, Chief Engineer Fred Wheeler requested damage reports from all engineering stations. Each station but one reported no damage. Contact could not be made with the after fire room, which had been filled quickly with heavy black smoke.

What happened there was revealed later, graphically described in a letter written by S1c. Thomas E. Abernathy, a survivor, to the mother of the officer in charge of the after fire room, Lt. Edward J. Vandenberg, who did not survive. Abernathy wrote:

> Dear Mrs. Vandenberg:
> I will do my best to tell you what happened in the after fire room when we were hit.
>
> First, trash started blowing through the blowers and then smoke, so we kept the boilers under control until the smoke got so bad we couldn't see the meters and then Mr. Vandenberg tried to get permission to leave the fire room, but he couldn't get anyone on the phone, so we started up the escape hatch and before we

could get the hatches opened they passed the word over the loudspeaker for all the engineers to lay up topside.

Mr. Vandenberg started up the ladder just ahead of me and about the time Cogdill got the hatch open, he passed out and I caught him in my arms. I called his name three or four times and he didn't answer, so I tried to climb the ladder with him, but I couldn't get up with him so I had to drop him, so I managed to get to the top of the ladder and three boys dragged and carried me to the sick bay and then a pharmacist took me to the topside and I gained enough strength to go down a line and get in the water and I was picked up in about an hour.

There were sixteen of us in the fire room and eleven got killed in the bunch. I will give you the names and rates of all that I can remember the names of out of the eleven that got killed, but I don't know their first names or addresses. Mr. [James G.] Steele, chief warrant officer; [Ralph S.] Zaick [Zaicek], WT2c.; [William J.] Spencer, WT2c.; [Robert R.] Harrold [Harrell], WT3c.; [Manuel L.] Peno [Pino], WT3c.; [Adrian L.] Adalph [Adolph], F1c.; and [Donald L.] Vinderly [Vendrely], F1c. I can't remember the other three names.

Mr. Vandenberg was a swell officer and all the boys liked him and enjoyed working with him.

The forward engine room also was filled, almost at once, by smoke so thick that crewmen were threatened with suffocation and plunged into darkness. Similar smoke conditions, as well as intense heat, were reported in both the forward fire room and the after engine room.

A high-pressure air line in the after engine room developed a leak, and this was mistaken for a steam leak. The blinding smoke, and the belief live steam was being sprayed into the compartment, forced evacuation of the area. Because of communications failures and confusion, no report was made to main engine control.

Because no phone contact could be made with the after fire room following the bomb hit, it appears the boilers there were secured within minutes and the area evacuated. For lack of steam, the after turbogenerators gradually slowed and then stopped completely. This meant there was no longer any electric power available aft.

Meanwhile, some access doors and hatches were opened in an effort to clear the smoke from the forward engine room and forward fire room. As engine personnel donned gas masks, ventilation supply blowers were slowed and dampers were closed. Even so, a series of explosions in other parts of the carrier forced dense smoke into the engineering spaces through the ventilation system. Heat and smoke also were pulled into the engineering compartments from the hangar blaze.

The major explosions that occurred in the hangar in a twenty-minute period shortly after 1000 blew out all the ventilating ducts, creating a wide open tunnel for smoke and fire.

With the after engine room already abandoned, the forward engine room was likewise vacated following a third explosion on the hangar. The ship's "power plant" was out of business.

With the heavy explosion that blew out the forward elevator and intensified the hangar fire, both of the *Princeton*'s gyro compasses went out and all internal communications were lost. The order was passed by word of mouth: "All hands topside."

On the bridge, the most serious injury involved a lookout who was struck by a flying four-by-four-inch timber. He was lowered to the flight deck, and then to the forecastle of the *Irwin*. He died the following day.

There were no remaining communication links with other ships, and conditions on the bridge worsened rapidly. Personnel were instructed to go to the forward flight deck. Because of intense smoke and heat, they were unable to use the ladder on the inboard side of the island structure. They were forced to descend over the forward side of the bridge splinter shield instead, and on down the pedestal of the flight deck crane.

One of those in the forward fire room was watertender John Malmen. He had arisen at 0330 and went on duty at 0400. Because the ship was at general quarters, his watch was not relieved at 0800.

Things seemed normal, and he settled down for coffee after asking a fireman on some grates above him to hand down his gas mask. This was hung on the bulkhead by the steam gauges.

"We all knew we were going into battle," Malmen said, "and we were used to it by that time. So far below decks there was nothing to see. We increased speed to launch our aircraft, but we rarely knew whether they were going on an attack or were taking off to guard the fleet."

After a period of calm, the engine crew was ordered to increase speed so the *Princeton* could get the necessary wind over the flight deck to successfully land planes. This meant an air flow of thirty to thirty-two knots, realized by turning into the wind and stepping up the ship's pace. If the surface wind was blowing at ten knots, the carrier had to travel at twenty to twenty-two knots for the desired landing conditions.

"There was an explosion," Malmen said. "It was not very loud, but the ship sort of shook. We looked at one another, and someone said 'I think we got hit.' A voice came over the PA system and informed us a bomb had hit the ship and knocked out the after fire room. We were asked to keep up steam pressure, which we tried to do. After awhile, we were told the ship was on fire. They said to secure all the boilers, but not to leave the fireroom."

While Malmen and his fellow crewmen were making certain the boilers were shut down properly, black smoke began pouring into the area from the ventilating system.

"It was getting hard to breathe," he said. "I was on the deck plates in the lower part of the fire room and said to myself 'Hell, I guess this is it' because I could hardly breathe.

"The voice came over the PA again saying 'People below decks put on your gas masks.' I reached up and got my mask, put it on and could breathe once more. Then word was passed for all hands to go topside. I yelled to the crew 'Let's go!' "

The chief, and those stationed on the fire room grates, headed for the main hatch, while Malmen and four others elected to go up an escape trunk.

"I went first, and when we reached the third deck, the wheel which opened the hatch was jammed. Luckily I found a short pipe and beat on the wheel until I got it loose. As we crawled out on the third deck level things went black. I mean it really gets black below deck when there is so much smoke. We lost each other in the dark, and I began feeling my way out."

The first hatch he encountered in the blackness was closed and felt warm to his touch. He knew he must be moving toward the damaged after fire room. He turned and felt his way forward. Suddenly the lights came on.

"I ran into five men who also were trying to get topside. We stuck together and found a ladder going to the hangar deck, but the escape hatch was closed. A couple of guys pushed me aside and ran to the ladder. The first man opened the hatch and raised it about halfway. Suddenly, there was a large explosion right above the hatch. Fire, men, and metal came crashing down on us. It was pitch black once more and I yelled 'Hey, is anybody alive.' Nobody answered."

Malmen got to his feet and started moving toward what he believed was the bow. The compartment he was in was getting warmer.

"In fact," he said, "the bulkheads were almost too hot to touch and once more I realized I was going aft, the wrong way again. I turned and made my way into a passageway just as the lights came on a second time."

Malmen realized he was in "officers' country" — that portion of the ship made up of the living and eating quarters of the officers aboard.

"I stopped to get my bearings," he said. "Some fellows came by and told me to turn left down the passageway. As I started I found a friend, a watertender named Dean Hirleman, but he was dead.

"After another turn of the passageway, I could see blue sky. About halfway to the outside there was a large explosion, which blew me off my feet. When I recovered a little, I made my way to the catwalk on the port side of the forward elevator. I took off my gas mask and one glove. The ship was a mess with the elevator on one side and smoke pouring out of the well. After I helped drag out some fire hoses, word came to abandon ship. I jumped onto the destroyer *Irwin*'s deck."

Another of the "plank owners" aboard the *Princeton* was Ronald Lyons. A survivor of the carrier *Hornet* sinking, he almost missed his *Princeton* assignment because he developed a case of the German measles and wound up in the Philadelphia Naval Hospital. He was discharged in time to embark on the shakedown cruise.

Lyons was in the repair four locker, a ten-foot wide compartment used to store emergency repair tools.

"Not long after they passed word of a bogey about twenty-five miles from us, I heard our guns start shooting, and then suddenly there was a big explosion just aft of where I was sitting on a tool box. The force lifted me off that box and landed me on my feet. I ran out of the repair locker and looked aft. The door in the passageway, about twenty feet away, was blown open, and smoke was pouring out pretty bad.

"The men of repair four, stationed on the third deck outside the laundry, came up and said the smoke was so bad down there they had to evacuate the area. We checked the nearby fire plugs, but none of them had any pressure. About that time, men began coming up from the engine spaces below with oil all over them. All the time there were explosions overhead in the hangar. Each time, the light would almost shake loose and go very dim. We thought we were still getting bombed, because we weren't getting word from anywhere."

When the abandon ship word was relayed, Lyons and others around him went to the *Princeton*'s bow, where he was able to use a line to swing over onto the *Irwin*.

Internally, the *Princeton* contained five decks. Two of these — the main deck, which was the topside deck of the original cruiser design, and the third deck — ran the entire length of the ship. The second deck, the first platform, and the second platform extended fore and aft of the engine and fire rooms.

On the third deck, above the after engine room, was the scullery serving as the crew's galley. It was in this area that the Japanese bomb exploded.

S1c. Henry R. Bellavance was in his repair five station, on the starboard side of the scullery, when he "heard a tremendous roar and the ship bounced."

"I was on my hands and knees," he said. "I looked up and saw all sorts of fire shooting out above me. Then I heard someone shout 'come down here and get away from the area. A bomb hit us.' There were no lights and the smoke was heavy. The gates used to lock up the soda fountain, when it wasn't being used, fell right off."

Bellavance's primary assignment in the event of enemy bomb or torpedo damage was to flood the nearby magazines, which contained 40-millimeter ammunition and torpedo warheads. He opened the valves and started aft.

"I ran into Lieutenant [Robert G.] Bradley, our division officer. He told me to make sure I had all the hoses lined out and to make sure we had water for the fire mains. I could feel the heat, and grabbed a cloth to hold over part of my face. Lieutenant Bradley told me he was going below to make certain all the men were out because there was no communication by then. He left, and I proceeded aft on the third deck."

Bellavance opened a hatch leading to the hangar deck and found himself looking at a blazing torpedo plane. He slammed the hatch shut and went on, groping his way through the heavy smoke, until he found a ladder, which he used to get to the port side gun wells.

"I figure it must have taken me at least forty-five minutes to make that trip from where I left Lieutenant Bradley to the topside. There were a lot of people in the water, and others were jumping off the *Princeton*.

"I heard a tremendous explosion. Fire went around my face, my arms. I felt something hit my hand, and as I jumped I saw a fellow in the water, apparently unable to swim and struggling to stay up."

As soon as he was in the water, Bellavance swam to the assistance of the man he had seen struggling to remain afloat.

"I didn't have a life jacket or gun. I had taken off my helmet before I jumped so I would not choke to death. I saw a piece of log or some kind of wood bobbing nearby and gave it to the other guy, but he was having trouble, going up and down. Then a life raft came by and I put him on that. I used the log myself, and continued on until one of our chief petty officers appeared near me in the water. His side was cut open, so I managed to get him over to the life raft and put him on it, too. I floated around on my log for quite a while until the *Gatling* picked me up."

Aboard the destroyer, medics removed shrapnel from Bellavance's neck and hands.

Meanwhile, Bradley, who was the carrier's assistant first lieutenant, led a repair party engaged in fighting fires on both the second and third decks. The intense heat and blinding smoke caused the party to fall back and retreat to the fantail. Once again, the heat and smoke from the advancing fires forced Bradley and his men into the water. Bradley was picked up by the destroyer *Morrison*.

In the crew berthing area, one deck above the scullery, John Wenger experienced a phenomenon that still lingers in his memory.

"When the bomb exploded," he said, "the overhead, or ceiling, came down a few inches as the expansion joints buckled. The overhead was painted white, and the paint chipped off from the force of the blast. It was like a snow storm. After the bomb hit, all these paint chips floated down just like a snow storm."

Wenger gradually groped his way to the fantail, and from

there went into the water with three friends. The four stayed together in their life jackets "in a kind of quadrangle." They had been on inflatable, belt-type preservers and found it difficult to stay upright.

"They had a tendency," Wenger said, "to throw you forward with your face in the water, or send you over on your back. There were three kinds of preservers used on board our ship. The people below decks were issued the sort I had, which was more or less like an inner tube. The people above decks had a kapok-type, and the aviators had a vest-type that blew up when you pulled a cord. Everyone was unhappy with the preserver he had. The kapok ones got waterlogged, and the fliers said their type rubbed against your chin until it got raw."

Wenger and his companions turned to five-inch powder cans to stay afloat, putting them against their chests and wrapping their arms around them. The cans had been stacked on the decks of the destroyers for just such an emergency, and were thrown into the water to help the *Princeton*'s survivors.

"Without those containers," Wenger said, "it would have been a pretty unhappy experience. As it turned out, we were among the last ones picked up by the *Morrison* because, with those buoyant cans, we were in such good shape they picked up a lot of others who were not as fortunate first."

Thomas H. Williams, a second class machinist mate assigned to the forward engine room, had a general quarters duty post with a thirty-member damage control party. Their station was in a crew sleeping area on the carrier's port side, above the engine room. This was two compartments forward of the galley area where the bomb exploded, killing many of the bakers and cooks.

"I had come off a midnight-to-4 A.M. watch," he said, "and went directly to my bunk, which was in the same compartment as my GQ duty station. During my watch, I had two or three cups of coffee, and when I lay down to sleep it became a very restless time. I had a very unusual dream.

"All I could see was fire and smoke, explosions, and the sides of the hangar deck being blown out, with dense smoke all around the ship. I was awakened by general quarters, got dressed and lay down on the flash cover I had put over my bunk. When we went to condition 'Baker,' I started to tell my buddies about my dream, and they all said 'forget it.' Have you ever heard the old wives' tale about telling of a dream before breakfast and it will come true? Well, I haven't told about a dream since then, because shortly after that the poop hit the fan.

"We were eventually picked up by the *Irwin*, and because of the crowded conditions, a lot of us slept on the destroyer's deck. I bedded down with a friend on a torpedo tube, and trying to be funny I said 'Benny, I just had another dream.' I almost got thrown overboard."

Like other "airdales," Larry Morgan not only served as a plane handler during flight operations, but also was assigned to ride herd on specific aircraft. His F6F was the last to come aboard the *Princeton* before the bomb struck.

"I was up on the wing, helping the pilot get out of the cockpit, when the guns opened up," he said. "I looked up and caught a glimpse of a plane approaching in a dive. Me and the pilot jumped off his plane and scurried into the conflagration station just off the catwalk.

"Soon the ship started to burn, and smoke was coming up thru the hole the bomb had made. We were instructed to start pushing fighter aircraft over the side. Then we were told to grab firehoses. Me and a couple of shipmates took a hose and went to the forward elevator, which had been lowered about two feet to let us play water into the hangar deck. All of a sudden, the water pressure dropped."

Morgan was told to go to the conflagration station to check on the situation there. All he could learn was that the water supply had shut down at the time of a series of explosions on the hangar deck. He returned to pass that word to the officer in charge of firefighting, near the forward elevator, when there was an ear-shattering blast.

"I was about ten feet away when the elevator went sky high," he said. "There were people killed and wounded all around me. I was knocked down, and I lay there on the flight deck watching the smoke curl up about two thousand feet. For a few seconds I thought the elevator was still up in the air and was going to come back down on me, but it didn't."

When told to abandon ship, Morgan went down a line from the forecastle, inflated his life belt, and joined a dozen or so fellow sailors in swimming away from the carrier.

"When I got a little distance off, I turned over on my back and looked up at the *Princeton*. The carrier was on fire from one end to the other, and debris was falling into the water everywhere. I rolled over again and swam as hard as I could in the other direction.

"You know, when you're an 18-year-old boy floating in the water like that and thinking you're going to die, you have a tendency to pray. Well, I prayed for my mom. The first thought that went through my head was of my mom. I prayed to God to be with her in case I should die. I knew my father would be all right, but I didn't want my mother to suffer. Well I didn't die, and I was picked up by the *Irwin*."

The explosion that almost cost Morgan his life, and the one which turned the after elevator upside down, were in themselves somewhat of a mystery. It was generally believed, at the time, the blasts were caused by detonating torpedoes still rigged to the TBMs on the hangar deck.

This theory was disputed later by two explosives experts who interviewed the *Princeton* survivors at Pearl Harbor. They contended it was impossible to make Torpex-loaded torpedoes explode by either fire or heat, and that extensive testing with acetylene torches proved their contention. Torpedoes containing Torpex, they stated, could be exploded only by means of detonators.

The crippling blasts on the *Princeton*'s hangar, they said, may very well have been produced by aviation gas vaporized by heat and mixed with air. The argument never was settled to everyone's complete satisfaction. The fact remained that the explosions were devastating and deadly.

On the burning carrier, Captain Buracker ordered all but 490 designated salvage control officers and men to abandon ship. Within a dozen minutes he had the word passed to set salvage control phase two in motion, leaving the stricken ship in the hands of 240 chosen firefighters.

With the *Princeton* lying dead in the running groundswell under a plume of smoke and surrounded by a covey of rescue vessels, Admiral Sherman turned the balance of his task group to the pressing business of pursuing the Japanese Fleet to the west.

CHAPTER XVIII

On Their Own

SCARCELY MORE THAN A HALF-HOUR after the *Princeton*'s flight deck had been pierced by the Japanese bomb, the main portion of the task group cleared the area.

It was an epic scene the participants would long remember. The other carriers, the battleships, the cruisers, and the destroyers disappeared toward the western horizon in formation. Behind them, the *Princeton,* under a gigantic pall of smoke, drifted aimlessly atop the deepest waters of the Pacific Ocean; incapable of joining the battle to retake the Philippines. The Battle of Leyte Gulf was rapidly spreading over a half-million square miles of land and sea.

David Evans, a photographer's mate assigned to operate a 35-millimeter movie camera from a vantage point near one of the *Lexington*'s anti-aircraft mounts, recalls the moments following the bomb hit:

"Flames were burning brightly on the hangar deck, but the *Princeton* at first continued to steam even with us and not lose power, so we were hopeful she could be saved. Another, much larger explosion took place on the hangar deck, and the *Princeton*'s interior was filled with billows of orange flame.

"She began to lose speed and drop back in the formation. I kept watching her fall further and further back until she was a hull down on the horizon, and her position marked only by a huge column of black smoke contrasting with the cloudy sky. The last I saw of the *Princeton* was that pillar of smoke gradually sinking out of sight of our stern."

The crippled carrier was left with a small band of encircling cruisers and destroyers. Initial members of this emergency-created squadron were the destroyers *Gatling, Irwin,* and *Cassin Young*. As they began picking up survivors in the debris-strewn sea, the cruiser *Reno* moved in to provide anti-aircraft protection. Moments later, the cruiser *Birmingham* was designated command ship for the operation and a fourth destroyer, the *Morrison,* was instructed to join the group.

As skipper of the *Birmingham,* Capt. Thomas B. Inglis became senior officer present. Under the circumstances, he wasn't given any specific orders other than to stand by the *Princeton* and, presumably, to use every possible means of saving the carrier.

Inglis had given some previous thought to the best way to assist a damaged flattop. As soon as he had assessed his "tools at hand," he started his plan into action. The cruiser *Reno*, being primarily an anti-aircraft, anti-submarine vessel, was ordered to fill that role in the developing situation.

The highly mobile destroyers were told to play down efforts to get hoselines over to the *Princeton* and concentrate on the task of picking up survivors.

The *Birmingham* obviously was the best-equipped ship present to handle the actual firefighting because of more personnel, more deck space, more fire-battling gear, and greater pumping capacity. The warship, ironically, was, under its steel skin, a sister of the *Princeton*. Before its conversion to a light carrier, the *Princeton* originally was designed to be the same class cruiser as the *Birmingham*.

Shortly before the salvage squadron went into action, steering control was lost in the *Princeton*'s pilot house. The ship's steering emergency alarm was sounded and steering aft took over, with conning or directional orders coming from the bridge by telephone.

Following the two hangar deck explosions, which blew out first one elevator and then the other, the order was passed by phone for all engineering personnel to go topside. The steering aft crew asked if they, too, should leave their posts. Because they still were maintaining steering control, and conditions were not then untenable, they were instructed to remain on the job.

In a matter of minutes, however, all telephone communications were lost, and steering aft received orders to abandon that station.

The second hangar deck explosion shook the central station area violently. The vibration caused a micro-switch in a generator to close and the general alarm began to sound. An electrician's mate was told to secure the alarm; and he did after three strokes of the alarm bell. However, the signal generator continued to function for fifteen more strokes. These were heard by some members of the crew and interpreted as the abandon ship signal.

A number of men already had been forced by heat and smoke to go into the water from the carrier's stern, including all of the after repair party and a majority of the engineering department personnel. Among the last to take this route was Bradley.

By then the *Princeton* was dead in the water, drifting across wind. As the destroyers scoured the waves to retrieve the men in the water, the *Reno* opened fire on two Japanese planes that had penetrated the defense perimeter. Both bogeys — identified as a torpedo bomber and a dive bomber — were shot down before they could reach their helpless target, the *Princeton*.

Almost at the same time, fighter planes from the departing task group intercepted four more enemy planes and shot down two. The others fled back toward the Philippine Islands, some sixty miles to the west.

Just before 1100, a fifth Japanese intruder was "splashed" by the combat air patrol, which had been provided by the carrier *Essex*. At that point, the *Essex* Hellcats were under orders to stay on station over the *Princeton* for two hours, but the pursuit of the enemy plane had used up precious gallons of fuel.

The *Reno*, which had moved up the *Princeton*'s starboard side, reported the cruiser's position untenable because of the intense heat and smoke.

Captain Inglis decided that it would be impossible to battle the fires on the *Princeton* from any distance, as the wind and ship movements prevented much water from reaching the flames. He gave orders to run the cruiser against the blazing carrier.

"The first effort," he said "was to hold the *Birmingham* alongside without the use of lines and keep a moderate separation to avoid damage. This soon was found to be impossible, because the *Princeton* had considerable more freeboard and drifted faster than the *Birmingham*. So lines were passed to the *Princeton* and our engines were maneuvered to bring the two ships closer together."

The *Birmingham* sidled up to the carrier's port beam. The conflicting rise and fall of the two vessels caused a bow line to part under stress. Heavy swells banged the *Birmingham* and *Princeton* against one another repeatedly, damaging gun platforms and sponsons protruding from the sides of both ships.

Some men carrying out their orders to leave the carrier made the mistake of trying to go down ropes and chains on the port side. Several were caught and crushed between the bobbing *Birmingham* and *Princeton*.

On the *Princeton*'s flight deck, those still aboard had to stay clear of the gaping elevator holes as 50-caliber ammunition used in the fighter plane and torpedo bomber guns exploded in the intense hangar deck heat and sent slugs zinging upward. Some of these deadly projectiles ricocheted off the upended forward elevator at wild angles.

The *Cassin Young* and the *Irwin* were told to join in the firefighting effort, so long as they weren't needed to pick up survivors in the water, and provided they did not interfere with the *Birmingham*.

The *Birmingham* lowered cargo nets over the sides to give swimming survivors a means of climbing aboard. Members of the cruiser's crew stood by to help.

Although the *Birmingham*'s skipper was experiencing difficulty in keeping his ship alongside the *Princeton,* hose lines began to cross from cruiser to carrier. After another bow line was set, along with a spring line amidships, a degree of coordination was achieved between the rising and falling vessels. Fourteen hose lines now linked the *Birmingham* with the *Princeton*.

While the wind and seas continued to create problems, the scattered clouds, ranging from two to six thousand feet over the area, provided a degree of concealment from enemy snoopers. The rain squalls that sprang up periodically were also welcomed by the men struggling to save the *Princeton*.

As the fires forward appeared to come under control, the *Birmingham* moved farther aft, using the cruiser's engines to maintain position and keep excess stress off the lines and hoses.

During this maneuver — and indeed, through much of the long day — communications had to be conducted with the *Princeton* by semaphore or blinker light. The carrier's navigator, Lieutenant Moitoret, played a major role in this, bringing into play the hand-flag system he had learned as a boy scout, long before his navy career began.

Among the cruisers and destroyers, however, radio communications continued. The radio logs of the various vessels later proved invaluable in reconstructing the chain of events. The cryptic transmissions reflected the difficulties of the situation and the manner in which the men involved rose to the occasion.

The *Cassin Young,* early in the rescue operation, radioed the *Birmingham*: "I am in position to go along port quarter now." The *Birmingham* replied: "Wait." Then from the *Birmingham* to all rescue vessels: "*Irwin* remains alongside *Princeton. Reno* pick up survivors. Also *Cassin Young* and *Morrison.*"

Moments later, from the *Cassin Young* to the *Birmingham*: "Believe if the *Irwin* would pull up a little bit we could help in fighting fire. Our boat is in water picking up survivors." From the cruiser to the destroyer: "Affirmative but keep clear of *Birmingham*."

Irwin to *Cassin Young*: "*Princeton* requests that you come closer aboard the starboard quarter" and the *Birmingham* interjected: "Comply with *Princeton* request," then added, " Please keep clear. I am coming alongside the port quarter of the *Princeton*."

Irwin to *Reno*: "*Princeton* requests you come alongside starboard side with water." The *Reno* answered: "*Birmingham* in charge and going alongside." The *Birmingham* radioed *Reno*: "Comply with *Princeton* request," and then to the *Irwin*, in a message that put things in proper command perspective: "Coordinate rescue work of destroyers."

On the *Princeton*'s starboard side, the *Irwin* moved in close enough to take aboard a score of casualties from the carrier's forecastle. Comdr. R. O. Sala, *Princeton* senior medical officer; Lt. A. R. Oesterle, one of two dental officers; and three pharmacist's mates remained aboard the carrier, helping to man hose lines when they weren't otherwise occupied with caring for wounded shipmates.

Below decks, a major portion of the fire appeared to be concentrated in the area of the torpedo workshop. A quantity of napalm, assigned to the *Princeton* for possible use in attacking land targets, had been stored, for lack of better space, aft of the hangar on the starboard side. This incendiary material now was burning fiercely.

A dozen men, under Air Officer Bruce Harwood, had proceeded down the catwalk on the port side. They continued working their way aft on the hangar deck, hoping to reach the open hangar curtain and get a hoseline from the *Birmingham*. Topside, another crew under Executive Officer Murphy used the cruiser's hoses to play streams of water from the flight deck onto the fire in the after elevator pit.

The *Reno* made several attempts to move close enough to the *Princeton*'s starboard quarter to pump water on the burning carrier. The cruiser was forced back each time by heat and smoke, sustaining damage to its 40-millimeter gun mounts and side plates as the two ships collided.

The *Reno* asked for, and received, permission to nose against the *Princeton*'s port quarter, just aft of the *Birmingham*. From that position, the *Reno* was able to spray water on the carrier's flight and hangar decks until forced once more to drift astern. Again, the *Reno* was damaged as the *Princeton*'s protruding flight deck struck the cruiser's topside structure and gun mounts. While these collisions were not in themselves devastating, any damage to anti-aircraft guns was a matter of considerable concern when these weapons might be needed at any moment to defend against enemy planes.

The day produced many unusual situations.

Lieutenant Commander Large, the *Princeton*'s air operations officer who had been on duty in air plot when the bomb hit the carrier, wound up helping with hose lines when all hands were ordered topside. Large said: "At one point, the captain asked me to go aft. This was when we were getting water from the *Birmingham*. Twelve marine volunteers from the cruiser climbed aboard the *Princeton* to man the hoses, led by a young navy officer.

"I greeted them, and assigned them to hoses at the after end of the elevator. Their leader, Lt. Alan Reed, turned out to be the son-in-law of my former boss in the banking business.

"At that time, an alert was sounded because two enemy planes were approaching. The *Birmingham* had to break away and Lieutenant Reed, with his party of marines, went back to their cruiser."

William Degenhardt, who had enlisted in the regular navy with his parents' consent when he was seventeen, had been at his duty post, the after gun mount on the *Irwin*, when the *Princeton* was hit.

He said: "It wasn't long after when we heard the order to go alongside. There was a lot of smoke and flame coming out of the carrier. You got to give Captain [Comdr. Daniel B.] Miller a lot of credit, the way he handled that destroyer, just like you'd take a speed boat into the side of a dock in a marina. He took it in hard. He headed the bow into the carrier and we collided with it. The stern was out and there was a big space where you could see a bunch of guys in the water. We threw cargo nets over the side. The crew from number four gun came down and all of us were going down ropes pulling guys out of the drink and putting them on deck.

"Every once in awhile you'd hear our props rev up and you had to scramble back up on deck because we were coming in again. One man I had but I lost him. He was a marine, and I had him by the hair, but I didn't have the strength to pull him in. Another sailor came along and accidentally hit my arm and the marine went back into the water. He was carried off by the ship's wake. When I talked to others later they said he was already dead in the water.

"We spent about a half-hour, or maybe forty minutes, doing this. Some of our guys were diving off the stern, pulling in survivors."

Degenhardt said that much of the time, there were five men on the *Irwin*'s cargo net helping to bring survivors aboard the destroyer. Most of them were members of his own gun crew, including a black sailor named Hayes Lee Wyatt, whose general quarters station was in the magazine "hole" passing up shells to the after five-inch gun. When he wasn't on that duty, he and seven other blacks were mess cooks.

"Several people off our ship got navy and marine medals for lifesaving that day," Degenhardt said. "This guy Wyatt should have gotten one. He was there saving lives on that cargo net."

Another man on the net was Harvey Haroldson, a Mississippi share cropper whose top pay before being drafted was fifty cents a day. Degenhardt said every pay day, Haroldson put his monthly salary of fifty-four dollars in his locker with the money from previous months.

"I told him he was liable to get robbed, but he'd never seen that much money. He sure earned his pay that day."

Like the other destroyers, the *Cassin Young* was involved in the rescue of survivors both by means of extended cargo nets and life boats. Aboard a *Cassin Young* boat were Jim Maars, a quartermaster on the destroyer, and Al Melville, who served as coxswain.

Maars said the *Cassin Young* was instructed to approach the *Princeton* and pick up men who had been blown into the ocean from the carrier.

"About that time there was another attack by enemy planes," he said. "There were Betty bombers and Val dive bombers coming in. Our combat air patrol shot down two or three of them, and we fired at the lead Betty making a run on the *Princeton*. Then we were told to stop firing because of our own fighters. The thing I remember is this Japanese plane was on fire, but it just kept coming. A couple of our fighters actually put their flaps and wheels down to slow enough so they could really hose that Betty. Finally it went into the water."

Maars said the *Cassin Young*'s captain was told to launch a life boat to help in the rescue work. Maars, Melville, and a third sailor, Johnny Ansa, manned the destroyer's boat as it was lowered away in the rolling sea.

"We took our first load of survivors alongside the *Gatling* because we had a wounded man aboard," Maars said. "They said they couldn't take any more on board then, but I told them we had a wounded man, a badly wounded man we had picked up on a life raft. It turned out he was a pilot. Well, we went along the stern and, while we were unloading this wounded guy, the other twelve or fifteen survivors in our boat jumped out and went onto the *Gatling*'s deck like a bunch of penguins coming out of the ocean on an ice slope."

Maars and his shipmates put about and went seeking more survivors.

"We just kept gathering up people. We took three boatloads to our own ship," he said. "Then, when we went alongside the *Gatling* again, they asked us to help their boat, which had been loaded and capsized. We did."

Melville said he and his fellow sailors had been trained for such emergency duty.

"When we put our boat in the water," he said, "we knew how many people we could safely handle, and we tried to stay within that limit. I remember seeing a picture later in the *National Geographic*. The caption said we were picking up survivors, but the picture actually showed us throwing men back into the water. We couldn't overload the boat, and we wanted to be able to take one bunch in, then come back for the others. That way everybody would get home safe."

"They all tried to climb in one side," Maars said. "Al yelled to me and Johnny to get some of them out. That picture was of us tossing men out the other side as fast as we could, just to keep our load within bounds."

Melville and his companions made trip after trip, "picking up as many as twenty-five people at a time, some of them being towed behind our boat.

"I remember Jim going over the side, swimming maybe 100 yards to pick up a very tired man and bring him back to the boat."

"We were not aware at the time," Maars said, "that he had been a prisoner in the carrier's brig who had been released to abandon ship. He had on no life jacket when we saw him floundering and yelling out there. Al said 'we ought to get that guy.' I had on a life jacket, so I grabbed a life ring and went to get him. I had grown up in Southern California waters and knew that if a guy got panicky and tried to grab me, he could drown us both. With a life ring, I could push it to him and we'd both make it."

Melville didn't lose his sense of humor through the ordeal of rescue work.

"We came alongside a couple of guys dressed in khaki," he said. "I asked them if they were marines or navy. They said marines, and I said we're only picking up sailors today. One of them had a shoulder holster, and I said I'd pick him up if he'd give me his gun. He told me he had lost the gun, but he'd let me have the holster. We picked him up."

"It was remarkable," Maars said, "there were few signs of uncontrolled fear in evidence.

"Many of these guys probably had taken only a couple of boat rides in their lives, and maybe they were on their first ship. They never had been in a small boat in the open ocean. Al, Johnny, and I, on the other hand, never gave it a thought. It was like getting in your car and taking a drive, but for some that day it was not a pleasant experience."

"The cargo net crew, and those with me on the boat, were at complete ease the whole time," Melville added. "There was no panicking, except maybe a little by those we picked up, and that was only when they were hustling to get onto the destroyers."

The trio of life savers went about their business with an apparent disregard of the conditions and the passage of time.

"There were moderately heavy seas," Melville recalled later. "There were breakers and waves. I couldn't even estimate the time period. At the time, it never really crossed our minds that the captain had told us if another attack developed, we might have to be left behind."

Maars shrugged off that possibility.

"They would have come back for us if they could," he said. "If there had been another big air attack, the ships would have had to go into defense positions, go to high speed, and come back through the area where we were later. If they didn't come back, we just have to say to ourselves, 'well, that's what they were going to do.'"

As for the passage of time, Maars said he learned from subsequent re-examination of ship logs that he and his companions had been on their lifesaving mission approximately six hours.

CHAPTER XIX

So Near to Winning

IN A TITANIC ARC TO THE north, west, and south of the *Princeton*, the biggest naval battle of all time was being waged around and amid the scores of islands that make up the Philippine Archipelago.

In all, sixty-four warships of the Japanese Imperial Navy were attempting to fight their way to Leyte and stem the Allied invasion drive into the central Philippines. On those ships were nearly 43,000 Japanese officers and men.

Standing ready to thwart them were two U.S. fleets — the Seventh Fleet of older battleships, cruisers, destroyers, and "baby" flattops under Adm. Thomas Kincaid; and Admiral Halsey's Third Fleet of fast carriers and accompanying battleships, cruisers, and destroyers. The Allied naval array included 216 combat vessels — two of them Australian, and the others U.S. On board were more than 143,000 officers and men.

The Seventh Fleet's job was to provide close support to the invasion force and repel any enemy attacks on it. Halsey's task was to supply any needed backup for the Seventh Fleet, but primarily to seek out and destroy the enemy's ships. In Halsey's mind, the number one target was Japan's under-planed and dwindling aircraft carrier force.

The enemy's master battle plan was cleverly conceived, but

the Japanese lacked the manpower, ships, and above all the planes, to carry it out successfully. Basically, the strategy involved naval units converging on the Philippines from the northwest and southwest, splitting into a two-pronged, pincer attack. One task group would cruise through the Sibuyan Sea and the San Bernardino Strait; and the other would sail through the Surigao Strait to strike the Allied invasion force and supporting naval units.

Meanwhile, the Japanese carriers were to deliberately make their presence known to Admiral Halsey and draw the Third Fleet off to the north, away from the planned annihilation of General MacArthur's invaders. For lack of trained pilots, the flattops carried few planes, at best, or no planes at all.

U.S. submarines intercepted the Japanese warships before they reached the western rim of the Philippines, sinking two cruisers. With other subs and PT boats joining the attack in the confined waters of the two straits, additional damage was inflicted as the Japanese pincer closed on the Leyte beachhead.

Although the enemy did break through to blast U.S. warships in Leyte Gulf, they were driven back, and remained under air, submarine, and torpedo boat attack as they painfully withdrew toward the Sulu Sea.

Their retreat was all the more painful because they lacked air support. Virtually every available plane under the Japanese command on Luzon had been mustered to go after Halsey's Third Fleet, including the lone bomber that scored the hit on the *Princeton*. Only a fraction of the Japanese aircraft made it back home.

Planes from Halsey's carriers pounded the battleship *Musashi* with bombs until the ship rolled over and sank. The battleships *Yamato* and *Nagato* took bomb hits. Carrier bombers heavily damaged the cruiser *Tone* and three destroyers.

As scout planes located the Japanese carriers north of Luzon, Halsey turned his attention in that direction, steaming at flank speed until the Third Fleet's fighters, torpedo planes, and dive bombers were within attack range of the enemy.

The sprawling air and sea battle moved toward a climax as the *Birmingham, Reno, Morrison, Gatling, Irwin,* and *Cassin Young* continued their efforts to save the *Princeton*.

By midday, two-and-a-half hours after the Japanese bomb plunged through the *Princeton*'s flight deck, the rescue crews appeared to be winning their bitter struggle against the flames, but not without cost.

The *Reno* was the first to suffer damage as it attempted to nose against the carrier to send streams of water across the constantly changing gap. Repeatedly, the cruiser and carrier slammed against one another in the heavy swells. The higher overhang of the *Princeton*'s flight deck and sponsons smashed one of the *Reno*'s 40-millimeter gun mounts and put it out of action.

Then, as the *Reno* was pulled back to maintain anti-aircraft protection for the beleaguered flotilla, the *Birmingham* took over the firefighting assignment. Again, the rise and fall of the sea brought cruiser and carrier into violent and repeated contact. Two of the *Birmingham*'s five-inch gun mounts were knocked out of commission.

The *Irwin*, teeming with rescued survivors who nearly tripled the destroyer's normal complement of 300, lost the use of one engine when floating debris fouled a condenser.

The *Morrison* sustained the heaviest pounding when the destroyer became lodged under the *Princeton*'s flight deck overhang near the carrier's stacks. For nearly an hour, the *Morrison* rode up and down with the *Princeton* as a single entity. During this grinding union, the smaller vessel's mast was broken off, the forward director was lost, and the stacks, along with the searchlight platform and the port side of the bridge, were crushed.

One of the principal causes of damage was a tractor, normally used on the *Princeton*'s flight deck to move planes, which fell over the side onto the destroyer's superstructure. Moments later, a jeep broke loose from its tie-downs and bounced off the *Morrison* into the sea.

Throughout this terrible ordeal, the *Morrison* and those aboard were subjected to waves of intense heat and smoke from the carrier alongside. One individual managed to take advantage of the locking together of the two ships. The *Princeton*'s navigator, Moitoret, salvaged some of the carrier's confidential publications from the bridge and chart house, as well as the ship's two chronometers. He and his quartermaster lowered them onto the deck of the *Morrison* with a length of signal halyard.

In typical western Pacific fashion, the weather was erratic. While the *Morrison* was painfully wedged between two of the offset stacks of the *Princeton*, a severe rain squall moved directly across the stricken carrier and her unwilling companion. The sea became even more choppy as the wind out of the northeast rose to eighteen knots. Damage to the destroyer was intensified, and the rescue operations were further hampered by nature.

Among the 300 to 400 *Princeton* crewmen who had been pulled aboard the *Morrison* was Machinist Mate Bob Reno, who had been stationed near the machine shop when the *Princeton* took the Japanese pilot's bomb.

When the wayward tractor fell onto the *Morrison* from the *Princeton*'s flight deck, Reno helped clear away the destroyer's damaged mast.

"The mast collapsed and fell astern," he said. "We finished the job of chopping it loose, and one of the destroyers got a line over to us, trying to back us off the *Princeton*, but the line snapped and that maneuver didn't work.

"As we got the mast down and free from the *Morrison*, the waves were kind of high and the sea was rough, but fortunately the *Princeton* didn't explode at that time, and seemed to be cooling off quite a bit."

It was then that the *Irwin* attempted to get a line across to the *Morrison*, and pull the latter free of the *Princeton*. This rescue effort was thwarted by the fouling of one *Irwin* engine in the debris-strewn sea. In this exchange, the *Irwin* was pounded against the carrier's side until the other engine could be used to get the *Irwin* moving forward and clear of the bigger ship.

Further complicating the problem were intrusions by enemy aircraft and submarine sound contacts.

Unidentified aircraft were reported a bare five miles to the southwest of the rescue operation. A short time later, a large formation of enemy planes was detected sixty miles out, and almost simultaneously the destroyer *Cassin Young* reported a possible submarine contact.

The rescue vessels left the *Princeton* and formed a defensive circle to fight off the attacks that appeared imminent. In pulling away from the *Princeton*, the *Birmingham* took back aboard most of the emergency crew the cruiser had sent over to battle the carrier's fires.

Pharmacist's Mate Pantages also wound up aboard the *Morrison*. After abandoning the *Princeton*, he joined other swimmers to increase his chances of being spotted by one of the rescue vessels searching the waters around the carrier.

He tried to stay afloat on his back to conserve energy and to provide as inconspicuous a target for roving sharks as possible.

"It seemed like hours," he said, "when suddenly, approaching our area, were a few destroyers looking for survivors. At last help had arrived, and I was plucked out of the water by the *Morrison*. I think all of our collective thoughts at that moment were of thanks to the Almighty and the crew of the *Morrison* for being at the right place at the right time.

"The first few moments were spent just lying on the deck from sheer exhaustion. For the first time that day, I began to feel some security — until word was passed we were headed back to the *Princeton* to offer assistance."

On the way, the *Morrison*'s five-inch guns opened fire. To Pantages and the other survivors aboard, the "noise was deafening" and he "felt real panic at the thought we were going to be under attack again." The *Morrison* and other ships in the rescue squadron were shooting at a lone enemy plane, which was downed by the *Reno*'s anti-aircraft before reaching a target.

"We made it back to the *Princeton*," Pantages said, "and pulled along the starboard side of the carrier. Our attempt to give aid, however, was short lived. The superstructure of the *Morrison* became entrenched under the flight deck of the *Princeton*, and all the maneuvering in the world didn't seem to be of any help in dislodging the destroyer. It was a situation which caused a lot of additional stress. The thought of the *Princeton* exploding, or fires spreading to the *Morrison*, I'm sure raced through everyone's mind."

For the next half-hour, Pantages dodged falling debris from the carrier and grasped any available handhold to keep from being jolted off the destroyer's deck into the sea.

"The *Morrison* made another attempt to back away from the carrier," he said, "and, in finally breaking free, ripped a large section of the destroyer's superstructure."

At this point in the long, long day, when the firefighters seemed to have victory within their grasp, the enemy again interceded. As the *Morrison* managed to break free from its tenuous union with the *Princeton*, the *Birmingham* was forced to pull away because of impending air attack and submarine contacts.

The fires on the *Princeton* appeared under control, and the smoke pall had diminished. There were serious preparations made to bring the carrier under tow. However, the intrusion of Japanese planes and the unfruitful search for an enemy sub gave the flames renewed life.

The *Birmingham* firefighting detachment had been recalled to the cruiser, and the *Princeton* again was floating helplessly, without water to battle the fires, without power, and without communications other than the signal flags of the ship's navigator, who was perched above the bridge of his derelict vessel.

Lieutenant Commander Large, the *Princeton*'s air plot officer, was among the small band still left aboard the carrier. To him and his companions, the break-off of fire fighting operations was "the development that cost us the ship.

"Japanese aircraft were spotted approaching the formation," he said. "The ships alongside had to pull away and man their guns, leaving us dead in the water with no means to fight the fire.

"The commanding officers of those ships had no other choice, and within a matter of moments their automatic weapons were in action. The *Birmingham* volunteers had returned to their ship; and it was a small, exhausted group that retired to the relatively undamaged forward part of the flight deck. We looked at this debris-strewn area as an island of safety. A dismal rain started to soak through our dirty uniforms."

The ensuing surface-air engagement "found us as weary spectators," Large said.

"There was a good deal of shooting, and at least one Jap was splashed. Without any way to fight the fires on our ship, we sat disconsolately on airplane chocks and watched the show. A Jap plane circled low overhead, apparently photographing our misery. There was an ominous increase in smoke at the after end of the hangar."

The *Princeton*'s chief medical officer, Commander Sala, provided a welcome break in the tension.

"He produced a number of small bottles of brandy — the kind provided pilots after a combat mission — and a cup was passed around," Large said.

With all communications gone, those on the carrier could not hear the radio traffic between the other ships.

The destroyer *Cassin Young* reported: "Am investigating possible sub contact." The *Reno* responded: "Develop contact and keep us informed"; and the *Birmingham* messaged the *Gatling*: "Give *Cassin Young* a hand with that contact."

Moments later, from the *Cassin Young*: "Contact now bears 185 [degrees] distance 2,000 yards from me." Then, "contact has been lost. Will attempt to regain." Sound contact was picked up again, but lost for a second time, and the search for an enemy underwater intruder eventually was abandoned.

By radio, the *Birmingham*'s captain requested reports from the *Reno* and other destroyers on the "approximate number of *Princeton* personnel on board."

Back came the count. "*Irwin* has approximately 500." "*Gatling* has between 175 and 200." *Cassin Young* counted 200 and the *Reno* reported "I have five on board."

By 1400, the fires on the *Princeton*, which had appeared to be practically out, regained considerable intensity. The carrier's skipper asked that a destroyer be brought along the port side to pour water on the flame while the *Birmingham* attempted to take the *Princeton* under tow.

Even before such a move could be effected, it was realized the fires were far too much for the hoselines of a destroyer to handle. So the *Birmingham* was asked to come within hose range of the carrier's port quarter while the *Reno* prepared to tow. Unfortunately, this plan had to be rejected, too, because the *Reno* had sustained severe damage to her towing gear in a kamikaze attack a few days before. Moreover, the captain of the *Birmingham* wanted to keep the *Reno* away from further damage in any tow attempt, and capable of repelling possible enemy air attacks.

A strong, fresh wind had sprung up, reaching a force of twenty knots. The *Princeton* gained momentum in her aimless drift, and the *Birmingham*'s crew found it increasingly difficult to edge up to the carrier. With painful slowness, the cruiser closed on the stern of the carrier. Aboard the *Princeton*, preparations were made to receive the *Birmingham*'s hoses.

After several attempts against the heavy wind, the *Birmingham* managed to get a bow line across to the *Princeton* — the first step in the firefighting link-up. Lieutenant Bradley and Ensign Christie led a party of men to the hangar deck to secure the bow line to cleats there, and to accept the hoselines as they came over from the *Birmingham*.

The *Princeton*'s air officer, Commander Harwood, took another group of men to the area under the damaged after elevator — dangerously close to the ticking "time bomb" represented by the bomb-filled after magazine and the other high explosives stored nearby.

CHAPTER XX

Fatal Blow

MORE THAN FIVE HOURS HAD elapsed since the initial crippling of the *Princeton*.

While over an enormous expanse of the western Pacific naval history was being written in blood, twisted steel, and oil slicks on ocean waters, to the men not directly involved with the *Princeton*'s dilemma, the relentless clock was primarily a matter of lessened attack capability. To those on the *Princeton*, however, the dwindling day was a growing concern spelled — s–u–r–v–i–v–a–l.

The winds had risen beyond the twenty-knot level, and the mounting seas were adding to the difficulty of the rescue operation.

Although Captain Buracker and his companions were acutely aware of the munitions stowed outside the after magazine, the general feeling was that the fires on the *Princeton* had lessened enough to warrant a tow attempt.

Slowly, the *Birmingham* eased up toward the port side of the *Princeton*. The cruiser's captain radioed the *Reno*: "Prepare to take *Princeton* in tow." The *Reno* repeated its earlier status report: "I have no tow line."

The *Birmingham* continued to inch closer to the carrier, while its skipper considered the idea of serving as a side-by-side "tugboat" to move the *Princeton* as far as possible away from the enemy's

Philippine airfields. Then, another vessel capable of towing the carrier to a safe port could be summoned.

The *Birmingham*'s crew stood ready to get lines and hoses across to the carrier. Hundreds of fellow crew members and *Princeton* survivors lined the cruiser's topside, swarming over every vantage point to observe the action. All of them about to be witnesses to, and victims of, an unanticipated horror.

On the *Princeton*'s hangar deck, Commander Harwood's party awaited the *Birmingham*'s bow line and hoses. A few scant yards farther aft, four hundred 100-pound general purpose bombs and sixty-five fragmentation "clusters," which had been literally baking throughout the fire-ridden day, neared the disaster limit.

At 1523, the *Princeton* was blown asunder by an explosion that survivors later were to recall in terms of an atom bomb. The entire stern of the *Princeton* — nearly one-fourth of the ship — was hurtled out of the water amid a lethal shower of jagged debris, ranging from small particles to huge chunks of steel.

The air was filled with shrapnel, sections of plating, bits of clothing, steel helmets, life jackets, gas masks, flight-deck timbers, CO_2 bottles, and shattered ammunition containers.

The incredible force of the blast shoved the great bulk of the *Birmingham* more than fifteen feet sideways through the water.

For what seemed more than an eternity, there were no sounds but the splashing of metal, and wood, and God knows what else, falling back into the water. Then, out of the acrid silence, there emerged a gory scene of destruction.

The *Birmingham*'s starboard side had been jammed with humanity, including men attempting to get lines and hoses to the *Princeton*, others helping wounded survivors from the carrier, but the overwhelming majority merely spectators.

Hardly a single square inch of the *Birmingham*'s exposed flank escaped undamaged. There were jagged holes everywhere. Rubble on the decks of both the carrier and the cruiser ranged from 50-caliber shellcases to the 150-pound tool chest that landed on one of the *Birmingham*'s gun mounts and remained balanced there.

As the *Princeton*'s stern section floated free, the rudder, the big screws, and the carrier's name, clearly visible across the fantail, pointed skyward.

Almost before the eye could take in the full extent of the damage, the ear was bombarded by the cries and the moans of the wounded. There were no cries or moans from twenty-odd members of Commander Harwood's firefighting party. Their tomb was the *Princeton*'s blasted stern.

The airwaves crackled with urgent messages from the instant of the explosion. The *Birmingham* radioed the *Reno*: "Take command." Then, "we have had many casualties on *Birmingham*. Take command," and the *Reno* answered, "Roger."

Even before the smoke started to clear from the immediate scene, the radio transmissions began to paint the dreadful picture for those too far removed to see for themselves what had happened.

"There was an explosion on the *Princeton*," the *Birmingham* told the *Reno*. "I believe it has its fantail blown off. See if you can get contact with Commander Task Group 38.3." A moment later the *Reno* was asked to "take guard for us on all circuits but TBS [Talk Between Ships, short range voice radio]. We have been unable to determine damage."

Birmingham to *Reno*: "Try to contact *Santa Fe* and tell him we need our other doctor as soon as possible."

Reno to *Birmingham*: "Do you wish one of our doctors?"

Birmingham to *Reno*: "Affirmative. Would like you to send over some corpsmen?"

After a brief pause, from *Birmingham* to *Reno*: "We have about 100 to 150 killed and about the same number wounded. Those casualties are very gravely wounded. Our commanding officer is a casualty."

Frank Popham, a machinist mate, second class, was one of the sightseers on the *Birmingham*.

"I was sitting on this blower about four-and-a-half to five feet high, just watching the goings-on. Earlier, the *Birmingham* had wiped off all the platforms on the side of the *Princeton* when they were banging together. All the hatches on the *Princeton* were knocked off, too, and we could plainly see the open bomb storage. They were training salt water hoses on them and you could see the steam coming off the bombs, they were that hot. It seemed to me they were only about twelve feet away, but youth is not too smart at times."

Popham was perched between two other members of the *Birmingham*'s crew, one of them his best friend, Vernon Trevethan.

"The three of us were blown into the air. I landed on my back.

They wouldn't tell me for four days what happened to my friend. I had nightmares. I almost bled to death," Popham said.

As for the death-dealing blast, Popham may have been the only surviving witness to the actual explosion.

"The three of us were sitting on that blower, having a ball watching, when one of the guys said 'Hey, look at the smoke coming out of there.' He was pointing to the bomb storage area on the *Princeton*. I turned around; at that instant she blew. I was looking right at it, and none of the pictures in the paper, or anywhere showed the way it started," Popham said.

"It was a plume, a narrow plume or jet of orange smoke that went 300 to 400 feet into the air, and at the same second I could see this concussion coming at me. You can see a concussion, the air is more dense or something. I went backward, and what probably saved me was that I threw up my hand. One of my fingers was blown off, but it could have been much worse.

"Suddenly, just like that, it was deathly quiet. I mean just nothing, and then the hot shrapnel raining down. Oh, yes, shrapnel can be red hot. It was burning the hell out of me, so I tried to stand up, but one leg wouldn't support me. It turned out that a piece of shrapnel had broken a bone in my leg and I wasn't able to stand on it. I tried to crawl under a gun turret to get out of the way of the rain of hot shrapnel. Even so, some of it burned me on the neck; and I wound up with shrapnel in my back, and my other leg was injured, too."

Popham managed to take a look at the scene around him.

"As far as I could tell, there were only two or three people conscious anywhere near me," he said. "Everybody else was either dead or unconscious. The working parties, the guys manning hose lines and trying to get a bow line to the *Princeton*, were completely wiped out in one terrible flash."

While he was lying under the gun turret, a friend emerged from the other side of the deck and came over to Popham, whose name had prompted the nickname "Pop."

"He was a black man, name of John Miksis. He came up to me and said, 'Pop, Pop, take it easy.' Shock had taken effect. He was excited, but I wasn't for some reason. He was yelling in my face and I said 'God damn it, John, cut it out,' and he said 'I'll get you help.' He went down below deck and came back with a bunk bed he had torn off the fittings somehow. He and another fellow used it for a stretcher, and they got me down to an aid station. John probably saved my life by getting me there so fast."

Popham wound up in the care of Tim Holt, who was performing first aid duty under the incredible conditions of those moments.

"He was talking to me," Popham said. "I heard from him later, and he said he had twelve guys die on him before he got to me, and he wasn't about to have a thirteenth. He made them take me to the chief petty officers' quarters, which was an emergency aid station. They poured blood plasma into me, and that kept me alive."

Popham eventually wound up on a hospital ship, and his right leg was amputated before he was shipped back to the United States. While he was recuperating at the Mare Island Naval Hospital, he learned the *Birmingham* was under repair nearby.

"I was able to get word to some members of the crew. When they were ready to sail, I managed to get aboard and tried to go along as a stowaway. It's pretty hard for a one-legged sailor on crutches to hide away aboard ship. They found me, put me on a whaleboat, and I was sent back to the hospital. Everybody had a good laugh about it."

Frank Peevey, a member of the *Birmingham*'s engine room crew, became a sightseer through a quirk.

"A friend of mine was off watch, and he was my relief," Peevey said. "He didn't want to be on deck. He came down and offered to relieve me so I could go topside and see what was going on."

Peevey was standing on one of the *Birmingham*'s forward 40-millimeter gunmounts, on the cruiser's starboard side, when the *Princeton*'s stern blew skyward.

"Funny thing," he said, "I don't recall hearing the explosion, no sound whatsoever, but I do recall the concussion. This all happened in a split second, obviously. My first thought was to fight the concussion, but it occurred to me I should let it blow me down. I probably couldn't have withstood the force of it anyway.

"It blew me down. Then I crawled over to the port side of the *Birmingham* and suddenly something, it looked like a burning piece of two-by-four hit me across the back. I kept crawling until I got to a bulkhead and I saw some big drops of blood, I mean big drops of blood — as much as a teacup in each one — and I thought, 'Well Jesus Christ, somebody really got hurt,' but it never hit me then the terrible disaster that actually had happened."

Peevey worked his way back to the 40-millimeter mount.

"Of the two guys I had been talking to when the *Princeton* exploded, some of the brains of one were on my shoes. The other guy had a leg blown off at the knee and it was hanging only by a single tendon. I pulled out a little navy knife I had and cut that tendon, then put a tourniquet around his leg. For a long time afterward, I couldn't get rid of the horrible feeling I put the tourniquet on wrong. He was leaving a stream of blood from the stump of his leg."

After dragging his wounded shipmate to a safe spot, Peevey went looking for morphine and sulfa powder.

"The whole ship was littered with dead and wounded," Peevey said. "I never got back to the man I had been taking care of. There were so many injured you never got back to anybody. You just went from one to the next."

Buhler "Buck" Glans was the chief quartermaster on the *Birmingham*. It was his duty to take periodic sun sightings to pinpoint the ship's position at sea.

"When it was time to take sightings, I went to the flying bridge with my first class quartermaster. Using my sextant, I was bringing the sun down to the horizon between the smoke stacks of the *Princeton* when the carrier blew up," he said.

"Looking up, I saw steel coming down, so I dove for cover toward the ladder to the lower decks. I made that descent hitting only two steps on the way down. Then I found I had been hit by shrapnel in the thigh, only a few inches from an important part of my body."

When the debris fallout stopped, Glans returned to the open deck to find his first class quartermaster dead.

"I tried to get those who were still alive. Wounded men lay all over the deck, not a pretty sight," he said. "The ship's captain, the navigator, and officer of the deck were wounded. They all asked that others be helped first. There were many heroic acts. Our specialist chief of physical fitness, who had lost both legs, told the corpsmen to help others first. He died from loss of blood. The *Birmingham*'s decks ran with blood."

Full impact of the *Princeton*'s high explosive eruption struck the *Birmingham*'s bridge, where Capt. Thomas Browning Inglis was bringing his vessel in to help the stricken carrier under the command of his naval academy compatriot, Bill Buracker.

"As we moved back toward the *Princeton*," he said, "she looked as innocent as could be with just a thin wisp of smoke visible. I thought to myself, 'we'd have the fire licked in no time and have her in tow.' Then the *Princeton*'s stern blew."

Captain Inglis was thrown against the far bulkhead.

"I was struck by fragments," he said. "My left arm was broken — a clean break as it turned out. I had been hit by shrapnel in the head, face, and at the base of my spine."

Initially, Inglis thought he had escaped serious injury, that the latest blast was just another in the series of explosions that had racked the *Princeton* from mid-morning.

"At first, I thought I was okay. I hardly knew I had been wounded. I kept command for some ten to fifteen minutes, and then I began to feel dizzy and not really competent to handle the task of running my ship and looking out for the safety of all hands aboard."

The *Birmingham*'s chief gunnery officer, Comdr. Francis R. Duborg, was on the bridge with Captain Inglis. Although also wounded by shrapnel, he was in far better shape than the cruiser's skipper. When it became obvious Inglis couldn't continue in charge, Duborg assumed command as Inglis was helped to his cabin.

A naval reservist, Lt. James H. MacArt, was the sole doctor aboard the *Birmingham* at the time.

"It wasn't for some time later," said Commander Duborg, "that MacArt was able to check on the captain and found out how bad he was. He sent down a pharmacist's mate with a splint. The repair job was really painful."

Before being forced to leave the bridge, Captain Inglis sent a message to the *Reno*: "We have had many casualties on *Birmingham*. Take over command. Report to CTG 38.3 that bomb magazine exploded. I consider it useless to salvage ship. Recommend that personnel be removed and ship sunk. In the meantime we are trying to inspect the damage on the *Birmingham*."

Because of damage sustained by the *Birmingham*'s short range radio equipment, the message apparently never was received by the *Reno*.

Comdr. Winston Folk, the *Birmingham*'s executive officer second-in-charge, also was on the bridge at the instant of explosion.

"I was standing on the starboard side of the signal bridge a few feet from the captain," Folk said. "We were both struck by debris and knocked to the deck. As soon as I recovered from the shock of the concussion, I got up and went to the captain to see how he was. He said he had been hit, but was all right."

Captain Inglis instructed Folk to make a quick on-the-scene survey of the ship's condition. Folk left the bridge to check damage and casualties.

"I was totally unprepared for the spectacle that greeted me," Folk said. "Still a bit dazed myself, I somehow thought the principal effects of the explosion had been in the bridge area. I found instead that the main deck, for 140 of our 150 frames — most of its length — strewn with dead, dying, and wounded, many of them badly hurt. Already the few unwounded were beginning to render first aid to their companions.

"The communications platform was in the same condition. It is impossible, even remotely, adequately to describe the grisly scene of human fragmentation that presented itself. I felt as if I were having a horrible nightmare and wished I would hurry and wake up."

Despite the horror of the situation, Folk retained a lasting impression of personal and collective unselfishness — of magnificent heroism when there was good reason to fear the massive blast might be followed by others at any time.

"There was not the slightest tendency toward panic," he said, "and many of those involved had never before been in close contact with violent death, seen decks covered with the blood of companions.

"Men with legs off, arms off, with gaping wounds in their bodies, with the tops of their heads furrowed by fragments would insist 'I'm all right. Take care of Joe over there,' or 'Don't waste morphine on me, Commander, just hit me over the head.' "

Folk completed his survey of the *Birmingham*'s toll and worked his way back to the bridge. He discovered Captain Inglis had given over his command, reluctantly, to the gunnery officer and placed the *Reno* in charge of the rescue flotilla.

As the number-two officer on the *Birmingham* under Inglis, Folk relieved the gunnery officer and took command of the cruiser.

The *Birmingham*'s communications officer, Lt. Edward Ryan, escaped injury because he was standing near the middle of the pilot house at the time of the explosion.

"When I heard the blast," he said, "I crouched down, and fortunately none of the fragments penetrated to where I was. The officer of the deck, Lt. [John L.] Marocchi, was standing on the right side and was quite badly wounded in the face."

When he stood up, Ryan had a broad overlook of the forward half of the *Birmingham*.

"There were people lying all over the place, and a lot of blood. Almost immediately, some of those not so seriously hurt were busy trying to administer first aid to others. The superstructure, except for the conning tower, was not armored and the sheet metal had been riddled in many places."

Ryan, who had only basic first aid training, left the bridge to do what he could to help the wounded.

"The officer who had come aboard to replace me," Ryan said, "was very badly wounded. Somebody apparently carried him to his cabin where we found him. We started to take him to a dressing station. He wasn't conscious, but he instinctively grabbed the door handle as we moved him by it. He died shortly after we got him to the aid station."

Turning his attention to other victims, Ryan prepared to inject morphine in a seaman's arm. The sailor pushed him away and said, "No, don't take care of me. Take care of those other fellas. They're worse off than I am."

"That," said Ryan, "was typical of the spirit you saw everywhere. I don't really have too coherent a recollection of what I did much of the time after that. Most of the injuries were so serious you really didn't know how to begin to help."

Ens. Robert C. Kerr, a naval reservist serving on the *Birmingham*, was one of many who gave the ultimate. The citation, which accompanied his posthumous award of the Navy Cross, read in part:

> Seriously wounded when a terrific explosion in the magazine section of the stricken *Princeton* hurled him from his position on the starboard catapult onto the steel hangar deck and killed or wounded half of the *Birmingham* crew, Ensign Kerr steadfastly refused medical attention, insisting that others be cared for first. Although still conscious and suffering intense pain, he obtained materials for a tourniquet and after applying it to his injured leg, injected himself and two other casualties with morphine syrettes. Still refusing assistance, he requested that others be evacuated below decks and, remaining in the danger area for more than an

hour while his ship was under constant aerial attack, bravely instructed others in the administration of first aid and comforted the wounded and dying.

Kerr died of his wounds the following day as the battered flotilla crept back toward Ulithi.

On the *Princeton*, the explosion had an incredible impact. For the author, one of those still aboard the carrier, the instant reaction was: "My God, I'm going to die. Nothing is left. No one will survive."

The bulk of the ship lurched sideward and upward, trembled for a terrible instant, then settled into a rocking reception of the deadly shower of debris. The ensuing stillness was totally devoid of any human sound, pierced only by the clank of metal on metal, shrapnel hitting water, and steam hissing from ruptured pipes.

Of the *Princeton*'s total complement of some 1,500 officers and crew, there were, at the time of the blast, only fifty-odd still aboard. The explosion instantly wiped out Commander Harwood's twenty-five-man party in the immediate vicinity of the exploding munitions. Of the remaining two dozen survivors, not one escaped some degree of injury.

When the lethal explosion erupted, Navigator Moitoret was sitting on a bomb crate atop the *Princeton*'s open bridge with a pair of semaphore flags "because I was the only means of communication we had with the other ships."

Moitoret's first class quartermaster, Jim Hunnicutt, was on the bridge with him.

"When that last blast came," Moitoret said, "stuff just fell out of the sky for minutes. I was knocked down, and when I got up I had blood running down my face. I was concerned about Jim, although he was one level below me at the air officer's station, where the crew had built some plexiglass panes to make an enclosure. The blast shattered those panes and there were splinters all over Jim's face."

Moitoret jumped down to Hunnicutt's level and realized there was something wrong with his right knee.

"All officers at that time carried a navy Colt forty-five as a side arm while at general quarters. On the same web belt, we had a first aid kit including some morphine syringes and packets of sulfa powder. I didn't need the morphine, but I broke open the sulfa powder. As I pulled out each piece of plexiglass in Jim's face, I poured sulfa powder on the hole. After I got him fixed up, I asked him to look at me."

Hunnicutt applied sulfa powder to a half-inch slash, above one of Moitoret's eyes, caused by a piece of flying shrapnel. Then Moitoret took a look at his own injured leg.

"What had hit me was a jagged hunk of steel plating from the armored flight deck, which broke an artery on the inside of my right leg above the knee. It caused interior bleeding and a king-sized lump."

The explosion rocked a small group standing amidships on the port side of the *Princeton*'s flight deck. Included were the carrier's commander, Captain Buracker, and the man who had just come aboard days earlier to assume command, Capt. John Hoskins.

Hoskins, a genial red-haired four-striper who was destined to become a navy legend, had remained aboard to help fight the fires, although he was under no duty compulsion to do so. During the long hours from the initial bomb hit to the final blast, he manned hose lines and pitched in wherever an extra pair of hands was needed.

Captain Buracker recalls the explosion as "terrifying."

"The after part of the ship was blown high and fell in the sea astern," he said. "Flying fragments, some huge, some small, burst outwards and upwards. Big chunks swept the *Birmingham,* causing many casualties in killed and wounded. Our ship also was showered with flying debris from stem to stern. Practically all left aboard were killed or injured. Commander Harwood and his party aft in the hangar were lost."

Buracker said his replacement skipper was standing with him at the time.

"When the blast came, we all started crawling and running forward for protection. Someone noticed that Captain Hoskins couldn't move. Going back, I saw that his right foot was hanging by a shred. He already had applied a tourniquet to his leg to stop the flow of blood."

Commander Sala, the *Princeton*'s senior medical officer, and Pharmacist Mate First Class Paul Robinson rushed to assist Hoskins.

"Dr. Sala had fallen heir to an amputation knife that was in a set when we put the ship in commission," Robinson said. "He had a sheath made for it. When Captain Hoskins had this problem, which was on the flight deck next to the island, I know there are people that say they were eye witnesses to my amputating the leg, but I didn't amputate it at all.

"His foot was blown off above the ankle. The ankle has many bones in it. Captain Hoskins was in great pain. I came upon him when Dr. Sala was already there, but he, also, was wounded. I gave Captain Hoskins a shot of morphine — one-half grain. One-quarter grain is a lot, and I think one-eighth grain now is the usual dosage for pain."

Robinson said he started to "clean up the wound."

"I didn't know how bad it was. I put a tourniquet just above it — a stricture rather than a tourniquet because I cut off all the blood supply and cut through to the Achilles tendon. The people who saw me do this thought I was amputating the leg and this is the reason for that story."

With Sala standing by, knife in hand, Robinson gave Hoskins another one-half grain of morphine.

"He just gritted his teeth," Robinson said. "By then, he had a full grain of morphine. This is an awful lot for one to take, but when you are in pain; it has been proven the more pain, the more morphine you can take. A full grain might kill someone, but not someone in his state of pain."

With the unsheathed amputation knife, Sala removed Hoskins's leg, surrounded by the small party of survivors on the smoke-shrouded flight deck of a battered aircraft carrier, seemingly waging its own bitter struggle to remain afloat.

"There is a way that you do an amputation under sterile conditions," Robinson said, "where you cut the bone back a little and you cut a pattern somewhat like a baseball cover so you put a flap over the end of the extremity that is being amputated. This was not the time or the place, and it wasn't sterile. Nevertheless, he survived that very well. He was a real man. Eventually, we lowered him into a whaleboat."

Hoskins later did not recall having been given morphine.

"We had fought the fires from nine o'clock in the morning to nearly 3:30 in the afternoon. Our sprinklers were knocked out, and I was knocked on my fanny three times. When the stern of the carrier was blasted off, all twenty or so of us on the flight deck were blown flat. Then everyone started to run, but I couldn't get up.

"There was my bare right foot — minus shoe and sock, hanging by a tendon, almost completely severed. They carried me forward and the doctor, himself injured, went to work on me with a sheath knife. In his dazed condition, he forgot to give me morphine. Cutting off that tendon was the worst pain I ever experienced."

The *Princeton*'s dental officer, Dr. Oesterle, had been standing beside Captain Hoskins.

"After the explosion, when I had regained some composure," he said, "I found Captain Hoskins sitting near me using a belt as a tourniquet around his injured leg. Dr. Sala came up and removed the foot with his sheath knife. Dr. Sala also had been injured in the groin by a piece of shrapnel."

Still-conscious Hoskins was placed in a Stokes (metal basket) stretcher and lowered from the forward end of the flight deck to the forecastle — an open portion of deck at the carrier's pointed bow.

"Before he was lowered into a whaleboat and taken to the *Gatling*, Captain Hoskins asked that he be given a knife to use in cutting himself loose from the stretcher in case he wound up in the water before reaching the destroyer," Dr. Oesterle said.

At that moment, Hoskins inserted his name in navy lore by saluting in the direction of Captain Buracker and saying:

"Request permission to leave the ship."

His words were those addressed to the officer of the deck by every officer or enlisted man in disembarking from a U.S. Navy vessel.

Then as his stretcher was lowered toward the bobbing whaleboat, Hoskins called to Buracker:

"Don't worry about me. I hope you save her. You deserve to."

Chief Boatswain's Mate Eugene V. Mitchell was one of those picked by Commander Harwood to go aft just before the magazine explosion. He escaped death because he and two other men were dropped out of the party to receive the *Birmingham*'s bow line.

"He put me in charge, with these two men, and the sea was getting rough," Mitchell said. "I didn't think I'd be able to handle an eight-inch line, which is pretty heavy. First, they send over a messenger line, and then the hawser. We'd handled that kind of line with other ships when it wasn't so rough and we had trouble."

Mitchell and his companions were positioned on the *Princeton*'s port side, just aft of the forward elevator well, where there were bollards and cleats to secure the expected hawser.

The remaining members of Harwood's party moved aft, some

running and others bringing up the rear at a slower pace, among them Mitchell's best friend, William Saxton. Saxton had abandoned ship earlier in the day, and then returned to the *Princeton* to help battle the flames and, hopefully, to assist in engineering efforts to restore power aboard the carrier.

"I thought I was going to need some more help," Mitchell said, "and I turned to holler to my friend to come help me. I intended to yell 'Sax, I need some help' but all I got out was 'Sax, I need' when all hell broke loose. The explosion lifted me up in the air and just put me right back down where I was. I couldn't believe it. I looked around to the other two men and they were on fire. I thought I was burning, too, because it felt like something oozing out of me from here to there. I figured this is it."

Mitchell took a quick survey of his condition.

"I looked down and my shoes were full of blood," he said. "My back and shoulders were like a sieve. My life jacket was demolished. I stood there for seconds, or maybe minutes, in a state of shock. I thought, 'the ship's going down and I'm going to die so it doesn't matter how badly I'm wounded anyway.'"

It turned out that most of his wounds were relatively minor, with the exception of a piece of shrapnel that lodged near his spine. As he realized he wasn't going to die on the spot, Mitchell took a life jacket from a dead shipmate.

"There was blood coming out of his eyes and nose. I checked, and he was dead, so I put on his life jacket and went down a dark passageway to a ladder up to a catwalk, near the pilots' ready room.

"When I got up on the flight deck, there were wounded all over the place, and debris, and wailing and moaning. Captain Hoskins was there with his foot dangling on. I tried to assist the best I could. We got the wounded over the side into whaleboats. Then the captain told us to abandon ship, and I went down a ladder into another whaleboat and wound up on the *Gatling*."

Robert G. Bradley, the *Princeton*'s assistant first lieutenant, was with Bruce Harwood at the end. Bradley, a native of Washington, D.C., had graduated from the naval academy after three years, rather than the normal four, because of the great need for trained officers at sea.

He was attached to the *Princeton* before the carrier was fitted out for combat duty, and served with the ship until its sinking. The citation, which awarded him posthumously the Navy Cross "for extraordinary heroism," told his story:

> Lieutenant Bradley led a repair party in the valiant effort to control fires on the second and third decks until the intense heat generated by those flames forced him and his men to fall back. After ensuring that no wounded men had been left behind during the abandonment, Lieutenant Bradley followed his men into the water at about 1005 and was picked up by the *Morrison*.
>
> Shortly after 1300 Bradley left the *Morrison* to rejoin his ship and the efforts to save her. At 1523, the flames touched off a mass detonation of four hundred 100-pound bombs stowed aft on the *Princeton*. This explosion literally blew off the carrier's stern, killing Bradley and every man in the repair party that had been in the vicinity.
>
> Bradley repeatedly had risked his life, entering the most dangerous areas below decks to ascertain the extent of damage and to fight the fires blazing on board ship.

Once the rocking effect of the blast's force had subsided, the *Princeton* miraculously rode the sea at an even keel and trim, not listing, showing no signs of final surrender to the constant punishment the carrier had received. Captain Buracker considered his ship's state and had Moitoret make one more request for a tow.

The request was denied. The *Birmingham* was unable to handle the task with hundreds of dead and wounded to care for and untold damage to assess. The *Reno* had no usable tow gear because of the previous kamikaze attack. The destroyers present were too small for the job.

Messages flashed through the air waves between the *Reno* and the commander, Task Force 38.3. The eventual decision was made by Fleet Command: Abandon ship and sink the *Princeton*!

Some of the walking wounded on the *Princeton* were dispatched to the hangar deck to look for possible survivors. There were none to be found, only twisted, torn bodies against the grotesque backdrop of the carrier's open blasted stern.

The searchers rejoined the party on the flight deck. The steel plating under their feet was ominously hot and some of them knew that below those plates was the forward magazine, with enough bombs to blow the rest of the ship out of the water. There also was beneath them a huge tank containing 100,000 gallons of high octane aviation gasoline.

Two whaleboats from the *Gatling* bobbed up against the *Princeton*'s bow. Into the first of these went most of the survivors, to be taken to the destroyer lying to nearby. At 1640 — seven hours after the Japanese bomb hit — into the second boat went the executive officer, Commander Murphy, followed by Buracker, in the navy tradition calling for the captain to be the last to leave his ship.

Just ahead of Murphy was Large, the air operations officer, who made it into the whaleboat the hard way.

"Murphy and I went down the Jacob's ladder, which didn't quite reach the water," Large said. The whaleboat was bobbing around, and there was a pretty good sea running. We had to let go and drop maybe the last fifteen feet. Murphy, who had been a naval academy football player, was a huge man and a wonderful officer. When I looked up and saw him there, I thought I better get out of his way. I let go and was caught by a sailor in the whaleboat."

Moitoret went over the side of the forecastle deck, onto a Jacob's ladder, and boarded the first whaleboat. On the way down, he paused briefly.

"When my head got level with the deck," he said, "I leaned over and kissed the *Princeton* goodbye."

The two boats pulled away, one heading for the *Gatling* and the other, with Captain Buracker aboard, toured the blasted stern of the carrier for one final look at the damage — and to make certain there were no signs of life aboard — then on to the *Reno*.

Of Harwood, Buracker said, "Like every man on the ship, he thought of saving it first and not of personal danger."

CHAPTER XXI

The Hatchet is Buried

WHEN HE HAD SCRAMBLED UP A ladder from the *Gatling* whaleboat to the deck of the *Reno*, Buracker looked back across the rolling water toward the *Princeton*, riding high and defiant despite the loss of her stern. Somehow, he still hoped for a miracle that would let him take his crippled command back home. This was not going to happen.

The carrier could not be left a dangerous derelict on the high seas, a possible prize, or a gold mine of vital information for a Japanese boarding party.

With the western Pacific sunset drawing rapidly close and the visibility diminishing steadily, the *Irwin* was ordered to torpedo the *Princeton*.

Carrying a normal complement of slightly more than 300 officers and men, the *Irwin* now was overrun with 600 *Princeton* survivors — nearly one thousand humans, occupying every inch of available space on the ship, topside and below decks.

Not only was the *Irwin* badly overloaded with humanity, the destroyer's torpedo director had been severely damaged banging against the *Princeton* during earlier rescue and firefighting operations.

The *Irwin*'s captain worked his ship cautiously to a position

2,500 yards on the port beam of the *Princeton*. He ordered the torpedo crew to fire a salvo at the carrier, using "local control" to aim the tubes — sighting down them as a hunter draws a bead on his quarry by looking down his gun barrel.

The *Irwin* fired two "fish." One missed its target completely. The other barely struck the forward tip of the *Princeton*'s bow. The stubborn target appeared to sustain no appreciable damage as a result.

Again the *Irwin* sailors took down-the-barrel aim and fired a pair of torpedoes. One went wide. The second ran erratically, and to the shock of those aboard the *Irwin*, started on a sweeping circle that brought the porpoising missile on a collision course with the *Irwin*. The destroyer's skipper ordered "flank speed" — "everything we are capable of and fast."

After the errant torpedo passed harmlessly by, the *Irwin* resumed position, and for the third time fired a brace of torpedoes by local control. As before, one missed and the second started back toward the *Irwin*. Again, the destroyer was forced to bolt like a scared rabbit to avoid being blown sky-high by its own weapon.

Tom Mooney had been fished out of the sea by the *Irwin*. After a half-hour of alternately lying on his back and crawling to the destroyer's rail to vomit sea water, Mooney was ordered to go below decks with the rest of the *Princeton* survivors.

"The ship was rolling, and because there was a lot of extra weight on board in the form of people from the carrier, there was a dangerous situation," Mooney said. "I went below with the others, and after a bit, a Catholic chaplain came along and asked me to help him talk to the men. This guy knew it was his mission to restore some form of sanity to these guys.

"I don't know how long it lasted, maybe an hour or two. We just walked around in circles and told people to stay cool, glad you made it, and all that. Then for some reason — I'm not sure why — I was allowed to go up on deck."

At that point, the *Irwin* was ordered to sink the *Princeton*. As a torpedo plane pilot, Mooney was familiar with the navy's "tin fish."

"I looked at the torpedo mounts on the *Irwin*," he said, "and I thought, 'Jesus, they don't look right. They look like they're bent or something,' and they were. They had been damaged in all the colliding with the *Princeton*."

Mooney was a spectator as the *Irwin* took a firing stance.

"There was the *Princeton*, this big beautiful ship that was my home, sitting in the water, looking like it could sail if there was someone on it, and they were going to sink it."

Mooney watched in fascination as the *Irwin* torpedo tubes were hand-cranked into position.

"I saw this one fish leap off and then, impossible to believe, it started turning. I thought, 'It's going to miss us,' but it kept turning, and pretty soon it was coming right back toward the Irwin.

"I looked up toward the bridge and thought, 'Jesus Christ, full right rudder, full speed,' and then the destroyer started shaking and trembling until it got up enough weigh to make a slight turn. There went this U.S. Navy torpedo right past us, and I thought, 'You know that's fantastic. This can't be happening.' "

The *Irwin*'s captain maneuvered approximately into the spot where the initial torpedoes had been launched. However, this time he maintained some weigh, some forward speed, just in case. He needed that insurance, because once more one of the *Irwin*'s torpedoes headed back toward the destroyer.

"It didn't go very far," Mooney said, "before it turned, too, and I thought, 'I'm going to die.' Well, it went right by. It seemed to me I could read 'U.S. Navy' on that fish. After that, I figured if they fired another one, we were going down. There was no question but we'd be going down."

Lt. Richard M. Jackson, another survivor aboard the *Irwin*, also was a wide-eyed witness of the abortive attempts to torpedo the *Princeton*.

"We stopped dead in the water broadside to the *Princeton*, about a mile away, and fired one. It apparently sounded, because nothing happened. The depth setting on number two was raised and the torpedo fired. This one was too shallow. It porpoised and broached consecutively more on each wave until it headed back directly for the *Irwin*. The captain rang up flank speed and hard left rudder. The fish passed about thirty feet away on a parallel course. Whatever morale had been left in the hundreds of *Princeton* survivors aboard vanished in those few seconds."

After another torpedo went into a deadly circle, the *Irwin*'s gunners tried to administer a death blow to the *Princeton* with the destroyer's five-inch guns. They succeeded in re-igniting the hangar deck fires, but the carrier continued to ride high and trim.

The *Reno* was ordered to move in and finish the task of destroying the *Princeton*. The cruiser took the *Irwin*'s place on the firing line. At 1746 — the middle of the night at home — the *Reno* launched one torpedo, then a second. It took them three seemingly endless minutes to reach their target. They struck the *Princeton* almost simultaneously, a dozen feet below the water line.

There were two tremendous explosions. Flames shot 500 feet into the air, and a dense mushroom-shaped cloud of smoke rose thousands of feet more. When the air had cleared enough to reveal the carrier's position, there was no more *Princeton* — only the smoke and burning fuel on the water.

The force of the blasts was not surprising, considering the "cargo" the flattop had been carrying. The torpedoes detonated the *Princeton*'s forward magazine. In that area had been stored thirty-three 350-pound bombs, one hundred and forty-four 500-pound bombs, one hundred and twenty-six 1,000-pound bombs, and ten 2,000-pounders.

Their mass detonation was combined with a blast involving 100,000 gallons of gasoline, in a huge tank next to the magazine. The bottom of this tank also served as the skin of the ship.

No vessel of the *Princeton*'s type and tonnage could have escaped total destruction from such a fearsome power.

Princeton crewman George Green witnessed the end of the carrier from the deck of the *Cassin Young*.

"When the *Reno* fired its two torpedoes, the *Princeton* literally disintegrated," he said. "It went up in a wall of fire. They said the *Princeton* disappeared immediately on the radar screens. Our position was two-and-a-half miles away, and my pant legs were flattened against my legs from the concussion. Some people said they could see part of the carrier sink into the sea, but all I saw were the flames, the fire, the mushroom cloud that formed. Later, when I saw films of the A-bomb explosion at Bikini Atoll, I remembered the *Princeton*'s finish looked just like that."

Marine Sgt. Adrian Chisholm was on the *Irwin*.

"We were about a mile away from the *Princeton*. I was a mess after being in the water a couple of hours. I'm standing there, looking at the carrier and thinking, 'My God, I've lost everything I owned and I don't even know where my boys are.'

"I saw the damn thing go down. I'm all alone in the middle of that little tin can. I had a couple of tears in my eyes and I saluted her. I don't think anybody saw me do that, but she was a good ship."

Chisholm was far from alone. One of those near him was *Princeton* shipmate, Larry Morgan.

"The *Reno*'s torpedoes made good runs, real true right toward the *Princeton*," Morgan said. "I could see their wakes, and when they disappeared it seemed like a minute until the old 'Peerless P' let go with a blast that looked like an ammunition dump exploding. When the smoke cleared, there was nothing left, nothing but water."

A *Princeton* survivor, thinking of the carrier's code name for her final combat operation, was heard to say: "Well, they've buried the Hatchet."

The *Princeton*, or whatever fragments were left, went down some eighty miles east of the Polillo Islands, into a massive ocean trench 2,700 fathoms deep — 16,200 feet, or more than three miles straight down.

The ship was the first fast carrier lost in two years of Pacific naval warfare. The last had been the *Hornet*, torpedoed during the Battle of Santa Cruz.

More lives were lost on the *Princeton* and *Birmingham* than during the Battle of Midway. One hundred and fourteen members of the *Princeton* ship's complement of 1,500 were killed. One hundred and ninety were wounded. Of the *Birmingham*'s crew of 1,253, there were 241 killed and 412 wounded, one-half seriously. In all, there were 957 killed and wounded on the two ships.

In her scant two years of existence, the *Princeton*'s pilots destroyed 186 Japanese aircraft in aerial combat. On the carrier's final day alone, her fliers accounted for thirty-four planes. Individual records that morning included: Ens. Tom J. Conroy (his 21st birthday), six-and-a-half Japanese planes; Lt. James A. Shirley, six planes; Lt. (jg) E. P. Townsend, five.

At the end, the *Princeton*'s island superstructure bore a painted silhouette representing each of those 186 planes, and the silhouettes of eight enemy ships sunk. The carrier had earned nine Battle Stars, each representing a major operation or engagement.

With all trace of the *Princeton* gone except for scattered floating debris, the *Reno* radioed the commander, Task Group 38:3: "This is *Reno*. Duty completed. Am rejoining." The three destroyers were assigned screen positions around the *Reno* for the return to the task group formation. The beleaguered *Birmingham* was told to follow at 1,500 yards, astern of the other ships. The cruiser still was able to maintain speed, even though one screw had been damaged by the *Princeton*'s floating stern section and had to be locked out of use.

At 2015, with full darkness at hand, the *Reno* made a status report by radio to the task group:

"*Reno* group has 134 officers and 1,227 enlisted personnel from *Princeton*. Damage to *Birmingham* topside casualties two 5-inch mounts, two 40-millimeter, four 20-millimeter smashed. *Reno* has one 40-millimeter smashed. *Morrison*'s mast gone, portside smashed. *Irwin*'s forward director out. *Birmingham* has about 85 killed, 300 wounded, 200 seriously. Casualties include captain. *Princeton* captain on *Reno*. *Irwin* limited to twenty-four knots." The casualty figures were to be revised upward during the night.

At 2242, the *Birmingham*, the *Morrison*, the *Irwin*, and the *Gatling* were separated from the main task group and designated Task Unit 38.3.6, with orders to proceed to Ulithi, rendezvousing with tankers en route to refuel. The *Gatling* was included because the destroyer had 221 survivors aboard. Its engineering plant still was in good shape, and most important the ship had the only completely operable radar in the group.

The *Reno*, with Captain Buracker and Executive Officer Murphy aboard, rejoined the task group, along with the *Cassin Young*.

There would be a long night ahead — and others to follow. At 2121 hours the commander, Task Force 38 had radioed Task Group 38.3: "You and your group have done a fine job today. I am proud to ride with TG 38.3."

Later, the *Birmingham*'s skipper radioed the task group commander: "*Birmingham* will do her utmost to return as soon as possible. Goodbye, good luck. Hit them hard for us."

The *Birmingham*'s own chief medical officer was back on board after temporary duty with the cruiser *Santa Fe*, and the *Birmingham* also had the services of the *Reno*'s doctor. Despite their incredible efforts, they could not save all the badly wounded, and many were beyond their help from the instant of the final explosion on the *Princeton*.

The *Birmingham*'s log contained stark notations that failed to tell the full story of those hours.

"At 0138 completed burial of four officers and sixty-seven men."

"0700, Resumed collection, identification and burial of the dead."

"1145, Completed burial services for three officers and 154 enlisted men."

From his initial haven on the *Morrison*, Pharmacist's Mate Pantages was transferred, with two of his shipmates, to the *Birmingham* the following morning when an urgent call was sent out for medical help.

"We changed ships by breeches buoy," he said, "and believe me, that's an experience. The lines between the ships kept sagging to the point where you could be dunked into the sea, and next they would be taut. The secret was to try to take off when you thought the two vessels would not be rolling too much."

The scene Pantages and his buddies found before their eyes "was without description."

"The deck of the *Birmingham* was a shambles, and sand had been spread about in places so you wouldn't slide about on the bloody mess. Below decks, much of the interior space had been cleared of bunks and other objects to make room for the wounded and medical supplies.

"The ship was divided up into sections, and each was given as many wounded as we expected to care for in the best possible manner. They had only three doctors aboard, and a few medical corpsmen, so all hands had to pitch in and do whatever was needed. My first night aboard the *Birmingham* really was the most critical and exhausting."

Pantages recalls applying splints to five men with compound leg fractures, "using Thomas splints and sufficient morphine to keep the men from suffering too much during the splinting.

"Probably the worst incident I encountered, as far as splinting was concerned, involved a sailor with his left leg at right angles to his body, about ten inches above the knee. It took all the strength and courage I could muster to straighten that leg and apply the splint. God and perseverance were on my side. I finally got the job done to my own satisfaction."

The name of the game that first night was two-fold — to save as many of the most seriously injured as possible and to make the others as comfortable as could be under the circumstances.

"Plasma was used by the hundreds of units," Pantages said. "Monitoring all the casualties was no easy matter. There were approximately one hundred wounded in the compartment I was assigned to. To the best of my recollection, we lost only one man in our group."

The performance of Pantages, and others like him, during the post-sinking hours and days was unbelievable.

"Most of us in the medical department labored around the clock for five days without any real sleep," he recalls, "at the very most, just a wink or two. Food was brought to us while we worked for the first couple of days. The center of the deck was a mountain of bandages and medical supplies, and thank God for the fact we had plenty to work with. I feel certain that meant the difference between making it or not for quite a few of the more severely wounded."

Some events were remembered in greater clarity later. One involved a patient "with a gaping hole in his chest."

"Air was bubbling from his lungs," Pantages said, "and it really looked like he was a goner. After trying desperately for some time to administer plasma, I finally found a vein suitable enough to get a needle in. The usual spots on his arms turned up only collapsed veins."

When the plasma had been injected, a doctor closed the chest wound.

"In about two hours," Pantages said, "the patient showed pretty good signs of recovery. After several units of plasma, he really rallied and ended up on the right side of the roster. Experiences like that on the *Birmingham* always will be etched on my mind."

Later, when medical officers came aboard the *Birmingham* at Ulithi Atoll, to Pantages' extreme gratification every splint he and his comrades had applied passed inspection without question. When the last patient had been transferred to a hospital ship, Pantages went to a corner of the deck and lay down.

"I went out like a light. I don't recall how long I slept but the call to reveille didn't faze me at all. Unfortunately, I didn't pay much attention to the sort of pillow I laid my head on. It turned out to be a pile of spun glass, and when I awoke my face was covered with microscopic cuts."

Pharmacist's Mate Robinson, who helped treat Captain Hoskins after the *Princeton* magazine blast, was taken aboard the *Gatling* with Hoskins and the carrier's chief medical officer, Commander

Sala. Although he had sustained a shrapnel wound in the groin, Sala completed the grisly task of removing Hoskins' lower leg.

"Commander Sala was peeing blood," Robinson said. "We didn't have any X-rays, and didn't have any way of knowing the extent of his injuries. He stayed in the wardroom, and anyone in extremely critical condition, we put them up there with Commander Sala."

Other wounded were treated by the *Gatling*'s own doctor and corpsmen, including Robinson, in the destroyer's mess compartment.

"We had a real good system," Robinson said, "and we didn't have any infections. We had sulfa and we had some penicillin, but not very much. It isn't for burns. Our big problem was burns."

Robinson instructed other pharmacist's mates to administer sleeping pills to those who needed them, and pain killers, including morphine, to those who needed such relief.

"We had a lot of casualties on the *Gatling,* including burn cases. We gave sulfadiazene to those patients. Rather than changing their bandages, if arms or legs were involved, where swelling might develop, we looked for blue finger nails or toe nails. In those cases, instead of taking the bandage off, we would just cut the bandage and put a new one on the outside. The odor was bad, but the serum oozed from the burns through the cut in the bandage and a lot of sulfa killed any bacteria. As far as I know, we didn't have any burn infections on the *Gatling*."

For those whose wounds had called for sedation, the night brought sleep and a few hours of forgetfulness. For those unhurt or less seriously wounded, it was a long and troubled time, brightened at least by the knowledge they were saved from something worse.

"Things on the *Irwin* were really crowded, and we had to sleep on deck," said Larry Morgan. "However, out in the Pacific in October it was warm, and we weren't too uncomfortable. Some of our shipmates who had died from their wounds were awaiting burial. They had been placed on deck in canvas bags. We laid down among them, wherever there was room."

In the morning, the crews of the *Birmingham* and the three destroyers somehow prepared enough food for everyone who wanted to eat.

"I know I didn't feel too much like eating," Morgan said. "We were all pretty much shook up. During the morning, we buried five of our *Princeton* shipmates."

Shortly before noon, a pair of Japanese twin-engine planes began shadowing the four cripples. Aviation Ordnanceman Peter Callan was on the *Irwin*'s deck when the enemy aircraft arrived on the scene.

"The gunners on the 40-millimeter mounts were pointing and training them by hand," he said, "because the electrical controls had been knocked out when the *Irwin* banged into the *Princeton*. Fortunately, the Japanese pilots were satisfied just to look us over and not attack. We would have been easy pickings, overcrowded as we were, and with no automatic gun control."

Larry Morgan watched the Japanese planes approach, and wondered when the *Irwin* and other ships would begin firing.

"I started to shake," he said. "My knees were knocking together and my teeth were chattering. Anyhow, the guns opened up and the two Jap planes took tail. After the guns stopped firing, I was okay.

"I talked about this later to one of the officers, and he said he had experienced the same sort of thing. He was laying on his bunk a couple of nights after we had been sunk. He said he started to shake and get sick to his stomach. He went to see a doctor, and the doctor told him that was quite normal under the circumstances. I felt better about it after hearing that."

There were repeated radar contacts throughout the day, both from the air and on the surface. All had to be treated as potential enemies until proven otherwise. To those who had lost their ship and scores of their shipmates, the suspense in each instance was nerve-wracking.

Most of the "blips" on the radar screen were discounted when identified as friendly. An exception was a bogey detected to the south of the formation, and sixty miles out. The apparent enemy came no nearer, and it didn't become necessary for the task unit to prepare for evasive action.

At 1214, the *Birmingham* radioed the three destroyers: "Have completed burial of dead. All units two-block colors." The flags on all four vessels had been at half-mast during the burials at sea, honoring the men who were not going to make it home.

Conscious of the ever-present possibility of Japanese submarine attack, the skipper of the *Birmingham*, who was in command despite his own injuries, reminded the other ships by radio: "Do not throw floatable trash over the side."

As morning became afternoon, the *Birmingham* established radio contact with the task group of three oilers that had been designated to refuel the cruiser and trio of destroyers. When the location of the oilers had been established, and a course set to effect a rendezvous, the *Birmingham* radioed:

"Request services two oilers to give drink [fuel] to one CL [cruiser] and three destroyers simultaneously. Please designate oilers and drinking-course speed and formation." Then a follow-up message: "One destroyer would like to get about 10,000 gallons of water."

Each of the damaged vessels was assigned a port or starboard position beside one of the oilers. The *Irwin* was granted permission to shift to a port approach because "my starboard side is smashed."

The scene that ensued was one repeated hundreds of times at sea during the war in the Pacific. To keep combat ships close to battle areas, they were supplied with fuel and other needs at sea. The "thirsty" ship, or ships, would take a position close beside the oiler. The two vessels would proceed in an identical direction at the same speed while a weighted line was fired from oiler to warship by means of a specially designed gun.

The initial line was attached to a heavier line, and then came the hose itself. Keeping the two ships properly aligned, in a rolling sea, with the hoseline linking them carrying highly combustible fuel, was a ticklish operation at best.

When the *Birmingham* and destroyers had their tanks filled, a radio poll was made of the oilers and their escort vessels, requesting doctor and hospital corpsman help, along with plasma, morphine, and other medical supplies.

In all, the oilers and their escorts sent two doctors and five corpsmen to the *Birmingham*, using destroyers to complete the transfer. Also turned over to the beleaguered cruiser were quantities of much-needed morphine syrettes, bandages, plaster of paris (for casts), and a variety of other items.

Finally, before the two groups parted company, bags of welcome mail were passed by line to the *Gatling* and *Morrison* — following the wartime delivery system in which mail moved from stateside origins to eventual destinations by leapfrogging from ship to ship across the ocean.

The *Birmingham*, via radio, expressed the feelings of all aboard the four ships of Task Unit 38.3.6: "We are eternally thankful to you for your assistance. We shall now proceed on our way."

From the commander of the oiler group: "Thank you and good luck."

The following morning, while the *Birmingham* group was still twenty-four hours from Ulithi, radio monitors picked up the text of a communique issued by General Douglas MacArthur's Philippine headquarters. Those aboard the cruiser and the three destroyers were astounded to learn the sinking of the *Princeton* had been revealed.

Mooney remembers his shock.

"When a Navy ship was lost at sea, there were no public reports until the next of kin were notified," he said. "The loss of the *Princeton* was announced the instant the battle reports came in to MacArthur. As a result, the relatives and friends of more than 1,200 men didn't know for days who had survived. It wasn't a matter of national importance, but in terms of the people involved, we were outraged."

Not until the four ships reached Ulithi were the survivors able to write brief notes to their families. These were flown back to the United States, but it still was five days or more before these reached the hands of wives, children, parents, sweethearts, brothers, and sisters.

Ulithi, the one-time Japanese stronghold, brought down the curtain on the *Princeton* drama. The dead had been given to the sea. The living were dispatched to various hospitals and other duties. They took with them a memory that would not be buried.

Epilogue

FOR JOHN MADISON HOSKINS, the demise of the *Princeton* marked the start of an all-out crusade.

To put it mildly, his navy career had gotten under way in low gear. After failing the written examination for the naval academy twice, and the physical exam three times, he passed the written test on a third try. An ear operation made him physically acceptable. In four years at Annapolis, he ranked at, or near, the bottom of his class, graduating in 1921.

The *Princeton* was to have been Hoskins's first major sea command. He had not been on board long enough to officially relieve Bill Buracker when the carrier was blasted out from under him. His reaction to the loss of his right foot and lower leg was remarkable.

At Ulithi, Hoskins was transferred to the hospital ship *Samaritan*. When a navy doctor, trying to be comforting, told him he was headed home to probable medical discharge, Hoskins exploded and declared he fully intended to be back on combat duty in short order.

Flown back to the United States, Hoskins pushed hard to master the use of an artificial limb. He told Admiral Halsey: "The navy doesn't expect a man to think with his feet. The blast didn't knock off my head." He also insisted that a one-legged captain, sleeping with one shoe on, could get to the bridge of his ship at sea faster than a skipper who had to don both shoes before going into action.

From his bed in the Philadelphia Naval Hospital, Hoskins followed closely the progress of a new *Princeton*, an Essex class carrier nearing completion at the nearby Philadelphia Navy Yard. He prodded hospital personnel to speed up his rehabilitation program, and he intensified efforts to win command of the carrier.

The telling effort came when he demonstrated, before a navy medical board, his ability to climb up and down a ship's ladders with his artificial foot.

His determination paid off. Hoskins was named commanding officer of the newly commissioned *Princeton*, the fifth navy vessel to bear that name. In his honor, airmen serving aboard the carrier emblazoned their planes with an emblem depicting Hoskins as a wood-legged pirate, with an aircraft carrier under one arm and holding a saber with the other hand. The pirate's wooden leg was a machine-gun barrel spewing bullets.

He later commanded Carrier Division Three, providing air support during the Korean conflict, rose to the rank of rear admiral, and then to vice admiral. At one point, he was acting commander of the Seventh Fleet. His decorations included the Navy Cross, the Distinguished Service Medal, the Silver Star, and the Purple Heart.

After his retirement from the navy, he served five years as director of the Office of Declassification, Department of Defense — riding herd on the removal of secrecy labels from documents no longer requiring them. He died in 1964, at the age of sixty-five, following a heart attack in his home.

Captain Buracker was awarded the Navy Cross for his "heroic and determined efforts" to save the *Princeton*. He also won the Silver Star, the Legion of Merit, and the Purple Heart for wounds sustained when the carrier's stern blew away.

He was to write later "it is difficult to express the feelings of a captain who has lost his ship — his home — with so many fine shipmates. Every captain believes his own crew is the best on any ship. I certainly feel that about mine."

Last to leave the *Princeton*, except for Buracker, had been Executive Officer John Murphy, a big man physically, but prior to the final day of the *Princeton*, very much a lesser character on board.

Murphy came to the *Princeton* from a Bureau of Aeronautics assignment in Washington. He reported aboard a ship that already had an enviable record in combat. The carrier was manned, in significant part, by officers and men who were reassigned after the sinking of the *Hornet*. As a newly arrived "fat cat" from the sheltered environment of stateside duty, Murphy was not readily welcomed by the seasoned crew he was supposed to govern.

A career "academy" navy officer, Murphy was fortunate to have aboard a chaplain with an extremely acute appreciation of his responsibilities to both God and man, especially to the crew of a combat vessel. Chaplain Otto Karl Olander happened to be Lutheran. He would have been welcomed by any denomination. The role of a chaplain in a combat situation brings out the best — or sometimes, unfortunately, the worst — in individuals. In Olander's case, there is little doubt he brought out the best in John Murphy.

Vic Moitoret was well aware of what was happening.

"Commander Murphy had come from Washington, where he had been 'flying a desk' in the Bureau of Aeronautics," Moitoret said. "Murphy was an intelligent man, quite intelligent, and basically a good man, but he had no recent experience in handling men. Now, here he was with 1,200 or more crew members he was supposed to be in charge of, right under the captain.

"The captain is occupied on the bridge most of the time and the executive officer runs the ship for him, with just policy guidance from the captain. All the rest, particularly the discipline, is handled by the executive officer," Moitoret said.

Murphy, for a variety of reasons, had not made a good start on the *Princeton*.

"The officers didn't think much of him to begin with," Moitoret said. "There was one incident when we were anchored in a lagoon and had a beer party ashore. All the pilots plied Murphy with beer, and then got him into a football game on the beach. They gave him the ball as much as possible so they could tackle him.

"The poor guy came back to the ship black and blue, and with a hangover. The next day, he didn't even emerge from his cabin. Some of the pilots thought that was a great way to get him, but Chaplain Olander used a more humane method."

He went to see Murphy in his cabin and "talked turkey." The chaplain told Moitoret later he "laid it on the line."

"Commander Murphy," Olander said, "do you realize there isn't an officer aboard this ship who respects you? Do you realize that the enlisted men on this ship have told me they purposely go across to the other side of the flight deck if they see you coming so they won't have to salute you? You need to take a serious look at yourself and how you're handling your duties on the carrier."

Moitoret said Murphy stayed very much by himself for a day.

"He apparently took a look at himself in the mirror, and when he came out of his cabin finally, he was a changed man," Moitoret said. "He had gotten the message. He was rather quiet for several days. He would come around and kind of meekly talk to the officers and men. He was remaking himself; and that's not an easy thing to do."

On the *Princeton*'s final day, Murphy was in the thick of the effort to save the carrier, manning hose lines, and assessing damage in flame-swept, and potentially explosive, areas of the ship. Alongside Captain Hoskins, he suffered shrapnel wounds in the final blast, but was able to help get Hoskins off the *Princeton*.

"More than one person remarked, 'Commander Murphy really earned his Navy Cross,'" Moitoret said.

Recognized as one of the U.S. Navy's leading aeronautical engineers, Murphy later was promoted to the rank of rear admiral.

The ships of the battered flotilla — *Birmingham, Morrison, Irwin,* and *Gatling* — returned to combat after repairs at Pearl Harbor and the West Coast. Six months after the *Princeton* went down, the *Birmingham* was the target of a Japanese suicide plane off Okinawa.

Carrying a 500-pound bomb — very similar to that which brought an end to the *Princeton* — the Japanese plane dove out of the sun, through the cruiser's anti-aircraft screen, and zeroed in on the number two gun turret. The bomb ripped through three decks and exploded in the sick bay. Both of the *Birmingham*'s doctors were killed. Nineteen of the twenty-four corpsmen aboard were killed or wounded, as well as a number of other crewmen.

Birmingham survivors were to credit experience gained in their earlier *Princeton* blood-bath with saving lives in the later Okinawa action.

From Ulithi, the *Irwin* sailed for overhaul at the San Francisco Navy Yard. Back in action in February 1945, the destroyer was involved in action off Okinawa, sinking one attacking Japanese torpedo boat, damaging another, and forcing a third to flee.

When U.S. Marines stormed ashore at Okinawa, the *Irwin*'s gunners shot down an enemy plane and rescued a member of the crew. In the following weeks of support duty, three more Japanese planes were accounted for by *Irwin* gunners.

The *Irwin* remained off Okinawa until hostilities ceased in August 1945, then escorted Allied occupation troops between Okinawa and Japan before being decommissioned and made a unit of the Pacific Reserve Fleet, in 1946.

The *Cassin Young,* named for a navy captain awarded the Medal of Honor at Pearl Harbor, and later killed while commanding the cruiser *San Francisco* at Guadalcanal, went on to further action after the sinking of the *Princeton*. The destroyer screened the American force that sank four Japanese carriers in the Battle of Engano.

The *Cassin Young* was twice damaged by kamikazes at Okinawa, and was awarded the Navy Unit Commendation. When the ship was decommissioned, in 1960, she was tied up at Boston Navy Yard as a floating representative of the ships built there during World War II, which served the navy with distinction for more than thirty years. Nearby is the famed frigate *Constitution*, "Old Ironsides."

The *Morrison*, while on radar picket station at Okinawa, was hit by two kamikaze planes simultaneously, and then, almost immediately, by two "antique" wood-and-canvas biplanes — the Japanese were hard up for kamikaze aircraft by then. The *Morrison* had to be abandoned quickly. Over half the ship's complement, 159 officers and men, were lost, with another 100 wounded.

In the navy tradition of naming warships after combat heroes, a new frigate — similar in size to a destroyer — honored the memory of Lt. Robert Graham Bradley, the *Princeton*'s assistant first lieutenant, who died in the final blast aboard the carrier. The USS *Robert G. Bradley* joined the Atlantic Fleet after commissioning ceremonies at Portsmouth, NH, in August 1984.

Bradley had been awarded the Navy Cross posthumously. The accompanying citation read in part: "Bradley repeatedly had risked his life, entering the most dangerous areas below decks to ascertain the extent of damage and to fight the fires on board ship." He had returned to the *Princeton* after being forced to abandon ship and being picked up by the *Morrison*.

After the reports of the *Princeton*'s crew and Air Group 27 were painstakingly re-created and completed, and the personnel given much-deserved leave, the air group was re-formed, with Fred Bardshar again commanding. There followed weeks of refresher training, at such unlikely spots as snow-covered Sanford, Maine, before pilots and crew went back to the southwest Pacific to board the carrier *Independence* in the Philippine Islands.

Flying off the *Independence*, sister ship of the *Princeton*, Torpedo 27 and Fighting 27 joined in the drive toward the Japanese homeland. In the final days of World War II, the air group's planes attacked enemy installations and ships in Tokyo Bay, itself.

On the day of the formal surrender, Air Group 27 participated in a multi-squadron flyover as the Japanese representatives signed the document of defeat on the battleship *Missouri*. One pilot used his radio to comment: "Too bad the *Princeton* isn't here."

Bardshar went on to command a carrier off Korea, and eventually attained the rank of vice admiral.

From those who had served on the *Princeton,* there emerged doctors, lawyers, a pharmacist, air line pilots, men of the cloth, and career navy men, representatives of a score of trades and professions.

Among them was George Pantages, the pharmacist's mate who played such a vital role in treating the wounded on the *Princeton* and *Birmingham.* Following his release from the navy, Pantages went home to California and worked for awhile in his former employer's pharmacy. Eventually, he was able to realize a lifelong dream — owning his own pharmacy.

The survivors of the *Princeton* in time rediscovered their common bond. In 1979, those who had seen duty on the *Princeton,* either as air group or ship's company, held their first annual reunion. Five years later, an initial Air Group 27 reunion brought together men who had not been in touch with one another since they shared that frightful peril forty years earlier.

Helping in great measure to keep that spirit flourishing was a U.S. Navy announcement that, 1988, a sixth warship was to bear the *Princeton* name — an Aegis cruiser (CG-59) with electronic weaponry capable of combating enemy aircraft, missiles, submarines, and surface ships.

Casualties

Princeton Personnel Killed in Action
24 October 1944

Officers

BRADLEY, R. G. Lt.
BURNS, J. P. ChMach.
CHRISTIE, A. A. Ens.
HARWOOD, B. L. Comdr.
HOECKER, E. H. Chief Pay Clerk
KASER, J. M. Lt (jg)
STEELE, J. C. ChElec.
SUAREZ, J. L. Mach.
THURMAN, R. E. Lt (jg)
VANDENBERG, E. J. Lt (jg)

Enlisted Personnel

ADOLPH, Adrian Lawrence F1c
ARSICS, Michael George EM1c
BENTLEY, John Steele MM1c
BLOECHER, Fred William Bkr1c
BLOMSTROM, Russell Carl S1c
BRUNELLE, Joseph Alberie S1c
BRYANT, Theodore Wayne SF1c
CARDOZA, David Frausto MM3c
CERNY, Joseph Lawrence WT3c
CHAGNON, Oscar Omer AM2c
CORUM, Paul Leroy S1c
DALY, Walter Leo EM3c
DOHERTY, James Bernard SF3c
FIORITA, Frank Edward SF3c
FLYNN, John Francis EM2c
FREDETTE, John Arthur F1c

GARRISON, Dorris Gwin RM3c
GLEN, Richard Harold F2c
GORMLEY, John Francis AOM2c
GRAVELL, William M. AMM2c
HARRELL, Robert Reed WT3c
HAUSER, Gary Ptr3c
HEISLER, Donald Ralph S1c
HILL, Donald Norman AM3c
HIRLEMAN, Richard Dean WT3c
HOLDEN, Paul Leo EM3c
JARRELL, James Clarence S1c
JONES, John Norbert WT3c
KOTLAS, Johnny EM3c
LAIRD, Richard Francis CM2c
LAMB, Lonnie Leo EM3c
LAWRENCE, Austin Levie Jr. Bkr3c
LETTON, James Wendell SC3c
LEWIS, John Selby S1c
LIND, Herbert James SM2c
MASON, Booker Thomas Jr. StM2c
MASON, Farrell Duane S2c
MAXSON, Henry Duayne MM2c
MEZA, Vicente Onesimo SKD3c
MILANO, Ralph Frank S1c
MIRANDO, Mario Gabe AMM3c
MOON, Bernard Paul S1c
MORRISON, Lewis Henry AMM3c
MORRISSEY, Fred Joseph AMM3c
McLENDON, Wallace Howard WT2c

McMAHAN, Jack Taylor S1c
NEWTON, Lester Frank F1c
O'LEARY, James Joseph AMM3c
PADULA, Joseph Michael S1c
PAGE, Nelson Keller F2c
PATTON, Jimmy Don S2c
PELLETIER, Lucien Ernest AMM2c
PINO, Manuel Lupe WT3c
PROBST, Herbert Lawrence PhM2c
REED, Wayne Markham S1c
REIMERS, Fred Lee Y3c
REYNOLDS, Earl Russell Ptr3c
RICKETTS, Henry Thomas S1c
RIGDON, David Mitchal Jr. S1c
RINGWELSKI, Frank S2c
ROBBE, Robert Raymond S1c
ROGERS, Everett Keith F1c
ROSS, Bernard Melvin F1c
SARGENT, William Thomas S2c
SASSENBERGER, James Anthony S2c
SAXTON, William Allen Jr. AM3c
SEABROOKS, Charlie Ck3c
SEDICAVAGE, Stanley Frank Bkr2c
SHANNON, William Jacob AMM3c
SMITH, George Thomas S2c
SMITH, Milford Hoyt Bkr3c
SPENCER, William Joseph WT2c
STEVENS, Russell Lowell S1c

STRAUCH, Adam CEM
STRICKLAND, Young Edward CWT
TANNER, William Joe S1c
TILLEY, Owen Edgar AOM3c
TOPORSKI, Edward S1c
VALLANTE, Pasquale F1c
VAN DUSEN, Robert Jay WT3c
VAN WINKLE, James Alex S2c
VENDRELY, Donald LaVon F1c
VICKERS, Lawrence Virgil BM2c
VINCENT, Ivan Ray S1c
VYDFOL, Fred Albert MM1c
WACHUNAS, Charles Stanley EM3c
WALKER, Ernest Eugene S1c
WALSH, David Samuel M1c
WESTFALL, Robert William MM1c
WHITE, Ralph Alexander CSF
ZAICEK, Ralph Steven WT3c
ZLATNIK, Henry Frederick MM3c

MARINES

BRUSTOSKI, Joseph John Pfc
GENTRY, James Everett Sgt.
KRALL, Henry Platoon Sgt.
NOLAN, Ernest LaVerne Pfc
NULPH, Harold Walker Pfc
RATTLER, Mark Jack Pfc

Princeton Personnel Wounded
24 October 1944

Officers
BECKETT, J. C. Lt.
BLANCHARD, W. A. Ens.
BRINTON, W. L. Lt.
COCHRANE, G. D. Lt(jg)
CRAWFORD, E. E Radio Elec.
DAVIS, A. H. Lt. Comdr.
DORR, E. L. Ens
HOSKINS, John M. Captain
HUGHES, P. Lt.
JACOBS, Richard B. Ens.

KELLEHER, J. N. Lt. Comdr.
MOITORET, V. A. Lt.
NELSON, W. J. Lt(jg)
SALA, R. O. Commander
SEARLES, G. B. Ens.
SMITH, C. A. Ens.
STASNEY, L. H. Lt.
STEBBINGS, Harry E. Jr. Lt. Comdr.
TURLINGTON, O. R. Gunner
WILLIAMS, L. D. Lt. (MC)

Enlisted Personnel

ADAMS, Elvin Leighton Cox
ARMENTA, Juan Calderon S2c
BELLAVANCE, Henry Roland S1c
BENWAY, Lee Walter S1c
BILLIET, Leopold Jr. S1c
BROWN, Merle D. MM2c
BYRNES, Stephen J. AM1c
CARRELLO, Nicholas SC1c
CAVANAUGH, Edwin Curtis ACMM
CHUN, Leong Jin RT2c
CLEVEN, Edward Joseph CSp
CONDA, Leonard R. S1c
COOK, Carl Dewayne AEM3c
COUCH, Bert Cline AMM1c
CUSICK, Thomas Vincent AMM2c
DAVIS, Edward C. EM1c
DESLONGCHAMP, Irving Edward S1c
DEGRE, Adrien Joseph SC3c
DITHEODORE, Nicholas M. MM3c
DUNBAR, Jack Frederick S1c
EAGLE, Jess LeRoy AM2c
EHRHARDT, Leo S1c
ELWING, James Edward S1c
EMMETS, Jacob Otto MM1c
EWING, Joseph Sherman S2c
FAGAN, William John S2c
FESH, John S2c
FOOTE, George Denton Jr. SC3c
FRAZIER, George Wesley Sea2c
FRANKLIN, Bobby Leo WT3c
FREDERICK, Franklin Clifford Jr. CM2c
GIDDLE, Lyle Burdette AMM1c
GILMORE, Charles Leo EM1c
GIROFALO, Joseph William MM3c
GIRVIN, Harold Hayes AMM1c
GOODE, James Franklin WT3c
GRABER, C. A. AOM2c
HARTGROVE, Harold R. S1c
HAVEMANN, Clayton John MM3c
HERRICK, Hiram Harold BM2c

HEYDON, Darrel Gene EM3c
HILL, William R. S1c
HITE, Bert Reilly WT3c
HOLLAND, Kenneth W. S2c
HOWARD, George Wendell S1c
HUNNICUTT, James Archie QM1c
JESSUP, Carl L. CMM
KASKO, John F1c
KERR, Thomas S2c
KINDT, Varon Robert S1c
KINGSFATHER, Harold Jr. S1c
KNAUB, Phillip Jr. MM3c
KUBIAK, Donald Joseph S2c
KUBICKA, Edward L. Y3c
INDT, Varon Robert S1c
LaFEVRE, Ivan Lyle AMM1c
LAUTENSSCHLAGER, Cloyd Emory S1c
LINSENMAIER, Richard Carl AMM2c
LITTLE, William Zack S1c
LOFTIS, William Franklin S2c
LUENEMANN, Victor Henry CBM
MANCHESTER, Edward Wilbur MS3c
MANUELS, Charles Thomas AMM3c
MARTIN, Frank William F2c
MATHEWS, Charles StMlc
MAZUR, Anthony Eugene AM3c
MEDEIROS, John Allen MM3c
MENTZER, Chalmers O. S1c
MILLER, Donald Bacon StM1c
MILLER, John A. AMM2c
MITCHELL, Eugene Victor BM1c
MOORE, Bird Anderson S2c
MOSES, Henry Lee StM2c
MUIR, George Marcel AMM3c
MULARCIK, Edward Peter AM3c
MULLEN, Carl l. PtrV1c
NELSON, Walter Elihu EM2c
O'CONNOR, George Gettios F1c
OTTERSON, Ralph Elbridge SK2c
PACKARD, James E. S1c
PALMER, Lawton Evans Jr. S1c

Casualties 191

PARKOLA, W. AMM1c
PHILLIPS, Joseph Jermiah AMM2c
PETER, Robert E. EM2c
PETERS, Gerald Joseph S1c
PETERSON, William George S1c
RADER, Russel E. MM3c
RALPH, Edward Anthony S1c
RAMOS, Julian Ambrose S1c
REID, John Johnston S2c
REISHUS, Orin Alden Bkr2c
RENO, Robert Jr. MM2c
RICKETSON, Fred Albert S2c
ROBINSON, Paul PhM1c
RUBIN, Seymour S2c
SCHROTT, Kenneth Henry MM1c
SMITH, James C. MM3c
SORGER, Joseph Robert SF3c
SOUZA, Joseph Gomes S2c
STOIAN, Thomas S1c
SUMRALL, Thomas B. S2c
TALABA, Paul GM3c
THERRIEN, Hector Normand S1c
TOLLEY, William Hubert S2c

TRAFFORD, Richard George AMM2c
TRUDEAU, Paul L. F2c
TUTINO, Anthony MM1c
VAN HORN, James Glen S2c
WADSWORTH, Glenn A. F1c
WALCK, Lloyd A. PhM2c
WALKER, Robert Ansel S2c
WENDEL, George Daniel Jr. S2c
WEYHMULLER, Alfred Victor Jr. ACMM
WHIPPLE, Albert Haywood S2c
ZABOROWSKI, Ralph S1c

Marines

CHISHOLM, Adrian C. 1st Sgt.
ANDERSON, Arthur A. Gy Sgt.
RUTKOWSKI, Frank S. Corp
HEUMANN, Carl W. FM Corp
CLAYPOOL, James C. Pfc
CONKLIN, Walter K. Pfc
HOLLAR, Frank W. Pfc
KEILMAN, Maurice F. Pfc
WALKER, Frank E. Pfc

Birmingham Personnel Killed in Action
24 October 1944

Officers
COOPER, Roland Lt.
EKSTROM, Stanley Edson Lt.
HOAGWOOD, George Holl Mach.
KERR, Robert Charles Ens.
McCORMICK, Donald Lt.
REED, Alan Lt.
PERKINS, Van Ostrand Comdr.
SMITH, Mirel Ralph Rad. Elect.

Enlisted Personnel

AGNEW, Charles Vincent RdM3c
AUSTIN, Carl Samuel S2c
BABBS, Marshall Lewis S2c
BABGER, Thomas Earl EM2c
BARRON, Samuel John S1c

BASSETT, Albert Joseph, Jr. S2c
BATES, Robert Harrison QM1c
BENZIE, Paul GM3c
BISHOP, Joseph Edward CEM
BLANCO, Anthony Perry S1c
BLANKENSHIP, Cleo S2c
BODNAR, John Paul SC1c
BOWERS, Harry Leroy CRT
BUCKINGHAM, Ernest Archie MM2c
BURCKHARD, Mike Thomas S1c
BURNHAM, Robert Lee S1c
BURNS, Rodger M. Cox
BUTKIEWICZ, Daniel N. S1c
BUTLER, Collie Harding S2c
CAPUTO, Vincenzo James RdM3c
CARL, Robert Paul S1c

CARMODY, Kenneth James GM3c
CARR, James Robert FS3c
CARROLL, John Francis S1c
CORBIN, Charles Oswald S2c
CORINI, Carlo Louis S1c
COSTIGAN, Joseph Frank S2c
COTTRILL, Harold Richard S2c
CRAMER, Winfred Lee S1c
CREAVEN, John Anthony Cox
CROCKETT, Thaddeus Hamp SC3c
CULOTTA, Dominic Peter S1c
DEAKIN, Billy Wayne MM2c
DEANE, Normin Goodrow CWT
DeCENZO, Frank Joseph F2c
DICKERSON, Alfonzo, Jr. S1c
DIETRICH, Howard Bill GM1c
DOBBINS, Robert Henry S2c
DOUGHMAN, Clarence Leroy S2c
DROSTE, Albert Henry SSML3c
DUKE, Robert Clayton S2c
DYMOND, Charles David S1c
ELKINS, Samuel Eli S2c
ELLISON, Harold Pond, Jr. S1c
ELSINGER, Francis Joseph S2c
ELSON, William, Junior F1c
ENGLERT, Harry Joseph S1c
ERICKSEN, Ralph John WT1c
ESTES, George S2c
EVANKOE, Steve F1c
FARISH, James William MM1c
FILIP, James William CSP
FLYNN, Gerard Edward GM3c
FOLKMAN, Leon J. SK3c
FORD, Simon Patrick Cox
FOWLER, Arthur Jesse GM3c
FRAZIER, Paul Dewitt S1c
FULTON, Richard E. MM3c
GERSON, Paul William WT3c
GIFFORD, Winford Bundy Cox
GILBERT, Charles Hugo, Jr. EM1c
GLUSCIC, Joseph John S1c
GOLITCO, Edward Paul S2c
GODIN, Vincet Richard Y2c
GRAHAM, James Paul S1c

GRAVES, Joe Earl S1c
GRIGER, Arthur Y3c
GWINN, Charles Parker S1c
HAAS, Edward Joseph S1c
HAHN, John Edward GM3c
HARTLE, Raymond Lewis S2c
HEDGES, Wilbert GM3c
HOEGERL, Anthony Joseph MM2
HOFF, Ralph William SSML3c
HOLLEY, Hubert Henry S2c
HOWARD, Henry Franklin S2c
HOWZE, James Edward QM3c
HUCKABY, Broudie David S2c
HUEY, Hubbard Pool S1c
HULS, Joseph Francis S2c
HUNTER, Norman Elwood S2c
JACKSON, David Elwood S1c
JAMES, Raymond S1c
JARAMILLO, William S2c
JONES, George Franklin FCO3c
JOHNSON, John Thomas, Jr. S1c
JOHNSTON, Richard Henry GM3c
KENLEY, Lee Charles F1c
KUMINGA, Chester Stanley M3c
KWITKOWSKI, Peter Paul BM1c
KWOLEK, John Joseph MM3c
LARGE, George Hathaway SC3c
LANDIN, Johan Ambrose F1c
LaTORRE, Joseph S2c
LaVALLE, John Arthur S2c
LAWSON, William Dallas M3c
LeBLANC, Osias Joseph S1c
LeCLAIRE, Ovila Joseph S2c
LEONARD, Daniel, Jr. SC3c
LETA, Domenico Michael S2c
LIBENGOOD, James Ralph QM3c
LIEBMAN, Marion Albert S1c
LOEBER, Edward Conrad SRT3c
LOEFFLER, Ernest Edward S2c
LONGKABEL, Gordon, Jr. S2c
LOW, Frederick John S1c
LOWE, Wimpy F1c
MAHIN, Charles William SK2cc
MARA, George Philip Cox

MARKER, Franklin Leroy GM3c
MARRIOTT, Oscar Ferdinand CEM
MARSLAND, Alvah Irwin MM3c
MARTIN, Wendell Linzy S1c
MAUTER, Paul Thomas F1c
MEDELLIN, Pedro Martinez S1c
MEDINA, Norberto RT3c
MENSENKAMP, Walworth Thomas S1c
MENIUS, Billy Odell MM3c
MENALLO, Nunzio Daniel BM2c
MICHALIK, George Edward S1c
MIERZEJEWSKI, Paul Raymond WT2c
MILLER, Joseph James Cox
MILLER, Robert William FC3c
MINAHAN, John Patrick S1c
MINKS, Everett Russel S2c
MITCHELL, Wallace Harry S2c
MOLZAHN, Albert Lester WT2c
MOORE, Carroll Edwin MM2c
MOOS, Robert Francis WT2c
MOUNT, James Watson S2c
MUGRIDGE, Paul Clayton Cox
McGEE, Donald Eugene S1c
McGINNIS, Arthur James S1c
McCLAIN, Charles Edward F1c
NEAL, Earl Arthur AMM3c
NELSON, Laverne Nels S2c
NELSON, Lowell Rainard GM3c
NETTLES, Edward Marvin S1c
NIELSEN, Kenneth Reher WT3c
OLESON, Harald Reio Arild CTC
OWENS, Luther Birchel S1c
PAYTON, Larus Elmer SF2c
PEREGUD, Harry S2c
PETERSON, Robert Hamilton EM2c
PIGGOTT, Tom Edward Bkr3c
PIRES, John Paul F1c
POPA, Emil S1c
POSTLE, Lewis Wiley, Jr. RM3c
POTE, Robert Lee S2c
PURVIS, John Mitchell GM3c
QUINN, Edward Joseph, Jr. S1c

RAMSEY, Charles Homer Cox
REED, Donald Otis S1c
RICHARD, Omer Adrian S2c
RICHIE, Eugene Anthony S1c
RITCHEY, Edward Gilbert MM2c
ROBERTS, Roberts Ewing CCSTD
ROD, Ernest David S1c
ROGERS, Harold Floyd S1c
ROGERS, Louis Richard S2c
ROLEDER, Howard Stanley MM2c
ROMO, Jesuse Antelno S2c
RUSSO, Anthony Thomas MM2c
SABINO, Peter Anthony S1c
SAMUELSEN, Laurence Albert S1c
SANDERS, Charles Ernest S1c
SAVAGE, Jack Milton CPhM
SAVEY, John Henry S1c
SCHAFFER, William Arthur MM3c
SCHIEBLE, Robert Frances S1c
SCHMIDT, John Mathew S1c
SCHOEN, Roy Adam BM2c
SCHULTZ, Alvin Leo Cox
SEARS, Billy D. S2c
SHAVER, Frank Jr. Bkr1c
SHEIL, Joseph Patrick S1c
SIDOR, John S1c
SIMKINS, Clarence Marcellus GM2c
SMITH, Harold Truman F1c
SOLANO, Isidro CST
SPILLANE, Charles William Cox
STAYMATES, Albert Harrison S2c
STEPP, Billie S2c
STUDDEN, Arthur MM3c
TAYLOR, Clair Elwood BM2
TAYLOR, Loyd S2c
TEAGUE, Jesse Zachaus S2c
THOMPSON, John Robert RT1c
THURMAN, Joseph Allen S2c
TICE, William Lester SC1c
TIPPS, Everett Shirman S2c
TONKA, George Joseph S2c
TOMLINSON, Frank Ellis S1c
TREVENTHAN, Vernon Ervin MM3c
TRUETT, James Melvin S1c

TRUJILLO, Daniel Carmen S1c
TURNER, Daniel Junior S2c
ULERY, Roy Levon MM1c
VAUGHN, Clyde Everett MM2c
VICKNAIR, Warren Joseph, Jr. EM2c
VOELKER, Delmer Oswald S2c
VOIGT, Ferdinand Max F1c
VOLK, Wendelin J. Cox
WADE, Jack Wayne S2c
WALDEN, Charles Orville S2c
WALKER, Paul Allen S2c
WALLS, William Howard S2c
WALTERS, James Trueman SK3c
WATERMAN, Lee F1c
WAYNICK, Delbert Lee S2c
WEAVER, Marlin Andrew S2c
WEAVER, Bruce Edward S1c
WEBB, Edward Perry, Jr. SC1c
WEDEKING, James Linard FC3c
WEIGAND, Ralph John S1c
WELLS, Paul Raymond SK3c
WEST, Clayton Clifford F1c
WESTFALL, Howard Venton S2c
WHITE, Fred Hoyt S2c
WILCZYNSKI, Tadausz Bernard S2c
WILSON, Max FCO3c
WOLFF, Warren William S2c
WOLLERMAN, Fritz August GM2c
WONG, Harry Bkr3c
WOOD, Russell Devere F1c
WYTRYKOWSKI, Henry Thomas F1c
ZESPY, Jerome Anthony GM3c

Marines
HOYT, Dale Hoel PlSgt
MAUCK, Wayne Vicent PFC
MAXWELL, Harry Guy, Jr. PFC
McGUIRE, Raleigh Maxwell PFC
TURCOTT, Charles Augustus PFC

Birmingham Personnel Wounded
24 October 1944

Officers
ADEY, Edward Alonzo, III Ens.
MAROCCHI, John Louis Lt.
REID, John Lt.
VOTTO, Frank V. Ens.
WINGFIELD, William Henry Elect.

Enlisted Personnel
ADAMS, Edward Berry EM3c
ADAMS, Smith Cantrell Jr. S1c
ALLEN, Richard Stephen ARM2c
ASKREN, Kenneth Lee S2c
AUSTGEN, William Ephrasm SSMB3c
BATTISTIN, Celeste Louis MoMM3c
BELCHER, John Lee S2c
BENNETT, James Claiborne RdM3c
BIERHAUS, Milford Leslie S2c
BLACKSTOCK, Clarence Edwin S2c
BOWEN, Clovis Armster S2c
BROWN, Charles Francis MM1c
BROWN, Bernard Jones BM2c
BROWN, Clyde O'Neil S2c
BROWN, Hansel S1c
BROWN, Mitchell RdM3c
BRYANT, Ellis Franklin S1c
BULL, Kenneth Arthur S2c
CAMPBELL, Jesse J Jr. Y2c
CARMEAN, Eugene Vernon Cox
CARMICHAEL, Harry Robert F1c
CARNEY, Kenith Lester S2c
CHANEY, John Russell S2c
CHOLEWA, Mitchell Joseph S1c
COLEMAN, Leon StM2c
COSTA, Antonio Thomas Cox
CRIPE, Lawrence R. S2c
CUPPETT, Leslie Joseph S1c
DANGLES, Christ S1c
DAVIDSON, Jewel Richmond S1c

DAVIS, Delbert Barney Cox
DAVIS, Eddy Junior S2c
DECKER, Richard Lawrence F2c
DEITCHLER, Harlan Hans S1c
DeJARNETT, Rudolph S2c
DELPH, Paul Donald S1c
DeMILLION, Vernon Edward S2c
DENTON, James Earl S2c
DeWITT, Harrell Lee F1c
DRZAZINSKI, Edward Joseph BM2c
DULL, John Carl S2c
DUNN, Merle Palmer S1c
DYER, Harry EM2c
ELEEW, Nathan F1c
ENGEN, Lawrence Allen FC3c
FISCHER, Robert Donald SK3c
FOX, Levin Thomas MM3c
FRANKE, Frederick L. Jr SF3c
FUTCH, Leonard Forrest Cox
GADDY, William Albert S2c
GANNON, Bernard Michael S2c
GARDNER, Raymond W. S1c
GAVGLER, Anthony Richard F2c
GEIGER, Martin Frank Jr. Bkr2c
GOLD, John Jay Y3c
GOULD, Wayne Emery S1c
GOWER, John Oscar GM3c
GRAVES, Robert Calvin SC1c
GREENE, Forrest Monroe S2c
HALE, Lloyd Mack ARM2c
HARRIS, Robert James S1c
HENSINGER, Neile L. CEM
HERRING, Bert Everett S2c
HERZBERG, William C. EM1c
HILL, Bertrand Louis S2c
HOLBERT, John Marvin S1c
HOLMES, Kenneth Roger Cox
HORNER, Nelson Robert S2c
HUDSON, Clyde Thomas S1c
JANKE, Grover Cleveland S2c
JENNINGS, Marvin Edgar S1c
JONES, James Martin S1c
JOSEPH, David Lee F1c
KALCK, Wendell August Jr. EM3c

KANE, William Donato S1c
KIMBLE, Volta Edison F1c
KLONOSKI, Edward James RM2c
LANTERMAN, Howard Melvin BM1c
LEARN, Wayne Emmett RM2c
LEDO, Philip Tavares F1c
LEE, Kenneth Sheldon S2c
LEWIS, Chester F1c
LLOYD, Ashby Wheeler Jr. S2c
LUCERO, Frank AMM2c
LYLE, Lewis Everette W. S1c
LYNN, Harry Charles QM3c
MANCUSO, Joe RdM3c
MANN, George Edward S1c
McCANN, Gordon Louis S2c
McCREARY, Robert Leroy EM1c
McLAUGHLIN, James SM3c
MELDRUM, Lynn Albert S1c
MEYER, William Joseph MM3c
MICHALAK, Henry Walter S2c
MILLER, Crockford MM1c
MILLER, Harold Ervine S1c
MILLS, Marion Carlile Cox
MILLS, Virgil Cox
MINTER, Harold Lee S2c
MISLEVY, Joseph MM2c
MONROE, Robert Walter S2c
MURPHY, Daniel James FC3c
NIELSON, Alton S2c
OCCHIPINTI, Saverio AM3c
O'KEEFE, Richard William S2c
OKRAY, Robert Nicholas S2c
O'NEAL, William Haynes F1c
PATRICK, William Lane S1c
PENNINGTON, Harold Walker S2c
PENNINGTON, Hollis Alvin S2c
PERKINS, Leslie James S1c
PICKENS, George Swope GM3c
PISOR, John Perry S2c
POLITO, Crist Tony S2c
POPHAM, Harry Junior MM2c
PORTER, Charles Edwin RM3c
PRINCE, Merle RdM3c
PUC, Adam Mike Cox

PURPURA, Francesco S1c
RAIMONDI, William Charles S2c
RAMON, William S1c
RASMUSSEN, Carl Sophus S1c
READNOUR, Robert S2c
REED, Ulessess Zellen S2c
REES, John Pursel MM1c
REIFF, Arvin Edward MM2c
RITTNER, Keith Haynes S1c
ROBERTS, Thomas Joseph Jr. RdM3c
ROBINSON, Emmet Ray FCO3c
ROBNOLITE, Charles Nelson S1c
RUNNION, Richard S1c
SCHAEFFER, Albert Andrew S2c
SCHOCH, Richard S1c
SCOLTOCK, John Joseph GM3c
SEARFOS, Melvin Raymond S1c
SHEARS, James Ck3c
SHERMER, Floyd Vernon S1c
SHULER, Irvin Alva MM3c
SIMMONS, Charles S2c
SMITH, Kermit Lyle SM2c
SNIADECKI, Francis Chester S2c
SPRINGMAN, William Walter S1c
STEELE, Irvin Robert S2c
STEELE, William Buford S2c
STEVENS, Eugene Leo S1c
STONEKING, Floyd Delbert Cox
STRAUB, Thomas Arthur S2c
SUMMERS, Charles Frederick Cox
SWINNEY, Robert Clyde BM1c
TAMLYN, Calvin Clealand F1c
THAWSH, Martin Frank S1c
THIESSEN, Russell Clark S1c
THOMPSON, George Bernard F1c
THOMPSON, Richard Ellsworth S1c
THORPE, Delbert Franklin S1c
TOTH, Sigmond William F1c
VADEN, Billy Earl S2c
VAGNIER, Robert Lee S1c
VEST, Jack Emerald S1c

VICARS, James McConnell S1c
VITULLO, Joseph Felix S1c
VOLCKE, Albert Maurice Y3c
WALLACE, Onnie Cyrous S2c
WALLO, John Joseph Jr. S1c
WALTER, Ralph S2c
WALTERS, Elmer George S2c
WALTON, George Raymond S2
WARREN, Dale Olin S1c
WEBB, Floyd Eugene F1c
WEGER, Martin Glenn EM2c
WEISS, William Arnoth MoMM2c
WHITE, Robert Edward S1c
WHITTINGTON, George Alvin S2c
WIANT, Edward Arnold S1c
WICKER, Philip William Cox
WIESZKOWIAK, Alexander GM3c
WIILIAINEN, Edward Ronald S2c
WILLIAM, Johnie Lee Jr. S2c
WILLIAMS, Homer Reed S2c
WILLIAMS, Kenneth Arthur F1c
WILLIAMS, Lynn WT3c
WILSON, Joseph Lloyd S2c
WILSON, Richard Lee Y2c
WIRKUS, Jerome Albert FC3c
WISNIEWSKI, Joseph Thomas S2c
WITKOVSKI, Russell Earl S2c
WOJTOWICZ, Joseph Chester S1c
WOLFORD, William Percival S2c
WOOD, LeRoy James S1c
WRINKLE, D. T. S2c
ZEA, Ward Homer S1c
ZIELINSKI, Michael Bruno S2c

Marines

CUNDIFF, William Henry Pvt
MAYNOR, James Lewis Corp.
SMITH, Opie Drexel Pfc
SPINKS, William John Pfc
VENDEMIA, James Anthony Pfc

Casualties

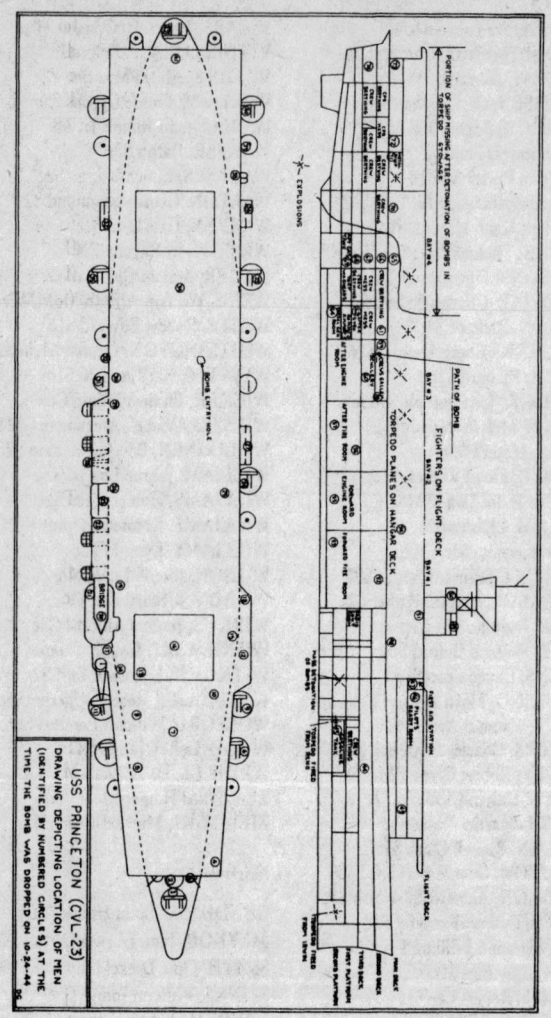

Chart showing location of men when the bomb hit the *Princeton*.
Numbers correlate to lists on page 199 and 200, and indicate positions of men on chart.
Locations of various explosions are also shown.

198   *CARRIER DOWN*

57	Abernathy, Thomas S1c	1	Addison, Lawrence S1c
57	Adolph, Adrian L. F1c	59	Arlequeeuw, Raymond SC1c
35	Arneson, Alton FC3c	60	Bellavance, Henry S1c
24	Blake, Russell S2c	69	Bowery, Robert AMM3c
59	Briskey, Richard PhM2c	59	Brockway, Ronald SC1c
26	Butler, Ed RdM2c	54	Byrnes, Steve AM1c
18	Callan, Peter AQM2c	43	Carson, F. R. Lt. (jg)
65	Chinn, Jack AQM2c	33	Chisholm, Adrian 1st Sgt.
49	Choquette, Edgar RdM1c	62	Christie, Joseph RT3c
57	Codgill, Richard S1c	4	Colby, Kenneth ACMM (PA)
42	Cook, Carl AEM3c	69	Cusick, Thomas AMM2c
9	Daniels, Kenneth Cox	15	DeVita, Alfred ACM (AA)
73	Diehl, Robert S1c	71	Doyle, James S2c
70	Drawbond, Clarence AMM2c	46	Drury, Paul Ens.
46	Fitzgerald, John Ens.	21	Flisher, Kenneth Y3c
38	Flynn, Ed S1c	27	Ford, Raymond Cpl.
71	Giddle, Lyle AMM1c	64	Gilmore, Charles EM1c
7	Gray, Russell S1c	2	Green, George Cox
8	Greer, James RdM3c	73	Guthrie, George SK2c
43	Hansen, William S1c	57	Harrell, Robert R. WT3c
67	Harrison, Roy S1c	46	Hautop, Fred Ens.
23	Herron, John S1c	31	Holmes, Merle S2c
27	Hosey, James Pfc	50	Hunnicutt, James QM1c
35	Johnson, Leland S1c	36	Johnson, Raymond S1c
71	Jones, Adrian AM1c	33	Keilman, Maurice Pfc
50	Kelleher, J. N. Lt. Comdr.	37	Kemler, Howard S2c
46	Kerr, William Lt.(jg) ACI	65	Kieri, Leo AMM1c
50	Knapp, Leonard Y3c	27	Knutson, Erling Pfc
48	Kohl, Harry S1c	14	Koukis, Nick S1c
71	La Breche, Joseph AMM1c	58	La Fevre, Lyle AMM1c
70	Leininger, Harold TMV2c	19	Levy, L. K. Lt. Cdr. MCVS
70	Linsenmaier, Richard AMM2c	60	Lyons, Ronald SF2c
22	Mace, William	53	Malmen, John WT2c
78	Manke (Mankiewicz), Ted S2c	19	Marchesini, Harry S2c
10	Martin, Melvin MM2c	8	Matusak, Leonard AOM2c
56	Mayer, Arthur MM3c	12	Mazziotti, Americo AOM2c
51	McVey, Jack AEM2c	71	Millar, James AM1c
3	Minervini, Sam S2c	16	Minyard, Jesse AMM1c
7	Mitchell, Eugene BM1c	6	Mitts, Harley S2c
50	Moitoret, Victor Lt.	46	Mooney, Thomas Lt.(jg) AVN
45	Moreland, James Lt.	5	Morgan, Lawrence AAM3c
38	Morris, Earl AMM3c	29	Mullen, Jack
46	Myer, William Ens.	44	Oesterle, A. R. Lt. (DC)
40	Page, Gerald S2c	41	Pantages, George PhM1c

Location of Men on USS Princeton

34	Pennington, Kenneth ACMM	57	Pino, Manuel L. WT3c
58	Plath, Frederick CCS	30	Puncerelli, Charles
67	Ramos, Julian S1c	53	Redfield, Frank WT3c
5	Robson, John AQM1c	48	Rubin, Lawrence SK1c
63	Russell, William RM2c	68	Samano, Peter SSMB3c
52	Sanders, Joe S2c	11	Scheer, Donald S2c
40	Schnatterly, Arden S2c	8	Schuyler, Norman Lt.
47	Shaffer, Luciano AOM3c	7	Shattenberg, Earl ACOM
32	Sherman, Percy AMM3c	14	Shirley, James "Red" Lt.
66	Slavin, Daniel S2c	39	Smith, Clifford Ensign
17	Smith, Russell S1c	20	Smith, William RT3c
57	Spencer, William J. WT2c	46	Stambook, Dick Lt. AVN
48	Staron, Max SK3c	57	Steele, James G. CWO
7	Swistak, Peter AOM3c	58	Tapsak, John SC3c
57	Tarullo, Samuel WT3c	47	Taylor, Ralph Lt.
43	Thompson, Charles AMM2c	73	Trevor, Robert AOM2c
74	Trosvig, Roy Y2c	13	Trout, Harry GM2c
25	Truett, Garland S1c	57	Vandenberg, Edward J. Lt.
28	Vanderkieft, Richard S2c	57	Vendrely, Donald L. F1c
19	Vittetoe, Richard S1c	57	Walborn, Archibald MM1c
44	Ward, Charles SF3c	46	Weekly, Robert Lt.(jg) AVN
55	Weidemann, Abel MM2c	61	Wenger, John CRT
55	Wheeler, Fred Lt. Cdr.	53	White, George WT3c
46	White, William Lt.	55	Williams, Thomas MM2c
57	Zaicek, Ralph S. WT2c	5	Zelent, Alfred F1c

Ens. Pete Burgess in his TBM Avenger on the Princeton's *flight deck.*

The Princeton *medical team consisted of doctors, dentists, corpsmen and pharmacist's mates.*

The first raising of the colors on the USS Princeton *(CVL 23). Signalman Second Class E. L. Templer and Quartermaster Third Class J. W. Powell hoisted the ensign at the commissioning on February 25, 1943.*

Broadside view of Princeton *during the shakedown cruise, before her camouflage paint was added.*

King Neptune's "queen," in a grass skirt performs a hula dance for the Princeton crew as the carrier crosses the equator.

King Neptune rules — The mythical monarch of the sea (with trident) struts the Princeton flight deck during an initiation ceremony that came with a crossing of the equator.

Officers of Torpedo 27, pictured near one of the squadron's TBMs at the Naval Air Station, Kahului, Maui, in the Hawaiian Islands, before going aboard the Princeton. *In the back row (from left to right) are: Lt. (jg) Henry F. "Doc" Manget, Ens. Cliff Rogers, Jr., Lt. John G. Dooling, and Ens. William H. Mayer. In the front row (left to right): Lt. (jg) Thomas B. Mooney, Air Combat Intelligence Officer Lt. (jg) William K. Kerr, and Ens. Byron J. Sample.*

Pilots and ground officers of VF-27 in front of an F6F fighter plane with unique Hellcat face painted on cowling. (left to right): Top Row — T. I. Bradshaw, H. F. Loveland, R. P. Butler, S. B. Leigh, R. M. Burnell, R. Stambook, J. L. McMahon, J. A. Shirley, and G. A. Stanley. Middle Row — H. F. Brotherton, H. F. Finnerty, L. A. Erickson, G. E. Arnot, E. A. Lynn, F. A. Bardshar, W. E. Woods, W. E. Lamb, H. D. Lillie, G. J. L. McCormick, S. J. Goodrich, J. D. Fitzgerald, and P. E. Drury. Bottom Row — F. D. Hautop, V. Buren Carter, W. H. Gregg, R. S. Taylor, C. A. Brown, R. B. Grove, F. P. Kleffner, R. M. Russell, and J. C. O'Connor.

Easter sunrise services aboard the Princeton *while anchored at Majuro Atoll, a captured Japanese base in the Marshall Islands.*

Princeton *"pollywogs," being initiated on their first equator crossing, perform an "octopus dance" on the flight deck.*

Command Group — (from left) Comdr. John Murphy, Princeton executive officer; Lt. Comdr. M. T. Hatcher; Capt. William Buracker; Comdr. Frank Miller, air officer; and Lt. Comdr. Henry Miller, Air Group 23 skipper.

Pilots and ground officers of VF-23. Shown in front row (left to right) are: Ens. John Redmon, Lt. Claude Schmidt, Lt. Comdr. Harold Miller, Lt. Harold Funk, (?), Lt. (jg) James Smith, and Lt. (jg) Leon Haynes. In the back row: Lt. James Rickard, Lt. Richard Hefler, Ens. Leslie Kerr, (?), Lt. (jg) Robert Tyner, Lt. (jg) David Olin, Ens. Oscar Cantrell, Lt. Charles Kenyon, Lt. (jg) Walter Kirschke, Lt. (jg) Joe Webb, Ens. James Syme, Ens. Jack Madison, and Ens. William Buckelew.

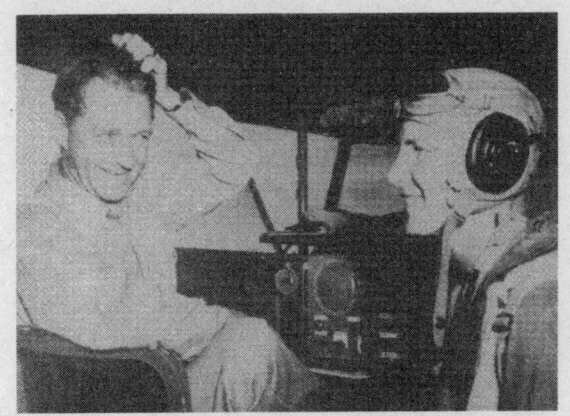

Ensign W. C. "Pete" Burgess (right) tells the Princeton's *skipper, Capt. William Buracker, how he used his torpedo bomber to force a Japanese plane into the sea.*

Aviation Machinist's Mate Ivan Lyle LeFevre stands by the Princeton's *superstructure, bearing a tally of air combat results; 4 enemy warships, and 3 merchant ships sunk; 131 Japanese airplanes destroyed; and 110 bombing missions against land targets. The scoreboard figures were increased later.*

With planes spotted aft on the flight deck, the Princeton *heads out to sea. The aircraft with their wings unfolded are SBD dive bombers, removed from the carrier's complement before the* Princeton *entered combat.*

The carrier strike "heard 'round the world" — Planes from the Princeton *and the* Saratoga *hit Rabaul in November 1943. Japanese warships frantically attempt to escape bombing, strafing, and torpedo attacks.*

One of a series of explosions rocks the Princeton, *sending aloft a mushroom-like cloud of smoke.*

Smoke pours from the Princeton *soon after the enemy bomb hit. The carrier has not yet been forced to pull away from the task group formation.*

A dense pall of black smoke, low on the water, shrouds much of the crippled carrier.

Amid the shambles of blasted elevators and a bulging flight deck, a handful of Princeton *crew members stand helplessly by as rescue ships pull away under enemy air attack alert.*

USS Birmingham *pulls directly against* Princeton *to provide firefighting aid.*

Watching lines being sent over from the Birmingham, *this group on the* Princeton *flight deck include (left to right) Comdr. John Murphy, executive officer (hands behind back); Pharmacist's Mate Paul Robinson (without helmet); Capt. John Hoskins (holding hose); Capt. William Buracker; Lt. Al Oesterle, dental officer; and Lt. Vic Moitoret, ship's navigator (without helmet).*

As the Birmingham *pulls alongside,* Princeton *officers and men still aboard stand by. Shown from left: Capt. William Buracker and Capt. John Hoskins (side by side); Vic Moitoret (with hose in back of group at center); Lt. James Kelleher (with head bandage); Comdr. John Murphy (third from right); Lt. Al Oesterle (behind Murphy), and James Hunnicutt (second from right).*

Smoke billows from blazing Princeton *as destroyer stands alongside, pumping water onto the fires.*

The destroyer Morrison, *with lines strung over to the* Princeton, *attempts to bring the fires aboard the carrier under control.*

A group gathers on the Princeton's *forecastle (left) as a rescue ship approaches. Other crewmen on the flight deck prepare to make their way down. One man uses a line secured to a torpedo bomber to descend to a gun platform with the help of comrades below.*

From the explosion-displaced forward elevator area, crew members work their way aft with a hoseline. The Birmingham *nears the carrier's port quarter in the background. The* Morrison's *damaged foremast shows to the left of the picture, along with the* Princeton's *collision-damaged radar antenna. A hoseline from the* Morrison *runs aft through the center of the hangar.*

Looking aft on the Princeton's *starboard side, the flight deck is a scene of destruction. The forward elevator is upended in its well (right). Beyond that and the "island" superstructure is the overturned after elevator.*

Princeton hangar deck, normally a bustling center for aircraft repair and servicing, is left a burned-out ruin. Just aft of this area, fires continue to work their way toward stored bombs and other munitions.

Flames from the hangar deck consumed the wooden flight-deck planking, exposing the supporting girders.

A hose from the Birmingham *(left foreground) is directed at the* Princeton's *charred, smoking mid-section. Firefighters on the carrier flight deck aim another hose at the open well by the forward elevator.*

VF-27 Pilot Frank Kleffner lands aboard the carrier Essex *after being waved away from his own flattop, the bomb-racked* Princeton *(in background). Kleffner's plane was taken below and the Hellcat face painted off under admiral's orders.*

Three Cassin Young *crewmen, James Marrs, Al Melville, and John Ansa bring a lifeboat, filled with* Princeton *survivors, alongside the destroyer. The men watch as a line is thrown to them.*

Cassin Young *boat picked up survivors from the water near the* Princeton. *Some of those already aboard leap back into the sea to help their comrades.*

Princeton *survivors provide necessary personal information after being taken aboard the carrier* Lexington. *Among those shown (left to right) are: Robert Anderson, YN1; Roman Kiefer, S2c; Robert Nutterfield, RM3c; Frank Redfield, WT3c; Sam Minervini, S2c; R. D. Ramos, S1c; and F. A. Perruna, S1c. A* Lexington *officer (with hat) watches the transfer.*

Index

A
Abell, Jack, Lt.(jg), 10, 16, 41
Abernathy, Thomas, S1c, 127–128, 199
Addison, Lawrence, S1c, 120–121, 199
Adolph, Adrian, F1c, 128, 199
Alabama, USS, 39, 42
Alameda Naval Air Station, 53, 56, 95
Albert W. Grant, USS, 43
Amsterdam, USS, 5
Ansa, Johnny, 144
Arlequeeuw, Raymond, SC1c, 49–50, 120, 199
Arneson, Alton, FC3c, 199
Arnold, Hap, General, 31
Auclair, Henry, Lt.(jg), 126
Aylwin, USS, 67–68

B
Babelthuap, 85
Baker, Herman, Lt., 56
Baker Island, 22–24, 25
Baltimore, USS, 36
Bancroft, USS, 25
Bardshar, Frederic, Lt., 53–54, 55, 57, 58, 59–60, 70, 72, 74, 82–83, 93–94, 187, 188
Barnes, USS, 57
Bataan, USS, 6
Becker, John, Lt., 9
Beckett, John, Lt., 101–102
Bell, Frank, Lt., 64–65, 98–99
Bellavance, Henry, S1c, 132–133, 199
Belleau Wood, USS, 5, 17, 19, 20, 21, 22, 23, 25, 69, 76
Birmingham, USS, iii, vii–viii, ix, 25, 62, 63, 88, 111, 138, 139–140, 141, 142, 148–149, 150, 154–164, 166, 168, 174, 175–176, 177, 178–181, 186, 188
Blake, Russell, S2c, 199
Blyth, Les, Ens., 72
Bonis, 28
Boston, USS, 36
Bougainville, 28, 29, 31–32
Bowery, Robert, AMM3c, 199
Boyd, USS, 22
Bradford, USS, 22
Bradley, Robert G., Lt., 132–133, 139, 153, 167–168, 187
Bradshaw, Thomas I., ACI (Author), xii, 53, 64, 96, 163
Brakeley, George A., 9
Bransfield, Charles, Lt.(jg), 26
Bremerton, Washington, 4, 34, 35
Brisky, Richard, PhM2c, 199
Brockway, Ronald, SC1c, 199
Brotherton, Hank, Lt., 71
Brown, Carl, Lt., xi, 55, 72, 89, 90–93
Brown, Larry, WT1c, 48–49
Buckelew, W. G., Lt.(jg), 10, 16, 36
Buka, 28, 29
Bullock, Robert, AMM, 73
Buracker, William, Capt., ix, 37–38, 44–45, 96, 98, 136, 154, 159, 164, 166, 168, 169, 170, 175, 183, 184
Burgess, "Pete," Ens., 72–73
Burnell, Bob, Ens., 59
Butler, Ed, RdM2c, 199
Butler, R. P. "Robin," Lt., 60
Byrnes, Steve, AM1c, 199

C
Cabot, USS, 5, 10, 69, 79
Caldwell, H. H., 30
Caldwell, USS, 25
Callan, Peter, AQM2c, 102–103, 179, 199
Canberra, USS, 36, 42, 87
Canton Island, 24
Cantrell, Oscar, Ens., 16
Caperton, USS, 43
Carson, F. R., Lt.(jg), 127, 199
Carter, Van "Castaway," 58, 71, 74
Carupano, Venezuela, 16
Cassin Young, USS, iii, ix, 43, 109, 123, 138, 140, 141, 143–144, 148, 150, 152–153, 173, 175, 186–187
Cebu, 4, 82

Chafee, George B., Comdr., 10
Charles Ausburn, USS, 43
Charon-Kanoa, 63, 66
Chesapeake Bay, 11–12, 13
Chester, USS, 7
Chinn, Jack, AQM2c, 199
Chisholm, Adrian, Sgt., 100, 173–174, 199
Choquette, Edgar, RdM1c, 199
Christie, A. A., Ens., 127, 153
Christie, Joseph, RT3c, 105, 199
Clifford, Edward L., Lt.Comdr., 11, 17, 47, 61
Cogdill, Richard, S1c, 128, 199
Coghlan, USS, 25
Cogswell, USS, 43
Colby, Kenneth, ACCM, 199
Colorado, USS, 34
Conroy, Tom, Ens., 174
Constitution, USS, 187
Converse, USS, 42
Cook, Carl, AEM3c, 199
Copahee, USS, 56
Cotton, USS, 43
Cowpens, USS, 5
Crews, Sandy, Lt., 23, 25
Crockett, Stanley, Lt.(jg), 30, 37
Curtis, W. L., Lt., 9, 119
Cusick, Thomas, AMM2c, 118–119, 199
Cyclops, 43

D

Daniels, Kenneth, Cox, 199
Dashiell, USS, 17
Dearman, Kermit, CY2c, 49
Degenhardt, William, GM2c, 142–143
Del Monte, 82
Delaware Bay, 11, 17, 19
DeVita, Alfred, ACM, 199
Diehl, Robert, S1c, 199
Dodds, Mrs. Harold, 6
Doolittle, James, Colonel, 10
Dortch, USS, 43
Doyle, James, S2c, 199
Drawbond, Clarence, AMM2c, 199
Drury, Paul, Ens., 95, 199
Duborg, Francis R., Comdr., 160
Dyer, Charles, 30
Dyson, USS, 43

E

Edwards, USS, 27, 28
Empress Augusta Bay, 29, 30
Engano, Battle of, 187
Engebi Island, 37
Eniwetok, 37, 39, 77–80, 82
Enterprise, USS, 7, 42, 44, 45, 54, 82
Erickson, Leif, 72
Espiritu Santo, 28, 33, 34, 39, 50
Essex, USS, 21, 88, 89, 93, 94–95, 97, 139
Evans, David, Photographer 3c, 137–38

F

Farenholt, USS, 28
Fitzgerald, John, Ens., xi, 114–115, 199
Flisher, Kenneth, Y3c, 199
Flynn, Ed, 199
Folk, Winston, Comdr., 160–161
Ford Island, 27, 34, 57, 60
Ford, Raymond, Cp1, 199
Formosa, 87
Fratus, William, 30
Funk, Harold, Lt., 23, 24

G

Gardiner, David, 2, 3
Gardiner, Julia, 2, 3
Gatling, USS, iii, ix, 43, 118, 133, 138, 144, 148, 152–153, 166, 167, 169, 170, 175, 177–178, 180, 186
Ghastin, Leo, xi
Gibbon, Robert, AMM1c, 118
Giddle, Lyle, AMM1c, 78–79, 104–105, 199
Gilbert Islands (Gilberts), 22, 34
Gilmer, Anne, 2
Gilmer, Thomas, 2–3
Gilmore, Charles, EM1c, 199
Glans, Buhler, C.Q.M., 159
Glidden, Germain, ACI, 59
Godson, "Junior," Ens., 25
Gray, Russell, S1c, 199
Great Western, 2
Green, George, Cox, xi, 100–101, 120, 122–124, 173, 199
Greer, James, RdM3c, 199
Gregg, Howie, 70–71
Grove, Bob, Lt., 55
Guam, 63, 65, 66, 67, 68, 69, 77, 81

Guest, USS, 20,
Guthrie, George, SK2c, 199

H

Hadley, S. M., Lt.Comdr., 54
Halsey, William "Bull," Adm., 29, 31, 33, 88, 147–148, 183
Hampton Roads, 13
Hansen, William, S1c, 199
Haroldson, Harvey, 143
Harrell, Robert, WT3c, 128, 199
Harrison, Roy, S1c, 199
Harrison, USS, 20, 25
Harwood, Bruce L., Comdr., 142, 153, 155–156, 163, 164, 166, 167, 169
Hautop, Fred, Ens., 83–85, 113–114, 199
Hazelwood, USS, 25, 28
Healy, USS, 43
Henderson, George, Capt., 7, 9, 14, 28, 37–39
Herron, John, S1c, 199
Hill, Robert, Ens., 72
Hirleman, Dean, 131
Hiroshima, vii
Hiyo (Japanese), 76
Hodgins, George, ARM2c, 73
Hollandia, 42–45
Hollister, California, 56
Holmes, Merle, S2c, 199
Holt, Tim, 158
Honolulu, Hawaii, 21, 27, 57
Hornet, USS, 7, 9, 10, 14, 48, 49, 69, 85, 97, 101, 107, 120, 131, 174, 184
Hosey, James, Pfc, 199
Hoskins, John, Capt., ix, 96, 164–166, 167, 177–178, 183–184, 186
Houston, USS, 87
Hunnicutt, James, QM1c, 163–164, 199

I

Iloilo, 4
Independence, USS, 5, 6, 21, 187
Indiana, USS, 42, 64
Indianapolis, USS, 39
Ingersoll, USS, 43
Inglis, Thomas B., Capt., viii, xii, 62–63, 138, 139, 159–161
Irwin, USS, iii, ix, 100, 106, 112, 114, 115–116, 122, 129, 131, 132, 135, 136, 138, 140, 141–143, 148–149, 150, 153, 170–173, 175, 178, 179, 180, 186

J

Jackson, Richard, Lt., 115–116, 172
Jaskilka, Sam, Lt., 78
John Rogers, USS, 25
Johnson, Leland, S1c, 199
Johnson, Raymond, S1c, 199
Johnston Island, 24
Jones, Adrian, 199

K

Kahului, 57–60
Kamikaze, 87, 97, 168, 187
Kaneohe, 27
Kauai, Hawaii, 59
Keilman, Maurice, Pfc, 116–118, 199
Kelleher, J. N., Lt.Comdr., 111, 199
Kemler, Howard, S2c, 199
Kennon, Beverly, 3
Kenyon, Chuck, Lt., 26–27
Kerr, Leslie, Lt.(jg), 23, 37, 41, 43
Kerr, Robert C., Ens., 162–163
Kerr, William "Bill," Lt., ACI, 53, 96, 199
Kiefer, Roman, S2c, 105
Kieri, Leo, AMM1c, 47, 50–51, 108–109, 199
Kincaid, Thomas, Adm., 147
Kirschke, Walter, Ens., 10
Kleffner, Frank "Smoke," Ens., 59, 66–67, 68, 74, 94–95
Knapp, Leonard, Y3c, 199
Knapp, USS, 43
Knutson, Erling, Pfc, 199
Kohl, Harry, S1c, 199
Koukis, Nick, S1c, 199
Kwajalein, 36, 37

L

La Breche, Joseph, AMM1c, 199
La Fevre, Lyle, AMM1c, 199
Lamb, William "Bill," Lt., 53, 55, 69, 71, 83
Langley, USS, 5, 35, 36, 39, 42, 61, 79, 88, 89
Lansdowne, USS, 28
Lardner, USS, 28
Large, Jim, Lt.Comdr., 40–41, 61, 64, 86–87, 96, 142, 152, 169
Leininger, Harold, TMV2c, 199

Levy, Louis, Lt.Comdr., 99, 199
Lexington, USS, 20, 21, 25, 34, 39, 42, 54, 82, 88, 89, 95, 101, 137
Leyte Gulf, vii, ix, x, 82, 137, 147, 148
Lillie, Hugh, Ens., 59
Linsenmaier, Richard, AMM2c, 199
Loesch, Dixie, Lt.(jg), 23
Louisville, USS, 39, 42
Loveland, Hugh, Lt., 71
Luzon, 4, 87, 148
Lyons, Ronald, SF2c, 131–132, 199

M

Maars, Jim, QM2c, 143–146
MacArt, James H., Lt., 160
MacArthur, Douglas, General, vii, 31, 148, 181
Mace, William, 199
Madison, Jack, Lt.(jg), 10, 26, 30
Majuro, 36, 39, 41, 42, 45–46, 61–62, 78
Makin Island, 25, 26
Malmen, John, WT2c, 129–131, 199
Manget, H. F. "Doc," Lt., 113
Manila, 82–83, 89
Manke (Mankiewicz), Ted, S2c, 199
Marchesini, Harry, S2c, 199
Mariana Islands (Marianas), vii, 39, 58, 62, 65, 67, 68, 69, 72, 75, 77, 81
Marocchi, John, Lt., 162
Marshall Islands, 34, 36, 37, 38, 39
Martin, Melvin, MM2c, 199
Masbate, 83
Massachusetts, USS, 39, 42, 83, 88
Matusak, Leonard, AOM2c, 199
Maui, Hawaii, 32, 46, 57–60
Maxey, Virgil, 3
Mayer, Arthur, MM3c, 199
Mazziotti, Americo, AOM2c, 99, 199
McKee, USS, 17, 25
McMahon, Patty, 55, 69
McVey, Jack, AEM2c, 199
Meade, USS, 28
Melville, Al, Cox, 143–146
Midway, Battle of, vii, 32, 174
Miksis, John, MM1c, 157–158
Millar, James, AM1c, 199
Miller, D. B., Comdr., 143
Miller, H. L. "Hank," Lt.Comdr., xi, 10–11, 17, 21, 23, 26, 27, 29–30, 33, 36, 37, 38, 39, 40, 41, 42, 43–45
Mindanao, 82
Mindoro, 89
Minervini, Sam, S2c, 199
Minyard, Jesse, AMM1c, 199
Mississippi, USS, 3
Missouri, USS, 188
Mitchell, Eugene, BM1c, 166–167, 199
Mitscher, Marc, V/Adm., 45, 68, 70, 76, 77
Mitts, Harley, S2c, 199
Mobile, USS, 25, 88
Moitoret, Vic, Lt., xi, 38, 96, 141, 149, 163–164, 168, 169, 185–186, 199
Molokai, Hawaii, 57
Montani, Edward, S2c, 108–109
Monterey, USS, 5, 46, 68
Mooney, Tom, Lt.(jg), AVN, xi, 72–73, 79–80, 97, 112–113, 126, 171, 172, 181, 199
Moreland, James, Lt., 199
Morgan, Lawrence, AAM3c, xi, 135–136, 174, 178–179, 199
Morris, Earl, AMM3c, 199
Morrison, USS, iii, ix, 106, 133, 134, 138, 141, 148–150, 151, 168, 175, 176, 180, 186–187
Moss, John B., Comdr., 35
Muhlfield, Frank, Lt.(jg), 41
Mullen, Jack, 199
Munson, Art, 72
Murphy, John, Comdr., 35, 126–127, 142, 169, 175, 184–186
Musashi (Japanese), 148
Myer, William Ens., 199

N

Nagasaki, vii
Nagato (Japanese), 148
Nauru, 33, 34
New Guinea, 33, 42, 43
New Hebrides, 28
Nichols Field, 82, 83
Nimitz, Chester, Adm., vii, 45
Norfolk, Virginia, 3, 9, 12, 13
North Carolina, USS, 39, 42, 64

O

Oahu, Hawaii, 21, 57
O'Connell, Richard, 30
O'Dell, Buddy, 79
Oesterle, A. R., Lt., 141, 166, 199
Okinawa, vii, 87, 186
Olander, Otto K., Lt., 30–31, 184–185
Oregon (gun on 1st Princeton), 2

P

Page, Gerald, S2c, 199
Palau Islands, 33, 40, 41, 82, 85
Panama Canal, 19
Pantages, George, PhM1c, 51–52, 65, 106–107, 150–151, 176–177, 188, 199
Parris Island, South Carolina, 8, 9, 10, 38
Peacemaker (Gun on 1st Princeton), 2
Pearl Harbor, Hawaii, vii, 20, 21, 22, 26, 27, 34, 35, 46, 47, 54, 57, 59, 61, 83, 136, 186
Peerless "P," 174
Peevey, Frank, F1c, 158–159
Peleliu Island, 82
Pennington, Kenneth, ACMM, 200
Pennsylvania, USS, 54
Phaler, Walt, Lt.Comdr., 7
Philippines, vii, ix, 4, 82, 83, 85, 87, 88, 137, 147–148
Pino, Manuel, WT3c, 128, 200
Plath, Frederick, CCS, 96–97, 107–108, 200
Ponape, 45
Popham, Frank, MM2c, 156–158
Portland, USS, 39, 42
Pritchett, USS, 42
Pullam, USS, 13
Puncerelli, Charles, 200
Pungo, 11
Puunene, 57

R

Rabaul, 29–32, 33–34, 37
Radford, Arthur, R/Adm., 22
Ramos, Julian, S1c, 200
Rapp, W. T. (Barney), Lt.(jg), 38–39
Redfield, Frank, WT3c, 200
Reed, Alan, Lt., 142
Reeves, J. W. "Black Jack," Adm., 42, 44, 45

Reno, Bob, MM2c, 150
Reno, USS, iii, ix, 87, 88, 138, 139, 141, 142, 148–149, 151, 152–153, 154, 156, 160, 161, 168, 169, 170, 173–175
Ringgold, USS, 13, 17, 20, 25
Rio Del Mar, 54, 56
Robbins, Albert, Ens., 9
Robert G. Bradley, 187
Robinson, Paul, PhM1c, 164–165, 177–178
Robson, John, AQM1c, 200
Roi, 37
Roosevelt, Franklin D., President, 10
Rota, 68, 72, 77
Rubin, Lawrence, SK1c, 200
Russell, Mr. and Mrs. John, 34
Russell, William, RM2c, 200
Ryan, Ed, Lt., 161–162

S

Saipan, 39, 62–63, 65, 66, 68, 69, 75, 77, 81–82
Sala, Roland, Comdr., 141, 152, 164–166, 177–178
Samano, Peter, SSMB3c, 200
San Bernardino Strait, 148
San Diego, USS, 28, 34
San Francisco, 186–187
San Jacinto, USS, 78–79
San Juan, USS, 28, 34, 40
Sanders, Joe, S2c, 200
Sangamon, 104
Santa Cruz, Battle of, 97, 174
Santa Fe, USS, 25, 88, 156, 175
Saratoga, USS, 7, 28, 30, 33, 34, 35–36, 54
Saxton, William, 167
Scheer, Donald, S2c, 121, 200
Schmidt, Claude, Lt., 37, 41
Schnatterly, Arden, S2c, 200
Schuyler, Norman Lt., 200
Scott, George, 30
Scott, Oliver, Ens., 83
Sea Bee's, 50–51
Selman, Richard, Ens., 9
Sentani, 43
Seventh Fleet, 147, 184
Shaffer, Luciano, AOM3c, 106, 200
Shattenberg, Earl, ACOM, 200
Sherman, Frederick, Adm., 136

Sherman, Percy, AMM3c, 121–122, 200
Shirley, James "Red," Lt., 55, 70–71, 89–90, 91, 95, 114–115, 174, 200
Shroder, USS, 25
Sibuyan Sea, 89, 93, 148
Sigsbee, USS, 20
Slavin, Daniel, S2c, 200
Smith, Clifford, Ens., 200
Smith, J. A., Lt., 30
Smith, Russell, S1c, 200
Smith, William, RT3c, 200
Solomon Islands, 28, 33
South Dakota, USS, 39, 42, 88
Spence, USS, 22, 42
Spencer, William, WT2c, 128, 200
Stambook, Dick, Lt., 55, 70, 200
Stanley, Gordon, Ens., 72
Staron, Max, SK3c, 200
Stebbings, H. E., Lt.Comdr., 125
Steele, James, CWO, 128, 200
Stevens, USS, 20, 25
Stevenson, USS, 11
Stockton, Robert F., Capt., 1, 2–3
Stockton, USS, 11
Sulu Sea, 148
Surigao Strait, 148
Swistak, Peter, AOM3c, 200
Syme, James, Lt.(jg), 26, 28, 41

T
Tapsak, John, SC3c, 200
Tarawa, 22, 24, 25, 26
Taroa, 33, 36
Tarullo, Samuel, WT3c, 200
Taylor, Ralph (Swish), Lt., 95, 114, 200
Taylor, USS, 42
Tennessee, USS, 34
Thatcher, USS, 42
Third Fleet, 39, 88, 147–148
Thompson, Charles, AMM2c, 200
Tinian, 39, 62, 65, 66, 77, 81–82
Tone (Japanese), 148
Townsend, E. P., Lt.(jg), 174
Trathen, USS, 22
Trevethan, Vernon, MM3c, 156–157
Trevor, Robert, AOM2c, 200
Trinidad, 13, 17
Trosvig, Roy, Y2c, 200
Trout, Harry, GM2c, 200
Truett, Garland, S1c, 200
Truk, 29, 31–32, 33, 39, 45, 61–62, 69
Tyler, John, President, 2
Tyner, Robert, Lt.(jg), 10, 16, 44

U
Ulithi, 78, 85–86, 87, 175, 177, 181, 183, 186
Upshur, Abel P. 3

V
Vandenberg, Edward, Lt., 127–128, 200
Vanderkieft, Richard, S2c, 200
Vendrely, Donald, F1c, 128, 200
Victorious, HMS, 21
Vittetoe, Richard, S1c, 200

W
Wadsworth, USS, 13, 20
Waikiki, Oahu, 21
Wake Island, 27
Walborn, Archibald, MM1c, 200
Ward, Charles, SF3c, 200
Wasp, 7
Webb, Joe, Lt.(jg), 44
Weekly, Robert, Lt.(jg), 200
Weidemann, Abel, MM2c, 200
Wenger, John, CRT, 133–134, 200
West, C. H. Comdr., 3
Wheeler, Fred, Lt.Comdr., 127, 200
White, George, WT3c, 200
White, William, Lt., 200
Wickes, USS, 28
Williams, Thomas, MM2c, 134, 200
Woleai, 41
Wood, Ernest "Woodie" Jr., Lt., 55–56, 57, 59–60, 66, 69–70, 74
Wotje, 33, 36
Wyatt, Hayes, SM1c, 143

Y
Yamato (Japanese), 148
Yap, 40
Yorktown, USS, 21, 39, 46, 61, 69
Young, Robert J., Ens, 9

Z
Zaicek, Ralph, WT2c, 128, 200
Zelent, Alfred, F1c, 200